V. L. BROWNSELL BSc, PhD
C. J. GRIFFITH BSc, PhD
ELERI JONES MSc, PhD

KU-509-563

APPLIED SCIENCE FOR FOOD STUDIES

Longman Scientific &
Longman Group UK
Longman House, Burnt Mill, Harlow,
Essex CM20 2JE, England
and Associated Companies throughout the world.

© Longman Group UK Limited 1989

All rights reserved; no part of this publication
may be reproduced, stored in a retrieval system,
or transmitted in any form or by any means, electronic,
mechanical, photocopying, recording, or otherwise,
without either the prior written permission of the
Publishers or a licence permitting restricted copying in
the United Kingdom issued by the Copyright Licensing
Agency Ltd, 90 Tottenham Court Road, London W1P 9HE.

First published 1989
Second impression 1990

British Library Cataloguing in Publication Data

Brownsell, V. L.
Applied science for food studies.

Longman
Scientific &
Technical

Longman Scientific & Technical,
Longman Group UK Limited,
Longman House, Burnt Mill, Harlow,
Essex CM20 2JE, England
and Associated Companies throughout the world.

First published 1989
Second impression 1992

British Library Cataloguing in Publication Data

Brownsell, V. L.
  Applied science for food studies.
  1. Caterers and catering   2. Food
  I. Title   II. Griffith, C. J.   III. Jones,
  Eleri
  641.1′024642   TX911
  ISBN 0-582-41367-2

Set in Linotron 202 10/12pt Times

Printed in Malaysia

APPLIED SCIENCE FOR FOOD STUDIES

Titles already published in this series:

Accounting in the Hotel and Catering Industry
Frank Wood and Peter Lightowlers

Purchasing, Costing and Control in the Hotel and Catering Industry
Frank Wood and Peter Lightowlers

Basic Restaurant Theory
M. Anker and V. K. Batta

Basic Science for Food Studies
V. L. Brownsell, C. J. Griffith and Eleri Jones

Title to be published in this series:

Mathematics for Catering Students
H. G. Davies

CONTENTS

PREFACE

Readers of this book would be advised to have an elementary knowledge of General Science (basic biology, physics and chemistry) either through appropriate GCSE or equivalent course(s), alternatively through having pursued a college-devised course covering B/TEC units U84/224 and U84/225 or having read *Basic Science for Food Studies* (V.L. Brownsell, C.J. Griffith and Eleri Jones, Longman Hotelwork and Catering Series, London, 1985).

Applied Science for Food Studies is a natural follow on from *Basic Science for Food Studies* and is intended to more than cover all the requirements of the B/TEC Applied Science unit 412C for Hotel Catering and Institutional Operations. In addition it should prove a suitable food science text and meet all the requirements for:

(a) National Diploma Catering students in those Colleges which have devised their own additional units in Food or Applied Science.

(b) Students who are studying for a B/TEC Higher National Diploma in Hotel, Catering and Institutional Operations.

(c) Home Economics students studying up to A level standard.

In line with the philosophy of B/TEC the areas of applied science covered lay particular emphasis on Food Handling, The Human Body and Catering Establishments. The book also contains all the food chemistry present in earlier B/TEC Applied Science units. The authors have deliberately retained this believing that food chemistry and nutrition are two different, but inseparable, sides of the same coin. Food is made up of chemicals, nutrition is the study of these chemicals in relation to human health and disease, food chemistry is the study of the same chemicals but in relation to the properties and uses of the foods containing them. With catering becoming increasingly technological a knowledge of both areas is desirable and relevant to caterers. However, the material in the book has been so arranged that students wishing to concentrate more on the nutritional areas and omit the more chemical aspects of the work can do so.

The book contains a small, separate section on food additives in relation to nutrition but the underlying reasons why chemicals may be added to foods is a theme running throughout the book.

A number of questions are found at the end of each individual chapter. The book also contains an appendix of wider ranging questions testing the student's ability to apply scientific facts to food-related problems and can be used for assignment-based assessment.

It is not suggested that hoteliers and caterers need to become scientists. They should, however, have sufficient scientific knowledge of the subjects dealt with in this book to help them keep abreast of current developments and to enable them to discuss science-related problems with experts, e.g. dietitians, environmental health officers, etc.

The scientific demand on caterers both in terms of healthy eating and safety of food and hotels has never been greater. *Applied Science for Food Studies* should provide a useful handbook to both students and practitioners alike.

AUTHORS ACKNOWLEDGEMENTS

The authors wish to thank Miss Julie Francis for preparing Figures A.1 and A.2. Thanks are also due to Mr John Hollingsworth, Mr Wyndham Boobier and Mr Iwan Davies for their constructive comments.

1

CARBOHYDRATES

1.1 INTRODUCTION

Carbohydrates are organic compounds of carbon, hydrogen and oxygen (with hydrogen and oxygen in the ratio of 2 : 1). Carbohydrates are an important group of nutrients and, with the exception of glycogen and lactose, are usually of plant origin, being produced as a result of photosynthesis. Thus, sources of carbohydrate are mainly fruits, vegetables, cereals and cereal products. Various approaches have been used in the study of carbohydrates, traditionally one based on their size and structure dividing them into sugars and polysaccharides has been the most frequently adopted. Increasingly, however, a method based on biological function is also being used – splitting them into available and unavailable carbohydrates. The available carbohydrates include various sugars and starches and can be used for the production of energy (see Ch. 4). Unavailable carbohydrate includes cellulose and related materials which are now collectively called 'dietary fibre'. In the nutritional labelling of foods carbohydrate components may be listed separately as sugar content and starch content or classed together as available carbohydrate, unavailable carbohydrate is usually referred to as 'dietary fibre' or 'roughage'. Lack of dietary fibre is now recognised as being a major factor in many diseases associated with an affluent Western society (see Sect. 1.5.1) but virtually unknown in less developed countries with high-fibre diets. Dietary fibre is of major importance to health and we are now urged to increase the amount of fibre in our diet. In addition, many everyday products, e.g. breakfast cereals, spaghetti and crisps, are currently being produced to different specifications so that high-fibre versions are available.

1.2 CHEMICAL COMPOSITION

The term 'carbohydrate' literally means 'hydrate of carbon' and most carbohydrates have the formula $C_x(H_2O)_y$. Hence, the ratio of hydrogen to oxygen in the molecule is 2 : 1. Available carbo-hydrates can be broken down to produce 16 kJ/g (3.8 kcal/g). For the purposes of investigation carbohydrates can be divided into three main structural groups: monosaccharides, disaccharides and oligosaccharides, and polysaccharides.

1. *Monosaccharides*, literally, single sugar units: sugars in which all the carbon atoms are joined by direct carbon–carbon bonds often in the form of a ring. Monosaccharides can be classified according to the number of carbon atoms in the molecule: trioses containing three carbon atoms are the simplest; tetroses have four carbon atoms; pentoses, important in nucleic acids, have five carbon atoms; hexoses, e.g. glucose, fructose and galactose, have six carbon atoms and are most important in food (see Fig. 1.1); heptoses have seven carbon atoms.

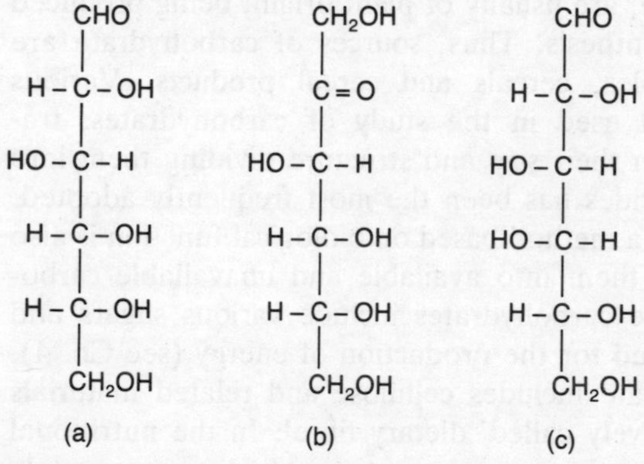

```
      CHO              CH₂OH              CHO
       |                 |                 |
  H – C – OH            C = O         H – C – OH
       |                 |                 |
  HO – C – H        HO – C – H       HO – C – H
       |                 |                 |
  H – C – OH        H – C – OH       HO – C – H
       |                 |                 |
  H – C – OH        H – C – OH       H – C – OH
       |                 |                 |
     CH₂OH             CH₂OH            CH₂OH

      (a)               (b)               (c)
```

FIG. 1.1 Common monosaccharides in foods: (a) glucose (b) fructose (c) galactose
Compare this 'straight chain' representation with the 'ring structures' used in Fig. 1.2

2. *Disaccharides and oligosaccharides*, sugars consisting of between two and ten monosaccharide units. Two monosaccharide monomers can link together by an oxygen bridge, and water is eliminated during the reaction producing a disaccharide (see Fig. 1.2). This type of reaction is a 'condensation' reaction. The three most commonly occurring disaccharides in foods are sucrose, maltose and lactose. Sucrose is composed of one glucose and one fructose unit, maltose is a disaccharide composed of two glucose units, and lactose consists of one glucose and one galactose unit (see Fig. 1.2). All sugars (mono- and disaccharides) are white crystalline compounds, soluble in water (especially when heated). Although all sugars are sweet they do not all have the same degree of sweetness (see Table 1.1).

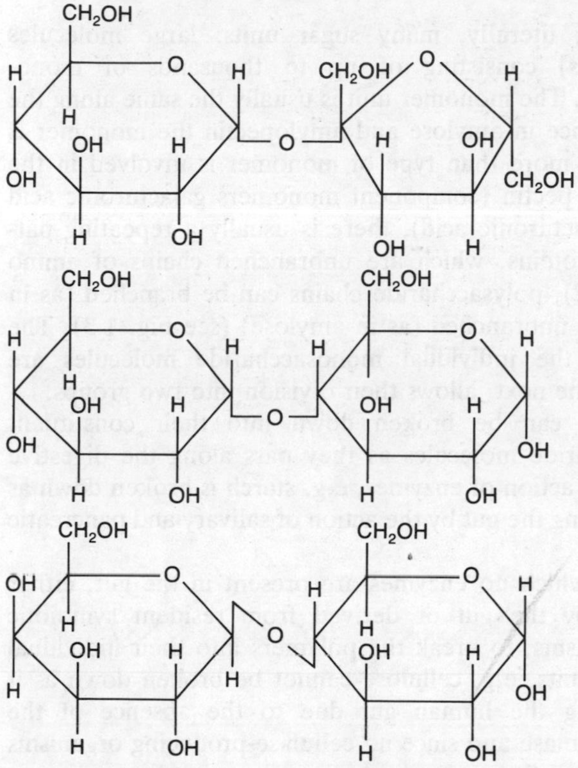

FIG. 1.2 Common disaccharides in foods: (a) sucrose: glucose-fructose
(b) maltose: glucose-glucose (c) lactose: galactose-glucose

TABLE 1.1 Relative sweetness of sugars and other sweeteners based on sucrose as 100

Sweetener	Relative Sweetness
Lactose	16
Maltose	33
Sorbitol	50
Glucose	70
Sucrose	100
Invert sugar	100
Xylitol	100
Fructose	120
Sodium cyclamate	3 000
Aspartame	18 000
Saccharin	40 000
Talin	250 000

3. *Polysaccharides*, literally, many sugar units: large molecules (macromolecules) consisting of up to thousands of monosaccharide units. The monomer unit is usually the same along the chain, for instance in amylose and amylopectin the monomer is glucose. Where more than type of monomer is involved in the molecule, as in pectin (component monomers galacturonic acid and methyl galacturonic acid), there is usually a repeating pattern. Unlike proteins, which are unbranched chains of amino acids (see Ch. 2), polysaccharide chains can be branched (as in amylopectin) or unbranched (as in amylose) (see Fig. 1.3). The way in which the individual monosaccharide molecules are linked, one to the next, allows their division into two groups:

(a) Those that can be broken down into their constituent monosaccharide molecules as they pass along the digestive tract by the action of enzymes, e.g. starch is broken down as it passes along the gut by the action of salivary and pancreatic amylase.

(b) Those for which no enzymes are present in the gut, either produced by the gut or derived from resident symbiotic microorganisms, to break the polymers into their individual monomer units, e.g. cellulose cannot be broken down as it passes along the human gut due to the absence of the enzyme cellulase and since no cellulase-producing organisms are harboured there.

glucose monomer

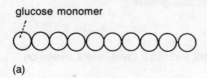

(a)

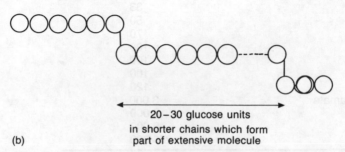

20–30 glucose units
in shorter chains which form
(b)   part of extensive molecule

FIG. 1.3 Polysaccharides: (a) amylose – straight chain of 70–350 glucose units – unbranched (b) amylopectin – branched chain of up to 100 000 units

Polysaccharides are large, non-crystalline molecules, insoluble in water and tasteless. Enzymic degradation decreases the size of the molecule resulting in the formation of sugars which can be absorbed across the wall of the gut and utilised for energy production by the body. There are, therefore, two important groups – available and unavailable polysaccharides. In addition, polysaccharides contribute to the textural properties of food (see starch and pectin, Sect. 1.3.3).

1.3 CARBOHYDRATES IN FOODS

1.3.1 MONOSACCHARIDES

The monosaccharides of greatest importance in foods are the hexoses – glucose and fructose.

1. *Glucose*, is also known as 'dextrose' or 'grape sugar'. As its name suggests it is found in grapes but also occurs in other fruits, honey (35 per cent) and to a lesser extent in some vegetables such as young peas and carrots. Glucose health drinks, which are prepared by hydrolysis of starch (and so contain glucose and other carbohydrates) are widely available and are used as energy supplements during illness and convalescence. Glucose sweets are used by athletes as a readily absorbable source of energy. In a combined form glucose is found in a number of polysaccharides.

2. *Fructose*, also called 'laevulose' or 'fruit sugar', has the same chemical formula as glucose but is its isomer (i.e. it contains a different structural arrangement of the atoms). Fructose is often associated with glucose in fruit and is also an important constituent of honey. It is sweeter than glucose and for this reason in some glucose syrups, glucose is enzymically converted to fructose to make the syrup sweeter. Some of these products are used in soft drinks.

3. *Galactose*, is another isomer of glucose. It is not important in the monosaccharide form but when combined with glucose it forms the disaccharide lactose (see Sect. 1.3.2).

4. *Sorbitol* is produced commercially by hydrogenation of glucose. It is absorbed from the gut much more slowly than glucose and although it is converted to glucose the blood glucose level does not rise as quickly. Sorbitol is widely used in the preparation of diabetic products such as jams, marmalade, tinned fruits, fruit drinks and chocolates.

5. *Inositol* is found in phytic acid which is present in cereal grains.

Phytic acid reacts with calcium and iron in the gut to reduce their absorption and hence availability from cereal products (see also Sect. 6.1).

1.3.2 DISACCHARIDES IN FOODS

The common disaccharides in foods are sucrose, lactose and maltose.

Sucrose

When most members of the public talk about 'sugar' they mean the disaccharide 'sucrose'. Sucrose, table, cane or beet sugar, is widely distributed in the plant kingdom, and can be purchased in many forms, both liquid and crystalline, at varying degrees of purity. Granulated sugar, castor sugar and icing sugar represent very pure forms of sucrose (see Table 1.2), whereas brown sugars are less highly extracted. In its most refined form sugar is the nearest thing to a pure chemical used in catering. A book entitled *Pure, White and Deadly* has been written about sugar by John Yudkin. Sucrose is the most widely used sugar in the food industry for sweetening and cooking with over 2 million tonnes being used per annum in Britain. About 33 per cent of this is derived from home-grown sugar beet. Approximately half of the sugar consumed is added to foods by the consumer, the other half added by manufacturers during processing (e.g. baked beans, All Bran, as well as confectionery items). Sugar not only sweetens products, it also helps to preserve foods, gives 'body' to foods and soft drinks. Many products to which sugar is added are not overtly sweet. The sugar we consume unknowingly as part of manufactured products is known as 'hidden sugar'. Food manufacturers are now being urged to show the content of sucrose and other sugars on product labels and while currently this practice is voluntary, it may well become a statutory

TABLE 1.2 Energy, iron and calcium provision of different sugars

Sugar	Energy (kcal)	Iron (mg/100 g)	Calcium (mg/100 g)
White: granulated	395	Trace	2
castor	395	Trace	2
icing	395	Trace	2
Demerara sugar	395	0.9	50
Muscovado	375	5	150
Golden syrup	300	1.5	25
Black treacle	260	9	400

TABLE 1.3 Sucrose content of some common foods

Food	Sucrose content (g)
Slice of cake (50 g)	25
Sweets (100 g)	60
Mars bar (65 g)	33
Ice-cream (one scoop)	12
Soft drink (330 cm^3 can)	25
Sugar (heaped teaspoon)	8

requirement before long (see Ch. 15). The sucrose content of some common foods is shown in Table 1.3.

As a sweetening agent sucrose has certain advantages and disadvantages when compared to others. Relative to other compounds sucrose is not that sweet (see Table 1.1) and is sometimes described as a 'bulk sweetener'. This is an advantage when it contributes to the physical properties of food but a disadvantage for calorie counters or healthy eaters. Because sucrose contributes calories it is described as a 'nutritive sweetener'. However, apart from calories, sugar has no other nutritive functions and they are thus described as 'empty calories' (see Sect. 4.6.1). Sweetening agents, e.g. saccharin, have no nutritive properties (hence the term 'non-nutritive sweeteners') and may be termed 'intense sweeteners' when much sweeter than sucrose. Some of these alternatives may not have exactly the same 'sweet taste' as sucrose. Saccharin has a bitter after-taste; thaumatin although intensely sweet, is slow to be detected.

Inversion of sucrose

Sucrose can be hydrolysed, or inverted, by boiling with acids or alkalis or by the action of the enzyme sucrase to produce invert sugar. Invert sugar naturally occurs in honey and is produced in jams during the boiling of sugar with fruit (due to their high acid content). Because sucrose contains one molecule of glucose and one molecule of fructose, inversion of sucrose produces an equimolar mixture of glucose and fructose. Invert sugar is sweeter and more soluble in water than sucrose due to the fructose content and can be used to control the texture of sweets, to control the crystallisation of sucrose and to modify equilibrium relative humidity (see below). These properties are important in the production of both jams and boiled sweets.

In jams, which must by law contain not less than 68.5 per cent soluble solids unless sold hermetically sealed, the sucrose : invert sugar ratio should be 1 : 1 and is carefully controlled to ensure maximum solubility and thus preserving properties. If too much sucrose is present the crystallisation of sucrose takes place; too much invert sugar and glucose crystallises. In commercial jam-making, invert sugar and sucrose are added to the fruit in the required proportions.

Hard-boiled sweets are another product in which invert sugar plays an important role. These are highly viscous, supercooled liquids. In order to prevent crystallisation of sugar on the surface of the sweet and deterioration of the product, a 'doctor', e.g. invert sugar or glucose syrup, is added at about 30 per cent. The 'doctor' increases solubility and reduces the hygroscopic proper-ties of sucrose. The hygroscopic properties of the product are known as the equilibrium relative humidity (ERH). If the ERH of a product equals the relative humidity then there is no loss or gain of moisture. If ERH is lower than the prevailing relative humidity, which is the usual problem with boiled sweets, then there is a gain of water and crystallisation takes place. The use of invert sugar increases the ERH of the product and reduces hygroscopicity. In very humid atmospheres glucose syrup is used in place of invert sugar.

Lactose
Milk sugar with its 'cool' taste, is only 16 per cent as sweet as sucrose. Cow's milk contains 4.5–5.5 per cent lactose, human milk 5.5–8.0 per cent. In milk, lactose is very easily converted by bacterial action to lactic acid (see Sect. 10.5.1) which gives the unpleasant taste and low pH to sour milk resulting in the curdling of milk protein.

Maltose
Malt sugar is produced by the action of amylase on starch. This reaction occurs both in the gut during digestion of starch and in the production of malt for brewing (see Sect. 10.4.1).

Syrups
Syrups are solutions of sugar in water, and depending on the concentration of sugar, vary in viscosity. Syrupy solutions with a high osmotic pressure can be flavoured with fruit or other extracts and used as cordials and squashes, or in the preservation of foods.

Perhaps the most familiar syrup is molasses, i.e. sucrose syrup formed as a by-product of sugar refining. Molasses has a distinctive flavour and in addition to sucrose contains certain trace elements, notably iron (see Table 1.2). Sucrose syrups from other sources include maple syrup from America and Canada.

Glucose syrups, made from hydrolysed maize or corn starch are finding increasing use in the food industry, replacing sucrose. This is due to their reduced tendency to crystallise out (see above, Inversion of sucrose). The action of heat and enzymes on the starch brings about hydrolysis resulting in sweet colourless liquids which vary in composition depending upon the degree of hydrolysis. Chemically they contain dextrins, maltose and glucose, the extent of hydrolysis being expressed by the amount of glucose or dextrose equivalent (DE). Syrups with a low DE contain little glucose, those with a high DE a lot. Increasing use is being made of glucose – fructose syrups where the glucose is converted by an isomerase enzyme into fructose (high-fructose corn syrup, HFCS).

Honey is a natural syrup and was widely used for sweetening before sugar extracts and refining became common. The main differences between various honeys are due to colour and flavour components extracted by the bees from the original flower source. Chemically, honeys contain about 20 per cent water, 65 per cent monosaccharides (mainly fructose and glucose), about 13 per cent disaccharides (mainly sucrose), and small amounts of wax, proteins, vitamins and minerals.

On a weight-for-weight basis honey (being 20 per cent water) is lower in energy value than sucrose and its high fructose content gives it marked sweetness.

1.3.3 POLYSACCHARIDES IN FOODS

The unavailable carbohydrates, alternatively known as 'dietary fibre', will be considered in Sect. 1.5.1. A wide range of polysaccharides are contained in foods and of these starches and pectin are of major importance to the textural properties of foods.

Starch
Starch is the storage polysaccharide of plants and enables storage of glucose with minimal effect on the osmotic pressure. Starch can be broken down to release glucose which can be used for energy production when required. It is typically found in seeds (especially cereals), roots, some stems (potatoes) and unripe fruit. Starch is not just one compound but is made up of two different polysaccharides, amylose and amylopectin, both based on glucose. Amylose consists of an unbranched chain of glucose units coiled in the form of a helix. Amylopectin is larger in size (i.e. it has more glucose units)

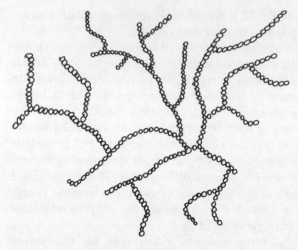

FIG. 1.4 Complex branched structure of part of an amylopectin molecule

and consists of large numbers of short connected chains forming a branched tree-like structure (see Fig. 1.4).

Amylose and amylopectin are neatly packed away for storage in the form of starch granules. Starch granules from different sources can be distinguished by their shape and size when examined under a microscope: potato starch granules are relatively large (about 100 µm) and rice granules relatively small (6–9 µm).

Gelatinisation of starch

Starch granules are relatively insoluble in water due to close packaging of molecules near their surface. Mixing the starch with water and heating results in the absorption of about 25–30 per cent water by weight. As the temperature approaches 60–70 °C the starch granules swell and take up a large amount of water, from three to ten times their own weight, although they still remain separate from each other. As the temperature continues to rise the uptake of water increases, to up to twenty times the weight of the starch until in the end the starch granule ruptures and spills its contents out into the surrounding fluid and the mixture becomes highly viscous. The starch paste is thus converted from a sol into a gel and the individual starch granules can no longer be differentiated. The actual viscosity of the gel depends on a number of factors. Cooling of the gel increases viscosity, e.g. thick custard and blancmange which set on cooling. Gel formation occurs through the trapping of water between the widely dispersed starch chains.

Factors affecting starch gels

Gelatinisation of starch is used in a variety of food products for two primary purposes – either as a thickening agent or as a gelling (solidifying agent). A variety of factors influence the strength of gelatinisation and these must be considered in relation to the overall desired effect.

1. *Type of starch used.* The ratio of amylose to amylopectin varies between starches and this is important because amylose enhances gelling by forming a more regular network in the gel. Hence high-amylose starches are used where a rigid gel is required. Low-amylose starches are used for thickening (as in gravy, sauces, etc.).

2. *Ratio of starch to water in the initial mixture.* Compare thick and thin custard.

3. *Sugar.* If sugar is added to the mixture, gelatinisation is modified, the sugar competing with the starch for water. The result is a more tender and less solid gel with syrup bound up in the starch network. Found in blancmange, vanilla and custard puddings.

4. *pH.* In puddings where acid is added e.g. in fruit puddings, gelatinisation is also affected, tending to form a viscous paste rather than a proper gel. This is caused by the acid hydrolysis of the starch to smaller polysaccharide fragments.

5. *Fat.* The presence of fat modifies the process of gelatinisation. The first step in the production of sauces is to form a roux by blending fat, or a commodity containing fat, with flour while heating. The whole process has to be carried out carefully to produce an appealing (and mobile) product. Uneven distribution of heat leads to uneven gelatinisation of the starch molecules and the formation of lumps. The fat helps to control the gelatinisation of the starch molecules by coating the granules. In the making of sauces, a stiff gel is not needed and low-amylose starches can be used.

6. *Stability.* On standing, starch gels contract, due to partial recoiling of the molecules, a process known as 'retrogradation'. As this occurs, water is lost from the gel and is known as 'syneresis' (weeping). Although amylose starches form gels more readily they tend to be unstable whereas high-amylopectin gels are more stable. This is important where starch bread products have to be stored and is of particular consequence in cook freeze catering (see Sect. 13.5.2). Here traditional recipes may need to be altered with the substitution of high-amylopectin starches (usually chemically, modified starch).

Gelatinised starch is easier to digest as it presents a more open structure for enzymic action and has smoother, more pleasing textural properties than the gritty texture of ungelatinised starch. 'Instant' products such as desserts and custard mixes are produced using gelatinised starches which have been dried. These powders gelatinise without heat treatment on the addition of water or milk.

Dextrinisation of starch

Dry roasting of starch produces low-viscosity, highly water-soluble decomposition products called 'dextrins'. On heating, these polymerise to form polydextrin which contributes to the brown crust of breads during baking and produces the pleasant flavours and colour associated with baked bread (see Sect. 10.3) as well as in malting.

Pectin

Pectin is the name given to a group of complex polysaccharides composed of galacturonic acid and methyl galacturonic acid monomers and found in fruits and vegetables as a structural material. During ripening or cooking pectin is converted into less acid breakdown products (contributing to the softer nature of ripe fruits). Pectin is also found in grapes and separated out in fermentation giving rise to an undesirable haze which may be difficult to remove.

Pectins are very important in the production of sugar – acid gels as found in jams and jellies. The gelling power of a pectin depends upon the percentage of pectin in the final mixture, the molecular weight of the pectin, the proportion of methyl galacturonic acid in the pectin, the amount of sugar and the pH of the product. Jams should be firm enough to maintain their shape on standing but soft enough to spread on bread and other products. About 1 per cent pectin will produce satisfactory firmness. Apples and quinces are fruits which produce particularly good pectin gels thus apples are often used as ingredient in fruit jams and apple pectin extracts are sold commercially for jam-making. Sugar is required for gel formation at a level of about 65 per cent. As mentioned above (see Inversion of sucrose, Sect. 1.3.2) some of the sugar has to be inverted to maximise solubility. Pectins form gels at pH 3.5 and below. Underripe fruit has a lower pH than ripe fruit and produces better jams and jellies. As the pH decreases equally firm gels can be produced with lower proportions of pectin. The use of citrus fruits in marmalade allows the production of very firm gels due to the low pH.

Glycogen
This is another polymer of glucose but of animal origin. It acts as an energy storage form of glucose and is especially found in liver and muscle tissue. It has an important role in muscle tissue in determining the quality of meat (see Sect. 2.6.3).

Cellulose
Another polymer of glucose found as structural material in plant cell walls, is important in dietary fibre (see Sect. 1.5.1).

1.4 BROWNING REACTIONS OF CARBOHYDRATES IN FOODS

1.4.1 MAILLARD REACTION – NON-ENZYMIC BROWNING REACTIONS

Non-enzymic browning reactions were first studied by Maillard in 1912 who observed that a brown coloration was produced when a solution of glucose was heated with the amino acid glycine. The reaction between the amino group, either of a free amino acid or a free amino group projecting from a protein, and the carbonyl (C=O) carbon of a reducing sugar, e.g. glucose, is known as the 'Maillard reaction' or 'non-enzymic browning'. The reaction is very complex and is not completely understood but eventually results in the formation of uncharacterised brown pigmented polymers. Nutritionally the Maillard reaction is important because certain essential amino acids (see Sect. 2.7), particularly lysine, take part and the products formed cannot be broken down by digestive enzymes and are thus rendered unavailable and of lower biological value (see Sect. 2.7.1). Foods containing free amino acids and sugars, such as cakes and puddings, are particularly susceptible and their nutritional value in terms of the availability of essential amino acids is reduced. However, the brown colour can enhance the appeal of foods such as cakes and puddings and its formation may be actively encouraged, e.g. by the use of an egg wash on baked goods.

1.4.2 CARAMELISATION

Caramelisation involves the degradation of sugars in the absence of amino acids and proteins. If sugars are heated above their melting points they darken to give a brown colour. Caramel is a very useful food colouring material and is used for the colouring of spirits such as whisky. Flavour changes also take place and although caramelisation can produce pleasant flavours used for the production of sweets and for desserts such as crème caramel, burned and bitter-tasting products can result if caramelisation is not carefully controlled.

1.5 CARBOHYDRATES AND HEALTH

1.5.1 DIETARY FIBRE

As mentioned earlier some carbohydrates, e.g. cellulose, cannot be digested as they pass along the gut and their energy remains unavailable to the body. Unavailable carbohydrates, and related polymeric compounds such as lignin which resist enzymic degradation in the gut, are classed together as 'dietary fibre'. Dietary fibre has been defined as a mixture of cellulose, non-cellulosic polysaccharides (e.g. pectin) and lignin (which is responsible for woodiness in plants) which is not digested by the endogenous enzymes of the gut. Although these compounds do not contribute nutritionally, they form an important component of diets. Modern Western diets which utilise highly refined carbohydrate products are termed 'fibre-depleted diets' and have been associated with a number of diseases of Western society, these are virtually unknown in communities eating more natural, less refined carbohydrate products. It is only in the last 150 years that milling of cereals has developed sufficiently for the large-scale production of low-extraction white flours. Until then highly refined products were extremely expensive and were only used by the rich. The introduction of steel rollers in place of the stone ones formerly used, and the improvement of steel meshes for the sieving of flours, allowed the more widespread use of low-extraction flours:

$$\text{Extraction rate} = \frac{\text{weight of flour produced}}{\text{weight of cereal grain used}} \times 100$$

The parts of the cereal grain removed (see Fig. 1.5) termed 'bran', are rich in dietary fibre. Thus the production of low-extraction flours reduces fibre content. A comparison of the fibre contents of various extraction rate flours is shown in Table 1.4. The reduction in the fibre content of the British diet over the last 150 years can be directly related to changes in the availability and use of low-extraction flours.

Dietary fibre can be divided into two groups, the water-insoluble fibres, which predominate in brans, cereal products and fibrous

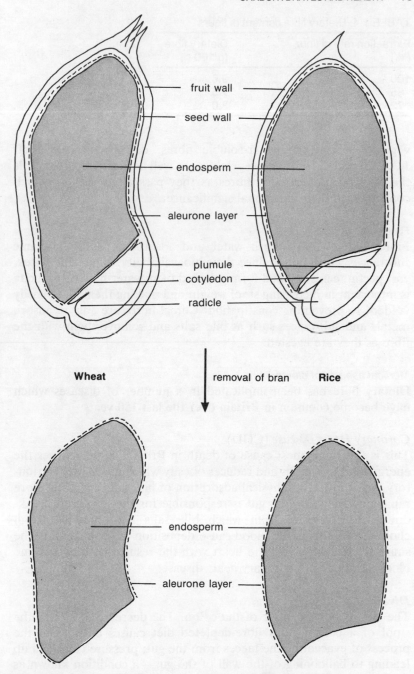

fruit wall

seed wall

endosperm

aleurone layer

plumule
cotyledon
radicle

Wheat   removal of bran   **Rice**

endosperm

aleurone layer

FIG. 1.5 Parts of cereal grains removed during refining

TABLE 1.4 Dietary fibre content of flours

Extraction rate of flour (%)	Dietary fibre (g/100 g)
100	9.6
85	7.5
72	3.0

vegetables, and the water-soluble fibres, e.g. pectin (see Sect. 1.3.3), found in fruits and vegetables, as well as pulses and oats. It is the physical properties of fibres as they pass along the gut which contribute to their nutritional significance.

Properties of dietary fibre
Fibres are able to absorb water and adsorb metals and organic substances which may reduce their bioavailability. Vegetable fibres, e.g. pectin, can swell and form gels and their water-holding capacity is important in increasing stool weight and making them more easily voided, so preventing constipation. Cereal fibres are able to adsorb metals and substances such as bile salts and remove them with the fibre as they are egested.

Medical aspects of dietary fibre
Dietary fibre has been implicated in a number of diseases which have become common in Britain over the last 150 years.

Coronary Heart Disease (CHD)
This is the commonest cause of death in Britain. Fibre reduces the energy intake of foods and reduces obesity which may be a contributory factor in CHD. Physical adsorption of bile salts and their more rapid removal from the gut is responsible for the increased breakdown of cholesterol from which bile salts are produced. High cholesterol levels in the blood cause deposition of cholesterol in the small arteries supplying the heart with the result that they become blocked, leading to coronary heart disease.

Diverticular disease
The commonest disorder of the colon. The decrease in size of the stool of a person on a fibre-depleted diet causes changes in the process of evacuating the faeces from the gut; pressure can build up leading to ballooning of the wall of the gut – a condition known as 'diverticulosis' (see Fig. 1.6). Infection of the diverticuli leads to diverticulitis.

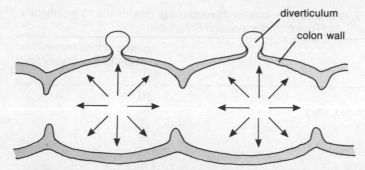

FIG. 1.6 Diverticulosis. Small faecal volume due to low-fibre diets, allows excessive segmentation of the colon. Build up of pressure force small balloon-shaped diverticula to form between the muscle fibres of the colon wall

Large bowel cancer

The most frequent cause of cancer in North America and the second most common cause in Britain. Dietary fibre sweeps away poisonous substances – implicated as carcinogens – which are produced in the large bowel by the decomposition of bile salts.

Diabetes

The commonest endocrine disorder. It is thought that dietary fibre reduces the rate of absorption of sucrose and other sugars from the gut and so minimises the massive rise in blood sugar level which occurs after a meal.

Obesity

The most general nutritional disorder in Britain where about one in fifteen persons are obese (i.e. more than 20 per cent above their ideal body weight for height). Decrease in fibre intakes results in more compact, less satisfying diets. Increases in energy intake result in increases in bodyweight.

Constipation

This is associated with a reduction in dietary fibre intake. Difficulty in voiding faeces results in straining at stool and a whole range of 'straining' diseases, e.g. haemorrhoids and varicose veins.

Sources of dietary fibre

Whole cereal grains, fruits and vegetables are rich sources of dietary fibre. It is estimated that the average fibre intake in Britain is 20 g/day and that for better health this should be increased to 30 g per day. A list of the amounts of various foods which would supply

TABLE 1.5 Amounts of various foods required to provide the 10 g of dietary fibre missing each day from the average British diet

Food	Amount of food required to provide 10 g of dietary fibre (g)
Bran	23
Apricots (dried, raw)	42
Rye bread	72
Peanuts	108
Wholemeal bread	117
Brown bread	196
Hovis bread	217
Carrots (cooked)	270
Runner bean (cooked)	298
Brussels sprouts (cooked)	349
White bread	370
Strawberries	472
Potatoes (baked in their jackets)	500
Tomatoes	735

the missing 10 g of fibre per day are shown in Table 1.5. Tips for increasing fibre intake include:

1. Change from white to wholemeal bread or high-fibre white bread.
2. Eat more high-fibre, whole-grain breakfast cereals.
3. Eat more high-fibre, whole cereal grains, e.g. brown rice, pasta, etc. Note, these may take longer to cook.
4. Use wholemeal flour in baking.
5. Eat more unpeeled fresh fruit and vegetables, e.g. baked potatoes.
6. Eat more dried fruits, e.g. dates, raisins. These can be mixed in with breakfast cereals.
7. Eat more pulse vegetables, e.g. peas, beans, lentils.

1.5.2 SUGAR

The sugar we consciously add to foods varies enormously from person to person. Those with a 'sweet tooth' may add vast amounts of sugar to breakfast cereals and beverages such as tea and coffee, others may use sugar very sparingly. Each teaspoonful of sugar supplies 8 g of sucrose. On average in Britain 2500 cups of tea and 750 cups of coffee are consumed per person per year. If two teaspoons of sugar are added to each cup then sucrose intake in tea and coffee alone is about 150 g/day. This amount of sucrose will increase the energy intake by 2400 kJ (574 kcal) per day. The significance of this energy for an individual in terms of bodyweight will obviously depend upon energy balance (see Ch. 4). Current healthy eating policies (see Sect. 7.3) recommend a reduction of 50 per cent in the amount of sugar consumed.

High sugar intakes are implicated in various diet-related diseases. Some, e.g. dental caries (tooth decay), are fairly obviously sugar-related. Others, e.g. obesity, coronary heart disease and diabetes, can also be caused by other dietary factors such as high fat intakes and low dietary fibre intakes, and therefore to point a finger at sugar alone is misleading. Even in dental caries, the form and frequency at which sugar is taken is very important. It is the long-term or frequent contact of sugar with the teeth, e.g. by sucking great quantities of sticky sweets or the use of syrups in babies dummies, which causes the problems.

For various reasons (e.g. bodyweight control and slimming regimes, diabetes, etc.) persons who wish to sweeten their foods may need to avoid the use of sucrose and other sugars (from which energy can also be derived) as sweetening agents. There are a whole range of alternative non-sugar sweetening agents, or artificial sweeteners, available. These do not produce dental caries, obesity or any of the other problems associated with a high sugar intake. The question mark of toxicity hangs over some of these alternatives, and one such sweetener cyclamate was banned as a sweetening agent in foods.

QUESTIONS

1. The following are the names of six sugars: lactose, glucose, galactose, fructose, sucrose, maltose.
   (a) Which one is the sweetest? ←
   (b) Which one is found in milk? ∟
   (c) Which one is grape sugar? G
   (d) Which one is household sugar? S
   (e) Which one is important in brewing? M
   (f) Name two that are disaccharides. S M
   (g) Name two that are monosaccharides. G F
   (h) Which sugar is obtained from sugar beet? S
2. (a) What is meant by the terms: (i) 'available carbohydrate', (ii) 'unavailable carbohydrate'?
   (b) Give an example of each.
   (c) By what other name is unavailable carbohydrate known and why is it important to include a proportion in the diet?

D. Fibre

    (d) Which foods would you include in menus to ensure that your diet is adequate in unavailable carbohydrate?

3. (a) What is meant by the term 'gelatinisation of starch'.
   (b) How do pectin gels differ from starch gels.
   (c) How do fruit acids affect each type of gel.
   (d) Name products in which each type of gel is important.

4. (a) Distinguish between the terms 'bulk sweetener' and 'intense sweetener'.
   (b) Name one example of each.
   (c) List three advantages of using sucrose as a sweetening agent and one disadvantage.
   (d) Describe the importance of invert sugar in the food industry.

2

PROTEINS

2.1 INTRODUCTION

The term 'protein' comes from the Greek (*proteus*) and means 'to come first' referring to its importance in the structure of body cells. Proteins are natural polymers, made up of monomers called 'amino acids' and are essential components of the human diet. During digestion, proteins are broken down to yield their constituent amino acids which are absorbed and then reassembled to form those proteins needed by the human body, e.g. for muscles, enzymes, etc.

2.2 CHEMICAL STRUCTURE OF AMINO ACIDS

There are about twenty different commonly occurring amino acids. They are all organic acids containing the elements carbon (C), hydrogen (H), oxygen (O) and nitrogen (N) – in addition some contain sulphur (S). Within each amino acid there is an amino group ($-NH_2$), a carboxylic acid group ($-COOH$) and a hydrogen atom attached to a central carbon atom. The final bond of the carbon atom is attached to a fourth group (usually designated $-R$) and is different for each amino acid (see Fig. 2.1a). Each of the twenty

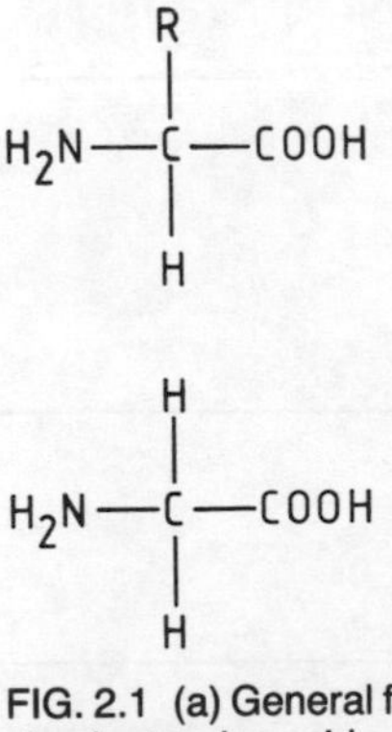

$$H_2N-\overset{\overset{\displaystyle R}{|}}{\underset{\underset{\displaystyle H}{|}}{C}}-COOH$$

$$H_2N-\overset{\overset{\displaystyle H}{|}}{\underset{\underset{\displaystyle H}{|}}{C}}-COOH$$

FIG. 2.1 (a) General formula of amino acids (b) aminoacetic acid (glycine), the simplest amino acid

Amino acid	Structure	Essential?
GLYCINE	HO—C(=O)—C(H)(NH₂)—H	NO
ALANINE	HO—C(=O)—C(H)(NH₂)—CH₃	NO
VALINE	HO—C(=O)—C(H)(NH₂)—C(H)(CH₃)—CH₃	YES
ISOLEUCINE	HO—C(=O)—C(H)(NH₂)—C(H)(CH₃)—C(H)(H)—CH₃	YES
LEUCINE	HO—C(=O)—C(H)(NH₂)—C(H)(H)—C(H)(CH₃)—CH₃	YES
PROLINE	HO—C(=O)—C(H)—C(H)—C(H)—H (ring with N—H)	NO
PHENYLALANINE	HO—C(=O)—C(H)(NH₂)—C(H)(H)—C₆H₅	YES
TYROSINE	HO—C(=O)—C(H)(NH₂)—C(H)(H)—C₆H₄—OH	NO
TRYPTOPHAN	HO—C(=O)—C(H)(NH₂)—C(H)(H)—H (indole ring)	YES
SERINE	HO—C(=O)—C(H)(NH₂)—C(H)(OH)—H	NO

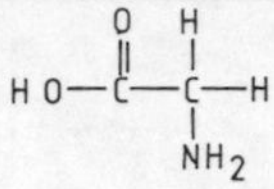

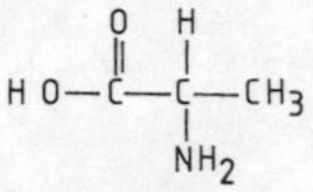

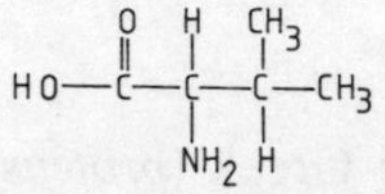

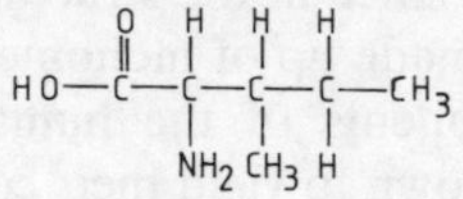

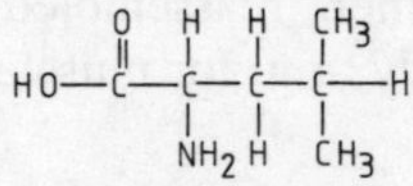

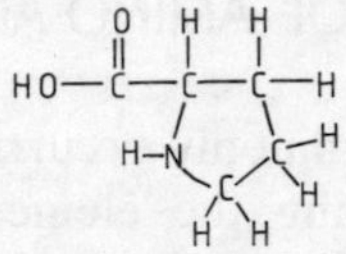

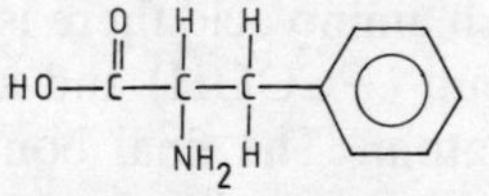

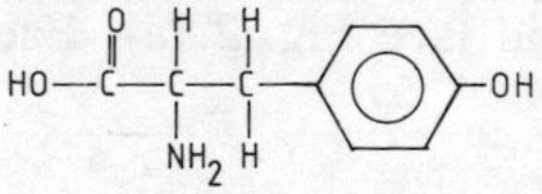

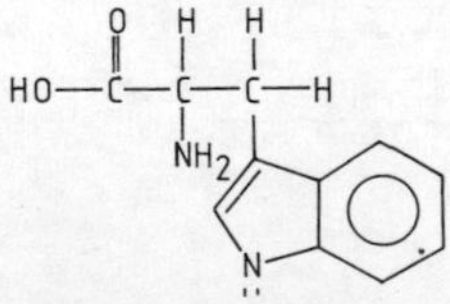

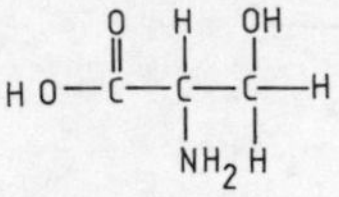

FIG. 2.2 Amino acids

Amino acid	Structure	Essential?
THREONINE	HO—C(=O)—C(H)(NH₂)—C(OH)(CH₃)—H	YES
ASPARTIC ACID	HO—C(=O)—C(H)(NH₂)—C(H)(H)—C(=O)—OH	NO
GLUTAMIC ACID	HO—C(=O)—C(H)(NH₂)—C(H)(H)—C(H)(H)—C(=O)—OH	NO
ASPARAGINE	HO—C(=O)—C(H)(NH₂)—C(H)(H)—C(=O)—NH₂	NO
GLUTAMINE	HO—C(=O)—C(H)(NH₂)—C(H)(H)—C(H)(H)—C(=O)—NH₂	NO
CYSTEINE	HO—C(=O)—C(H)(NH₂)—C(H)(H)—S—H	NO
METHIONINE	HO—C(=O)—C(H)(NH₂)—C(H)(H)—C(H)(H)—S—C(H)(H)—H	YES
HISTIDINE	HO—C(=O)—C(H)(NH₂)—C(H)(H)—(imidazole ring)	YES, in children
LYSINE	HO—C(=O)—C(H)(NH₂)—C(H)(H)—C(H)(H)—C(H)(H)—C(H)(H)—NH₃⁺	YES
ARGININE	HO—C(=O)—C(H)(NH₂)—C(H)(H)—C(H)(H)—C(H)(H)—N—C(NH₂)=NH₂⁺	YES, in children

FIG. 2.2 contd

commonly occurring amino acids contains a different fourth group. In the simplest one, aminoacetic acid (glycine), the fourth group is a hydrogen atom (see Fig. 2.1b). The structures of the twenty different naturally occurring amino acids are shown in Fig. 2.2.

2.3   PEPTIDE LINKS

The amino group of one amino acid can react with the carboxylic acid group of a second amino acid producing a molecule consisting of two amino acid units linked by a peptide bond, a −CO−NH− link (see Fig. 2.3). This type of linking together with the release of a small molecule such as water is called a condensation reaction and in this case the molecule formed is called a dipeptide. At one end of the dipeptide is a carboxylic acid group and at the other end is an amino group capable of undergoing further reaction to increase the length of the amino acid chain. Thus molecules of increasing length (tri-, tetra-, pentapeptides) can be produced. Polypeptides (poly-many) consist of many amino acid groups linked by peptide link-

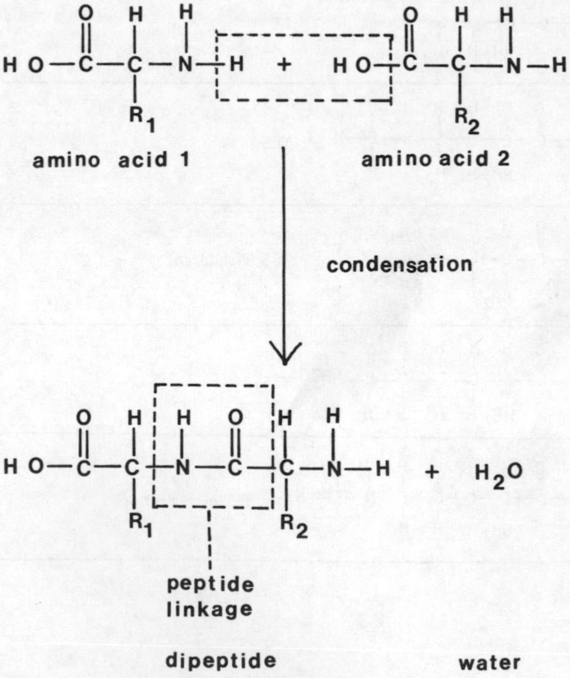

FIG. 2.3   The reaction of two amino acids to form a dipeptide

ages, the order and number of amino acid groups in the chain will obviously vary between different polypeptides.

A protein may consist of one or more than one polypeptide chain. Insulin, the hormone controlling blood glucose level, is one of the simplest proteins and consists of two polypeptide chains, one of 20 amino acids, the other of 31 amino acids, giving a total of 51 amino acids. Insulin was the first protein to have its amino acid sequence characterised (by Frederick Sanger in 1953). Most proteins are far more complex than insulin and consist of thousands of amino acid units. Keratin, the structural protein of skin, hair and nails, has its thousands of amino acid units arranged within three coiled polypeptide chains.

2.4   IMPORTANCE OF AMINO ACIDS AND PEPTIDES IN CATERING AND FOODS

In addition to their function as building blocks in proteins some amino acids and peptides play a vital role in their own right.

A significant amino acid in the body is glutamic acid – a dicarboxylic acid because it has not just one carboxylic acid group but two. L-Glutamic acid may be added to foods or can be converted into its sodium salt forming monosodium glutamate (MSG). Although this has a slight sweet – salt taste of its own, at low levels it acts as a flavour enhancer or intensifier. For this reason it is added to a large range of foods especially meat, fish and vegetable dishes to bring out their flavour, at concentrations between 0.1 and 0.3 per cent in convenience foods such as packet soups, pot noodles, potato snacks, etc. Although glutamate occurs widely in food proteins – meat, pulses, etc., and in the human body (approximately 20 per cent of body proteins), consumption of high levels may lead to illness. MSG is widely used in oriental cooking and it has been implicated as a cause of 'Chinese restaurant syndrome' – giving rise to nausea, headaches, dizziness and increased blood pressure. Moreover, its use in convenience foods is now so common that concern has been expressed. MSG in baby foods is banned, for it is feared that excessive use may be damaging to young infants.

One of the most important dipeptides is aspartame (trade name Candarel or Nutrasweet). This dipeptide consists of the amino acids aspartic acid and phenylalanine in a slightly modified form. Aspartame is approximately 100 times sweeter than sucrose and is now replacing saccharin as an artificial sweetener in a number of products. It was hoped that its 'natural' character might preclude the possibility of harmful side-effects. However, some claims have been made that toxic by-products may be formed on storage and doubts have been expressed concerning its use. Irrespective of toxicity claims it should not be consumed by children suffering from phenylketonuria (see Sect. 7.6.1). Aspartame is finding increasing use in confectionery, ice-cream, low-calorie desserts and soft drinks.

The tripeptide glutathione has a function in the transport of amino acids into cells, as an activator of certain enzymes and in the protection of lipids against rancidity (autooxidation) (see Sect. 3.4.2).

2.5 PROPERTIES OF PROTEINS

2.5.1 SHAPE

Proteins can be classified, on the basis of their shape into two groups: fibrous proteins and globular proteins.

Fibrous proteins
Examples are keratin in skin, fibrin in blood clots, myosin in muscles and elastin in connective tissue. Fibrous proteins are composed of polypeptide chains closely packed together, an arrangement which makes it difficult for water to penetrate. Thus, they are insoluble in water and are relatively unaffected by acids, alkalis or moderate heating. Fibrous proteins can be further sub-divided into elastic and non-elastic proteins.

Elastic proteins are polypeptide chains which are coiled like a spring and can be stretched into straight chains. The molecule will regain its original coiled shape when the stretching force is removed. Important elastic proteins include elastin, this is contained in the walls of arteries allowing them to stretch as blood passes through. In addition, it is found in connective tissue including ligaments which join bones together. Elastin is well suited to bearing sudden stress, although if this is too violent the ligament may not be elastic enough and will tear. Another fibrous elastic protein is gluten (see also Sect. 7.6), one of the proteins in dough which stretches as carbon dioxide accumulates in it to form pockets of gas. These pockets can be enlarged and 'set' by the action of heat giving the characteristic structure of leavened bread (see Sect. 10.3).

Non-elastic proteins occur naturally in an extended chain which resists stretching. These proteins provide great strength but no elasticity. Collagen is an important non-elastic protein found in tendons which attach muscles to bones and is thus like elastin found

associated with meat (see Sect. 2.6.3). Muscles contract and relax to pull on tendons so controlling the movements of bones.

Globular proteins

In contrast, globular proteins are soluble in water and are thus easily dispersed. The structure of a globular protein is far more complex than that of a fibrous protein with the polypeptide chains folded loosely to give a complex three-dimensional structure which is held in position by weak linkages. The protein is described as 'native' protein when it is held in this three-dimensional shape. Water easily penetrates the molecule and small changes in pH and temperature can disrupt the three-dimensional structure unfolding the chains – a process known as 'denaturation'. Most proteins in body cells are globular in nature, e.g. haemoglobin and myoglobin (see Fig. 2.4).

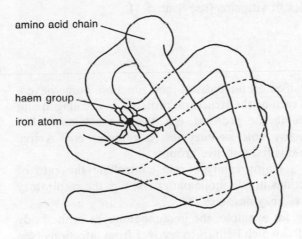

amino acid chain

haem group

iron atom

FIG. 2.4 The structure of a myoglobin molecule

2.5.2 CHEMICAL COMPOSITION

Some proteins contain only amino acid molecules and are termed 'simple proteins'. Others termed 'conjugated proteins', are linked to special groups, called 'prosthetic groups', e.g. lipids and carbohydrates, which give the molecule particular properties important in their biological activity. Thus the iron-containing part of the haemoglobin molecule is critical to its role in the transport of oxygen in the blood. Conjugated proteins are sub-divided on the nature of the prosthetic group.

1. *Lipoproteins*: proteins associated with a lipid molecule, usually a phospholipid, e.g. ovalbumin in egg (see Sect. 2.6.2).
2. *Glycoproteins*: a carbohydrate molecule is associated with protein, e.g. mucin in saliva and egg white (see Sect. 2.6.2).
3. *Nucleoproteins*.
4. *Metalloproteins*: contain metallic ions, e.g. Cu^{2+} and Zn^{2+}. Many enzymes have metallic ions as prosthetic groups, e.g. ascorbic acid oxidase, a copper-containing enzyme in plant tissues which oxidises ascorbic acid and thus reduces the vitamin C content of foods (see Sect. 5.4).
5. *Chromoproteins*: these proteins incorporate a coloured group which contains a metallic ion, e.g. haem in haemoglobin and myoglobin.
6. *Phosphoproteins*: contain phosphate groups, e.g. caseinogen in milk and vitellin in egg (see Sect. 2.6.1 and 2.6.2).
7. *Dehydrogenases*: contain coenzymes derived from the water-soluble B complex of vitamins (see Sect. 5.3).

2.5.3 FUNCTION

Proteins can be classified on the basis of their function. Some have a passive role in cells such as the structural proteins, e.g. collagen and keratin, and the membrane proteins, e.g. the lipoproteins. Other proteins play an active role as enzymes, hormones, etc. Active proteins can be sub-divided into five groups:
1. *Enzymes*: have a major catalytic role controlling the rate of biochemical reactions in metabolic pathways, e.g. the respiratory enzymes, digestive enzymes, etc.
2. *Immune proteins*: for example, the immunoglobulins in the body acting as antibodies which help us to recover from infections (see Sect. 12.10.2).
3. *Carrier or transport proteins*: the entry and exit of certain substances across the cell membrane is controlled by carrier molecules many of which are proteins. Haemoglobin transports oxygen in the blood.
4. *Regulatory proteins*: for example, the protein hormone insulin controls the level of sugar in the blood. The inability of a person to control their blood sugar level results in a condition known as diabetes. Individuals who are diabetic must carefully control their carbohydrate intake (see Sect. 7.6.1).
5. *Contractile proteins*: for example, actin and myosin the proteins in muscle which allow contraction of muscles (see Sect. 2.6.3).

2.5.4 NATIVE, DENATURED AND DERIVED PROTEINS

Native and Denatured protein
Protein which has not had its unique three-dimensional structure required for biological activity altered in any way by changes in pH or temperature is known as 'native protein'. As stated, proteins are complex interlinked three-dimensional structures and thus some of them are vulnerable to attack by heat, acids, salt and various chemicals which cause unfolding of the protein chain, a process called 'denaturation', resulting in a change of shape of the molecule. Denatured protein has had its three-dimensional structure altered but still possesses its full complement of amino acids and prosthetic groups. The change is usually irreversible and the protein becomes less soluble – the term 'coagulation' describes this loss of solubility. Denaturation can be caused by heat, as in cooking or blanching (see Sect. 11.4.2 for its use in denaturing spoilage enzymes). Cooking of protein foods should make them more digestible as a consequence of denaturation due to increased susceptibility to breakdown by digestive enzymes. Colour changes in meat on cooking are due to denaturation of myoglobin (see Sect. 2.6.3). Alteration of pH, as in the souring of milk by the development of lactic acid during cheese making (see Sect. 10.5.1) and in the addition of vinegar to eggs during poaching (see Sect. 2.6.2). Addition of salt to boiling and poaching eggs increases the rate of coagulation. Violent agitation in the beating of egg white can lead to denaturation (see Sect. 2.6.2). Denaturation of bacterial proteins by heat, as in cooking, or by acids, as in the very low pH environment of the stomach, contributes to the death of bacteria.

Derived proteins
Alterations in the original protein molecule result in the loss of amino acid groups or prosthetic groups which may or may not lead to loss of protein activity. Pepsinogen (an inactive protein or zymogen) is converted to pepsin in the acid conditions of the stomach and is so able to convert protein to peptides during digestion (see Sect. 2.8).

2.6 PROTEINS IN FOODS

An understanding of the properties of proteins and their susceptibility to denaturation helps to explain many of the characteristics of protein foods. Examination of proteins in milk, eggs and meat will illustrate this.

2.6.1 MILK

Milk is an oil-in-water emulsion containing about 3.8 per cent fat (dissolved in the fat phase are fat-soluble vitamins (see Sect. 5.2)). The water phase contains mineral salts, lactose, water-soluble vitamins and proteins.

About 80 per cent of milk protein is made up of caseinogen, which is not one protein but a mixture of three fractions: α, β and κ casein. Caseinogen is dispersed in milk in the form of colloidal particles which are called micelles. These spherical micelles which are stabilised by minerals are mainly responsible for the opalescent white of milk. In this form the caseinogen is less sensitive to heat than other milk proteins but is susceptible to denaturation by an acidic pH or by appropriate enzymes (see Sect. 10.5.1). As milk sours the pH falls and at about pH 5.2 the milk curdles and caseinogen is precipitated out in the curd. Caseinogen is also sensitive to the enzyme rennin which at a reduced pH converts the caseinogen into the coagulated form, casein.

The two other important proteins in milk, lactalbumin (14 per cent) and lactoglobulin (5 per cent) are not affected by rennin but are more susceptible to heat. When milk is heated the proteins coagulate to form a skin on the surface. This skin traps gas bubbles underneath it resulting in a build up of pressure which eventually causes the milk suddenly to boil over.

In addition to the proteins mentioned, milk contains low levels of immunoglobulin (about 2 per cent).

2.6.2 EGGS (HEN'S EGG)

Eggs consist of three main parts – a shell, a white and a yolk (see Fig. 2.5). The shell forms an outer protective layer (see Sect. 11.3.1) and is composed mainly of calcium carbonate. Variations in shell colour are mostly due to the breed of the laying hen and make no difference to the nutritional value of the egg.

Inside the shell is a colourless, viscous fluid called the 'egg white' and consists of approximately 12 per cent protein, 87 per cent water and small quantities of dissolved salts and riboflavin (see Sect. 5.3.3). At least nine different types of proteins are present in egg white (the major five are listed in Table 2.1).

Near the centre of the egg is the yolk, a complex dispersion of lipids and proteins. Being yellow–orange in colour the yolk is an oil-in-water emulsion stabilised by lecithin (see Sect. 3.5.1). Chemically the yolk is approximately 33 per cent fat, 50 per cent water and 16

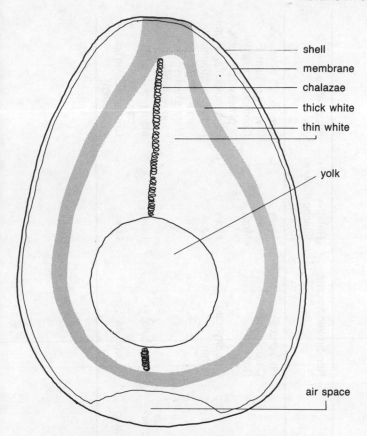

shell
membrane
chalazae
thick white
thin white

yolk

air space

FIG. 2.5 The internal structure of a hen's egg

per cent protein as well as mineral salts, vitamins and cholesterol
(see Table 2.1). The lipids and protein are combined to form
lipoproteins – responsible for the gummy quality of frozen egg yolk.

Heat coagulation of egg proteins
The proteins in egg yolk can be coagulated to varying degrees
depending on temperature, pH and salt concentration. When eggs
are heated, as in boiling, poaching or frying, the egg white proteins
coagulate. Egg white coagulates first at about 60 °C then the yolk at
about 66 °C.

When eggs are boiled the duration of the cooking determines the
degree of denaturation, in lightly boiled eggs the yolk is not fully
coagulated but is runny. Prolonged boiling brings about complete
coagulation and a hard-boiled egg is the result. Note, a little salt

TABLE 2.1 The major proteins in egg

Egg fraction	Protein name	Protein type	Non-protein fraction	Relative susceptibility to heat	Importance
Egg white	Ovalbumin	Fibrous	Phosphate	More	Approx. 70 % of egg white protein
	Conalbumin	Fibrous	Carbohydrate	More	Contributes to skin of baked products
	Ovomucin	Conjugated	None		
	Lysozyme	Globular	Carbohydrate	More	High molecular weight
			None	Less	Natural antibacterial agent found in tears
	Avidin				Makes biotin unavailable
Egg yolk	Lipovitellin	Phosphoprotein	Phosphate	Less	Main proteins (30 % in egg yolk)
	Lipovitellinin	Phosphoprotein	Phosphate	Less	Combined with lipid (lecithin)

should be added to the cooking water used for boiling the egg, then if the shell cracks egg white will not be lost. The salt helps to coagulate the escaping proteins thus 'sealing up' the crack.

In poaching, the presence of salt and vinegar speed up the coagulation of the egg white proteins while the yolk, owing to higher denaturation temperatures, is not fully coagulated.

In making scrambled eggs and omelettes, where egg white and yolk are beaten together, lower quality eggs can be used. In scrambled eggs, milk (88 per cent water) is added to dilute the egg protein. Seasoning is added according to taste. Stirring and the use of low heat is required to prevent the formation of large pieces of denatured protein which would result in a rubbery texture. The preparation of omelettes requires the beaten egg mixture to be fried at a high temperature in a shallow pan without stirring. The high temperature coagulates the outer proteins quickly and gives surface browning leaving the centre soft and almost liquid. The lightness of the omelette is determined by the degree of aeration during whisking prior to cooking.

Mechanical aeration

Mechanical aeration, such as whisking of egg white, brings about partial denaturation of the protein chains and the entrapment of air, the foam formed being influenced by a number of factors. Foams made from high-quality eggs are stronger but overwhisking can lead to collapse of the foam. Egg white foams are used in the preparation of meringues, angel cakes and other products.

2.6.3 MEAT

In legal terms, meat is the flesh, including fat, skin, rind, gristle and sinew, as well as other parts of the carcasses of animals and birds. Parts regarded as meat include the pancreas, head meat, tail meat, heart, kidney, liver and tongue but exclude brains and parts of the alimentary canal and reproductive systems. This assortment of animal products allowable as meat often causes confusion and food manufacturers are being pressed to label products with the lean meat content. Lean meat is the muscular flesh or tissue of animals, free when raw of visible fat and is structurally different from the other parts mentioned. In the United Kingdom the bulk of the animal meat protein is derived from cattle, sheep, pigs and poultry, although in different regions of the world a variety of other animals are used. There is considerable variation in the composition of the flesh of these animals and it is possible to distinguish chemically between them. This is important as some unscrupulous meat traders may try to sell off horse meat or even kangaroo meat labelled as beef. There is even chemical variation between different breeds of animal and even within breeds depending on their diet.

Composition of meat

Generally speaking lean meat is composed of about 70 per cent water, 20 per cent protein, variable quantities of fat, and small amounts of vitamins and minerals.

If raw meat is examined it is found to consist of muscle blocks, each block being made up of fibres. Each fibre is a long narrow cell containing many nuclei. Some of these fibres can be quite long reaching up to 30 cm in the muscles of some larger animals (see Fig. 2.6). Inside the fibres are myofibrils which consist of two types of parallel filaments (see Fig. 2.7). The thicker filaments are composed of the protein myosin while the thinner filaments are composed of the protein actin (see Table 2.2). It is the sliding action of these two proteins which is responsible for the contractile nature of muscle tissue. The whole arrangement is held together by two types of connective tissue, one containing a greater proportion of the protein collagen the other containing more of the protein elastin. Dispersed through the meat will be varying quantities of fat, known as 'marbling', as well as blood vessels and nerves. The red colour of the meat is due to the presence of myoglobin (see Fig. 2.4). The amount of myoglobin in the muscle tissue varies with the amount of

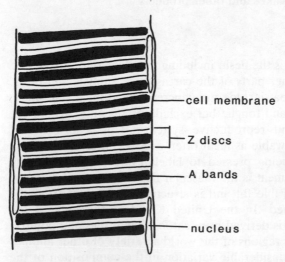

cell membrane

Z discs

A bands

nucleus

FIG. 2.6 Section of multinucleated skeletal muscle fibre showing stripes

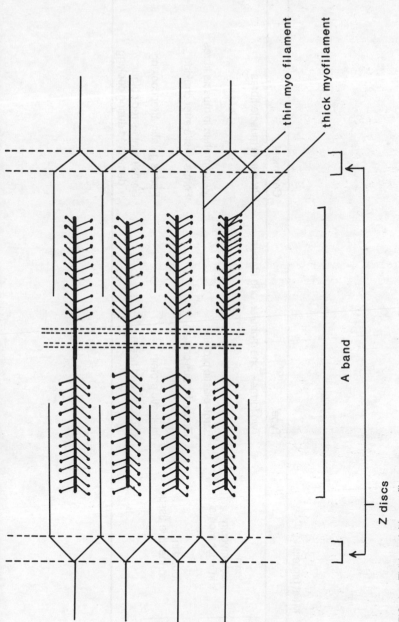

FIG. 2.7 Thick and thin myofilaments

TABLE 2.2 Meat proteins

Protein		Type	Comment
Actin	} form actomyosin in rigor mortis	Two forms – one globular, one fibrous	Protein in muscle fibres
Myosin		Large elastic protein	Major protein in muscle fibres
Elastin	} found in connective tissue	Elastic fibrous protein	Forms gristle after cooking
Collagen		Inelastic protein	Forms gelatin after cooking
Myoglobin		Globular and haem	Gives meat its red colour; denatured during cooking

use the muscle receives; active use of a muscle causes it to be darker and tougher. This distinction is best typified by comparing poultry breast with leg muscle, or veal with beef.

Tenderness and quality

Meat will vary in its tenderness (probably its most important property) depending on its muscular origin, its handling and preparation, and method of cooking.

Before slaughter

Tenderness of meat is greatly influenced by the history of the animal before slaughter and the usage the muscle tissue receives. Less used muscle is composed of small narrow fibres and is more tender than well used muscle containing larger thicker fibres. In addition, the more use the muscle receives the greater the amount of connective tissue, thus the tougher the meat becomes. Fillet steak, for example, contains only about one-third of the connective tissue found in shinbeef (stewing steak). Muscles in older animals also contain more connective tissue than those found in young animals, compare mutton and lamb. It is important that animals are rested prior to slaughter to maintain an adequate level of muscle glycogen (see Sect. 1.3.3). Meat derived from animals under stress, or exercised just prior to slaughter, will be tougher and 'gummier' and not have the same keeping quality as that from rested animals. One way of increasing tenderness of meat is to inject the animal with proteolytic enzymes just prior to slaughter.

Handling after slaughter

Within a few hours (varies from 1–12 hr) after death muscular tissue starts to stiffen – known as rigor mortis. This is due to the cross-linking of the contractile proteins actin and myosin to form rigid chains of actomyosin. Rigor mortis is likely to persist for several days therefore meat needs to 'hang' or be conditioned to allow the effects to wear off. Meat used in cooking while still in rigor mortis would be tough and unpalatable. Cold shortening is a term used to describe toughness in meat caused by cooling the carcass too quickly after slaughter. This can be overcome by electrical stimulation of the carcass. The chemistry of hanging or conditioning is quite complex but one of the main reactions involves the conversion of muscle glycogen to lactic acid thus decreasing the pH of the meat from about 7.2 to between 5.5 and 6.5. The fall in pH plus the activity of autolytic enzymes (see Sect. 11.4.2) causes protein coagulation and increased tenderness of the meat. Note that thicker, tougher fibres are less susceptible to coagulation. The hanging time varies with different types of meat, for beef typically between 10–20 days while pork, which is more susceptible to rancidity (see Sect. 3.4.2), is usually hung for only about 4 days.

Preparation for cooking
Meat suspected of being tough can be tenderised in a number of ways which affect the muscle fibres and protein state.
1. *Mechanical means*: the use of a steak hammer to pound the meat (especially thin pieces) helps to break up the muscle fibres and connective tissue and increases the chances of protein coagulation on cooking.
2. *Enzymes*: steak peppers and similar products contain proteolytic enzymes, such as papain, which degrade muscle fibres and connective tissue.
3. *Marinades* may contain lemon juice (citric acid), vinegar (acetic acid) or yoghurt (lactic acid) which helps to coagulate proteins. The addition of salt or alcoholic beverages to meat dishes apart from contributing flavour will also affect the proteins present. However, care needs to be taken not to over-tenderise meat otherwise it will become mushy and lacking in texture.

Cooking
Meat is cooked to make it safer (see Sect. 13.4) as well as more tender, easily digested and appetising. During cooking various changes take place – depending upon the type of cooking method used:
1. Further muscle fibre protein coagulation takes place and the meat shrinks.
2. The shrinking results in loss of liquid or juices containing water, melted fat, vitamins and minerals as well as volatile flavour substances. The latter contribute to the aroma of cooking meat.
3. Colour changes: the red colour of fresh meat is due to the myoglobin content. During cooking the myoglobin is denatured and often the protein part of the molecule becomes detached from the haem part which is oxidised and as a result the meat turns brown.
4. Connective tissue binds the muscle fibres together. Connective tissue high in collagen is denatured (especially in the presence of water) and is hydrolysed to form gelatin. As a result the meat becomes more tender and more digestible since digestive juices are better able to come in contact with the myosin. Connective

tissue containing elastin is not so readily affected by heat and forms gristle which is not easily digested.

Method of cooking
This is of considerable importance. Moist cooking methods e.g. stewing, braising, etc., result in greater breakdown of connective tissue than do the drier methods, e.g. grilling and roasting. Thus they are particularly suitable for cheaper cuts of meat, such as shin beef, which contains greater quantities of connective tissue. Dry methods of cooking are used for those cuts with less connective tissue such as sirloin and topside.

The rate of conduction of heat through the meat is relatively slow. Muscle proteins start to coagulate at about 40 °C but to be well done a temperature of about 78 °C needs to be achieved (see Sect. 13.4.2).

2.7   NUTRITIONAL VALUE OF PROTEINS

Some amino acids can be manufactured in the body and do not, therefore, need to be supplied 'ready made' in the diet – these are termed 'non-essential' amino acids although the term 'nutritionally dispensable' may be less misleading. Other amino acids cannot be made in the body and have to be supplied as building blocks within the protein of the diet – these amino acids are termed 'essential' amino acids (see Fig. 2.2). Of the twenty amino acids provided by the diet eight are essential in adults and ten are essential in children (histidine and arginine are not synthesised in children).

The amino acids provided by the diet must therefore fulfil the requirement for essential amino acids and must provide enough additional amino acid material to enable production of non-essential amino acids required during protein synthesis. The quantities of each of the essential amino acids required daily by an average human adult are shown in Table 2.3. The non-essential amino acids, cysteine and tyrosine, can be synthesised from the essential amino acids, methionine and phenylalanine, respectively. Supplying these non-essential amino acids in the diet spares the essential amino acids, reducing their requirement by up to 30 per cent for cysteine and 50 per cent for phenylalanine.

The composition of a protein or the relative amounts of each of the component amino acids is called its 'amino acid profile'. In nutritional terms the importance of a protein is based on its ability

TABLE 2.3 Essential Amino acid requirement
(mg/day) for a 70 kg adult

Essential amino acid	Requirement (mg/day)
Lysine	840
Methionine and cystine	910
Threonine	490
Tryptophan	245
Isoleucine	700
Leucine	980
Phenylalanine and tyrosine	980
Valine	700

to supply the particular amino acids needed by the body cells, i.e. a matching of the dietary protein with the amino acid profile of the protein content of human cells. A dietary protein which closely matches the amino acid requirements of the human body will be of most value. No one naturally occurring protein entirely matches the human amino acid requirement. Egg protein probably comes closest to human needs and is used as a standard or reference protein with which the amino acid profile of other dietary proteins can be compared.

Several factors control the ability of a dietary protein to provide this balance of amino acids:

1. The amount of the protein ingested.
2. The amount of each amino acid provided by that protein. The lowest nutritionally essential amino acid with respect to the amino acid requirement is called the 'limiting amino acid'. In cereals, lysine is the limiting amino acid whereas in legumes (for example, peas and beans), it is methionine. Proteins which contain high quantities of all the nutritionally essential amino acids are termed 'high biological value proteins'. Proteins which are deficient in one or more amino acids are termed 'low biological value proteins'. Complementation of two low biological value protein foods containing different limiting amino acids within the diet enables the overall provision of the required amino acids. There are many examples of protein complementation within traditional diets, e.g. rice and beans, beans on toast. Protein complementation is particularly important in vegan diets.
3. The digestibility of the protein as it passes along the digestive tract. A range of food preparation and cooking methods are available to increase the digestibility of proteins (see Sect. 2.6).
4. Chemical changes between proteins and other food components

which take place on the heating of foods may reduce availability of certain amino acids by virtue of the Maillard reaction (see Sects 1.4.1 and 11.4.4). It has been estimated that bread loses up to 15 per cent of its lysine during baking and a further 8 per cent on toasting.

2.7.1   METHODS OF ASSESSING NUTRITIONAL VALUE OF PROTEINS

Various methods are available for the assessment of the quality of a protein in nutritional terms.

Chemical scores

Chemical methods, e.g. the use of amino acid analysers, are available for the determination of the amino acid profiles of proteins. These methods enable the comparison of amino acid profiles of test proteins with the known human amino acid profile; they enable the limiting amino acid, if any, in the test protein to be quickly assessed. It is thus possible for the complementation of protein foods to be performed on a theoretical basis in order to determine their suitability for human dietary requirements. The method has disadvantages in that there is no assessment of the digestibility of a protein or the presence of toxic substances in the test material. Amino acid analysis is a usual first step in the assessment of the suitability of new ('novel') materials for human foods, e.g. in the assessment of microbial, the so-called single-cell, proteins (see Sect. 10.6).

The essential amino acid profile of egg, beef, fish and peanut protein is shown in Table 2.4 with the limiting amino acid for peanuts indicated with an asterisk. The chemical scores of each protein is shown at the bottom of the table.

TABLE 2.4 Amino acid profiles of food proteins

Amino acid	Beef	White fish	Egg	Peanuts
Isoleucine	320	330	350	210
Leucine	500	530	520	400
Lysine	570	610	390	220
Methionine	250	250	310	150
Phenylalanine	520	480	570	550
Threonine	290	300	320	160*
Tryptophan	80	70	110	70
Valine	330	360	470	260
Chemical score	100	100	100	65

* Limiting amino acid

Protein efficiency ratio

Young rats are fed measured amounts of protein and weighed regularly. The protein efficiency ratio (PER) is determined as follows:

$$PER = \frac{\text{weight gained}}{\text{protein intake}}$$

The method has the advantage of allowing the assessment of digestibility of the test protein and gives an indication of the presence of any toxic factors in the test material. However, the amino acid requirements for rats will not be the same as for humans. The amino acid requirements for growth also differ to those required for maintaining adult tissues.

Net protein utilisation

This method requires the use of nitrogen balance studies which involve a comparison of the protein consumed over a set period of time and the nitrogen (N) passing from the body during the same period. The major routes of nitrogen loss from the body are via the faeces and the urine. The net protein utilisation (NPU) can be calculated as follows:

$$NPU = \frac{\text{N retained}}{\text{N intake}}$$

Thus NPU is defined as the percentage of dietary protein converted into body protein.

Biological value

To assess biological value (BV) two nitrogen balance studies are undertaken. During the first study, no protein is consumed and the nitrogen lost from the body via the urine and the faeces is measured. During the second study, an amount of protein slightly below that required by the individual is consumed and nitrogen losses are again assessed. A comparison of the results allows calculation of the nitrogen absorbed by the body and the nitrogen retained by the body.

$$BV = \frac{\text{N retained}}{\text{N absorbed}} \times 100$$

The method has the advantage of allowing studies to be made on humans and allows an assessment of the digestibility and hence availability of the test protein. **Thus BV is defined as the percentage of absorbed protein converted to body protein.**

2.8   DIGESTION OF PROTEINS

Dietary protein is broken down as it passes through the gut. Gastric juice is a mixture of hydrochloric acid and the inactive zymogen, pepsinogen. Pepsinogen is converted to its active form due to the low pH in the stomach. Denaturation of dietary protein takes place in the low pH conditions of the stomach and breakdown of the protein into large polypeptides is initiated by pepsin. The major site of protein digestion is, however, the small intestine where the protein is attacked by the proteolytic enzymes trypsin and chymotrypsin. Peptidases convert peptides to free amino acids which are then absorbed across the wall of the ileum into the blood capillary in the villus.

During their absorption some of the amino acids are converted into others, e.g. aspartic acid and glutamic acid are converted to alanine (see Fig. 2.2).

2.9   USE OF PROTEIN IN THE BODY

After absorption amino acids are carried via the hepatic portal vein to the liver. One of three fates awaits amino acids arriving at the liver:
1. The amino acids may pass on directly to the tissues via the bloodstream where they will be used for growth or repair.
2. The amino acids may be used for the synthesis of liver and plasma proteins and other amino acid containing molecules such as haemoglobin.
3. When insufficient energy is available from other dietary components, e.g. carbohydrate and fat, or when excess protein is eaten, the protein will not be used for growth and repair but will be used for the production of energy. Amino acids reaching the liver are deaminated (i.e. the amino group is removed and converted to urea), and the rest of the molecule is used either for immediate energy production or used in fatty acid synthesis for longer term energy storage. A quantity of 1 g of protein will provide 17 kJ (4 kcal) of energy. Normally in the United Kingdom, at least 10 per cent of the energy comes from protein. However, this rises in individuals who diet by reducing carbohydrate and fat intake. Thus for most people carbohydrate has a protein-sparing capacity, i.e. prevents proteins from being used too much as a source of energy and allows them to be reserved for their main functions of growth and repair.

2.10 HUMAN PROTEIN REQUIREMENTS

Proteins are required by the body for the growth and repair of tissues. Obviously the requirements for protein will alter at various ages and will be larger in children where growth and repair is taking place than in adults where protein is used for the maintenance of tissues. Adult protein requirements will be increased during pregnancy and lactation, during illness and in convalescence, and after illness and surgery. The recommended protein intakes for various age groups are shown in Table 2.5. Typically adults require 1 g protein per kilogram bodyweight and children require 2 g protein per kilogram bodyweight.

TABLE 2.5 Recommended protein intakes for various age groups and conditions (g/d)

Age or condition	Males	Females
1	30	27
2	35	32
3–4	39	37
5–6	43	42
7–8	49	47
9–11	57	51
12–14	66	53
15–17	66	53
18–34	72	—
35–64	69	—
65–74	60	—
18–54	—	54
55–74	—	47
75 and over	54	42
Pregnancy	—	60
Lactation	—	69

2.11 SOURCES OF PROTEIN IN THE DIET

Table 2.6 illustrates the contribution made by some foods to the protein intake of a typical British diet along with the biological value and net protein utilisation of each protein.

2.12 TESTS FOR PROTEINS

The presence of proteins in foods can be determined by using simple

TABLE 2.6 Contribution of certain foods to the protein content of the Typical British diet

Food	Percentage protein contribution to British diet	Biological value (%)	Net protein utilisation (%)
Egg	5	97	96
Meat	30	82	78
Fish	4	79	77
Milk	18	77	71
Soya products	Low	73	61
Bread	20	49	48

biochemical tests. The main ones used are the Biuret, Millon's, and the Xanthoproteic tests.

QUESTIONS

1. (a) Draw a diagram to show the generalised structure of an amino acid.
   (b) What is meant by the terms 'essential amino acid' and 'non-essential amino acid'?
   (c) Name one example of an essential amino acid and one of a non-essential amino acid.
   (d) What is meant by 'chemical score of a protein'?
   (e) What is meant by 'complementation of proteins'?
2. (a) What food is the main source of protein in the British diet?
   (b) Approximately what (in grams per kilogram bodyweight) is the protein requirement of: (i) an adult, (ii) a growing child?
   (c) List three groups of adults who have increased protein requirements.
   (d) Explain why symptoms of protein deficiency may be seen in persons consuming low-energy diets which contain the recommended daily allowance of protein.
3. (a) Explain why milk curdles on souring?
   (b) Why does a skin form on the top of custard and milk-based sauces?
   (c) Why does meat quality improve after hanging?
4. (a) What is meant by: (i) protein efficiency ratio, (ii) net protein utilisation, (iii) biological value of a protein?

3
LIPIDS

3.1 INTRODUCTION

Lipids (Greek *lipos*, fat) are a very large and diverse group of chemical substances. They are made up of carbon, hydrogen and oxygen (no fixed ratio). Although they have quite different chemical structures they all have two properties in common – their solubility in organic solvents (e.g. petrol and chloroform) and their relative insolubility in water. The lipid fraction of a food can be separated for analysis by extraction with a suitable solvent, such as ethyl or petroleum ether, and is termed the 'ether-soluble fraction' or 'crude fat'. The most important group of lipids in foods are the true fats, as well as other lipids, e.g. waxes, complex lipids, e.g. cholesterol, derived lipids, many pigments, hormones and volatile odours. Only certain lipid substances are essential components of our diets for health. These are certain polyunsaturated fatty acids such as linoleic acid, and the fat-soluble vitamins A, D, E and K.

Fats in foods can be visible fats, for example, butter and margarine, lard and vegetable oils, suet and beef dripping, which can be used in cooking or eaten as they are. Invisible or hidden fats may not be obviously apparent in foods, for example, the fat in cheese and other dairy products (Cheddar cheese contains 35 per cent fat), chocolate (33 per cent fat), cakes, nuts, fish and eggs. Almost all foods contain some lipid material with flesh meats and fowl, milk, milk products and eggs making the largest contribution to our lipid intake; even fruit and vegetables contain a minimum of between 0.1 and 1 per cent total lipid, although the avocado pear which contains 22 per cent fat is particularly high for a fruit.

3.2 CHEMICAL STRUCTURE OF FATS AND OILS

Fats and oils are chemically similar, differing only in their physical state at normal room temperature: fats are solid at room temperature whereas oils are liquid. Both fats and oils are mainly composed of triacylglycerols (triglycerides), these are esters of long-chain carboxylic acids (fatty acids) and glycerol (a trihydric alcohol, i.e. an alcohol with three hydroxyl groups) (see Fig. 3.1). In mono-acylglycerols, glycerol is combined with only one fatty acid, in diacylglycerols glycerol is combined with two fatty acids. Natural fats are complex mixtures of a range of triacylglycerols containing up to twenty different fatty acids (see Table 3.1).

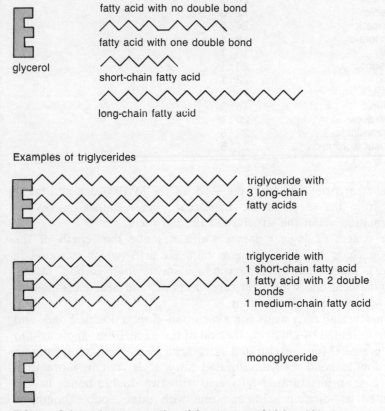

glycerol

fatty acid with no double bond

fatty acid with one double bond

short-chain fatty acid

long-chain fatty acid

Examples of triglycerides

triglyceride with
3 long-chain
fatty acids

triglyceride with
1 short-chain fatty acid
1 fatty acid with 2 double
bonds
1 medium-chain fatty acid

monoglyceride

FIG. 3.1 Schematic representation of the structure of triglycerides

3.2.2   NAMING OF FATTY ACIDS

Fatty acids (see Table 3.1) are often described by common or trivial names which are related to the source from which the fatty acid was first isolated, e.g. palmitic acid was isolated from the seeds of the

TABLE 3.1 Fatty acids commonly occurring in natural fats

Common or trivial name	Chain length and number of double bonds
Butyric	4 : 0
Caproic	6 : 0
Caprylic	8 : 0
Capric	10 : 0
Lauric	12 : 0
Myristic	14 : 0
Palmitic	16 : 0
Stearic	18 : 0
Arachidic	20 : 0
Behenic	22 : 0
Lignoceric	24 : 0
Palmitoleic	16 : 1
Oleic	18 : 1
Eicosenoic	20 : 1
Erucic	22 : 1
Linoleic	18 : 2
Linolenic	18 : 3
Arachidonic	20 : 4
Clupanodonic	22 : 5
Docosahexaenoic	24 : 6

Palmae, myristic acid from the seeds of the Myristaceae and lauric acid from the seeds of the Lauraceae. These names convey no information about the structure of the fatty acid.

A system of logical names which describe the length of the carbon chain can be used, e.g. butanoic acid (which is found in butter) represents a carboxylic acid with four carbon atoms, octanoic acid one with eight carbon atoms, and hexadecanoic acid one with sixteen carbon atoms.

Unsaturated fatty acids contain carbon–carbon double bonds and are represented by changing the end of the name from -anoic acid to -enoic acid. Monounsaturated fatty acids, e.g. oleic acid, contain one double bond, polyunsaturated fatty acids contain more than one, e.g. an unsaturated fatty acid with two double bonds is represented as -dienoic acid, and one with three double bonds as -trienoic acid. The position of the double bonds is indicated by numbering the carbons of the carbon chain with the carbon of the carboxylic acid group taken as being carbon atom 1, palmitoleic acid which has sixteen carbon atoms and one double bond between the ninth and tenth carbon atoms is described as 9-hexadecenoic acid.

Thus, fatty acids differ due to:

1. The length of the carbon backbone, e.g. butanoic (butyric) acid

has four carbon atoms in its carbon chain whereas eicosanoic (arachidic) acid has twenty carbon atoms in its carbon chain (see Table 3.1). Most of the fatty acids contained within natural fats have an even number of carbon atoms in them.

2. The number and position of any double bonds. Stearic, oleic, linoleic and linolenic acids each have eighteen carbon atoms in their carbon chain. Stearic acid has no double bonds and is a saturated fat; oleic, linoleic and linolenic acids each of which are unsaturated fatty acids have one, two and three double bonds, respectively (see Fig. 3.2).

3. The configuration of any double bonds. Two configurations are possible, i.e. the *cis*-configuration and the *trans*-configuration (see Fig. 3.3). Only unsaturated fatty acids of the *cis*-configuration are of any physiological benefit. During margarine manufacture,

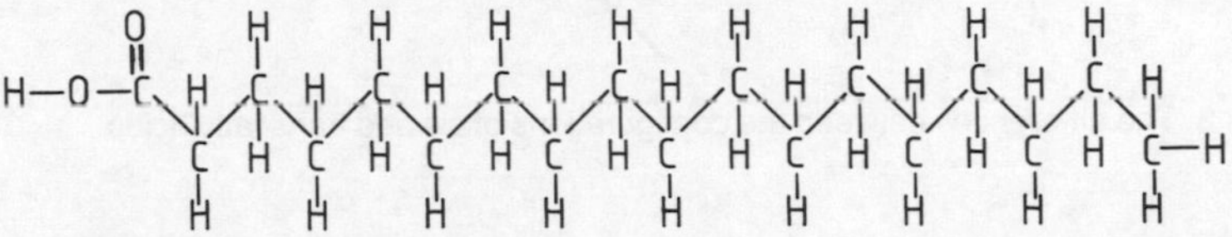

stearic acid (18:0)

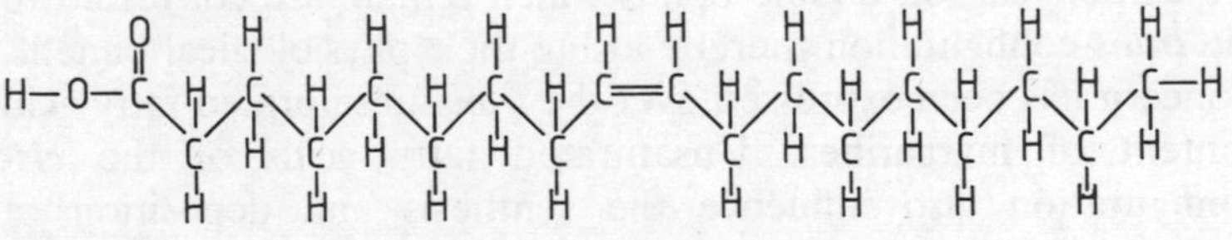

oleic acid (18:1)

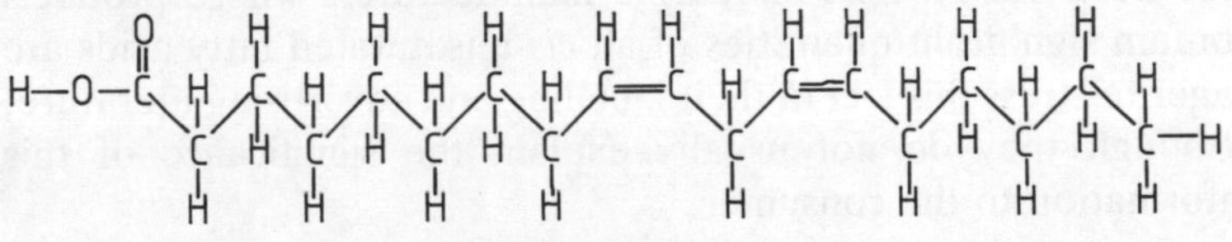

linoleic acid (18:2)

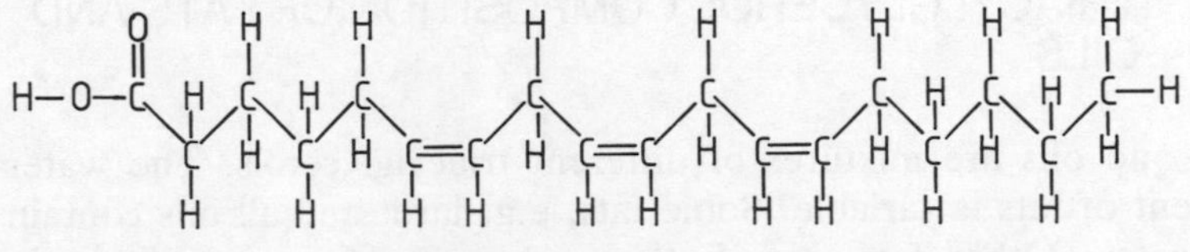

linolenic acid (18:3)

FIG. 3.2 The structure of stearic, oleic, linoleic and linolenic acids

configuration   structure   shape of molecule

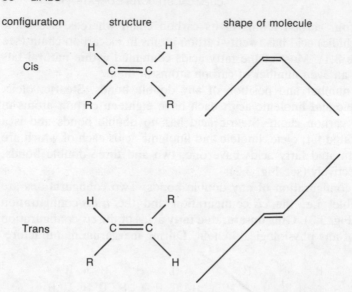

Cis

Trans

FIG. 3.3 The differences between the configurations of cis and trans fatty acids

saturated fatty acids are produced by the hydrogenation of (or the addition of hydrogen to) unsaturated fatty acids and many of the carbon–carbon double bonds which remain are converted to the *trans*-configuration thereby losing their physiological benefit. Concern has been expressed over the *trans*-unsaturated fatty acid content of margarines. Unsaturated fatty acids of the *cis*-configuration also influence the synthesis and deposition of cholesterol in tissues and thus may reduce the possibility of coronary heart disease, a major 'killer' in the Western World (see Sect. 1.5.1). Soft margarine manufacturers whose products contain significant quantities of all *cis*-unsaturated fatty acids are eager to stress this fact in their labelling and advertising literature, although they do not usually explain the significance of this information to the consumer.

3.3   TRIACYLGLYCEROL COMPOSITION OF FATS AND OILS

Fats and oils are mixtures of different triacylglycerols. The water content of fats is variable. Some fats, e.g. lard, and all oils contain no water. Other fats, e.g. butter and most margarines, contain about 20 per cent water. Low-fat spreads have their fat content reduced by emulsification with water and have a water content of about 60 per cent (see Fig. 3.4), emulsifying agents are added to maintain a homogenous product (see Sect. 7.7). Animal fats tend to have triacylglycerols with a higher proportion of saturated fatty acids than oils derived from fish and vegetables, which are usually higher in polyunsaturated fatty acids. However, some vegetable oils are much higher in polyunsaturated fatty acids than others, e.g. sunflower oil. Triacylglycerols are extracted from raw plant or animal material fairly easily. Plant oils are generally extracted from seeds and nuts using solvents, whereas animal fats, e.g. lard and dripping, are 'extracted' by gentle heat and this is termed rendering.

3.4   PROPERTIES OF FATS AND OILS

3.4.1   MELTING POINTS

Pure compounds melt sharply at a particular temperature. Since natural fats are mixtures of triacylglycerols of varying degrees of unsaturation they do not have sharp melting points and melt over a range of temperatures. A fat may be considered to have completely melted when in fact the higher-melting point components of the mixture are merely dissolved in the lower-melting point components. Hence, the term 'solution point' is a preferred description. Melting and softening points of fats are particularly important in the selection of fats for catering use.

A number of different methods are available for the determination of the melting range of fats are available. These include:

1. *The softening point or slip point*. A melted fat sample is placed in a capillary tube open at each end, it is chilled and then attached to a thermometer and placed vertically in a water bath below the level of the surface and warmed gently. The temperature at which the fat rises in the tube is measured.

2. *The shot melting point*. Small lead shot are placed on top of a hardened sample of fat in a beaker which is warmed slowly on a water bath. The temperature at which the shot settles to the bottom of the container is measured.

Generally speaking, the longer the chain of a saturated fatty acid the higher the melting point, e.g. butter which has a large number of short-chain fatty acids has a low melting point. The more double bonds, the lower the melting point, thus vegetable oils which have a higher content of unsaturated double bonds are liquid (one exception to this is coconut oil).

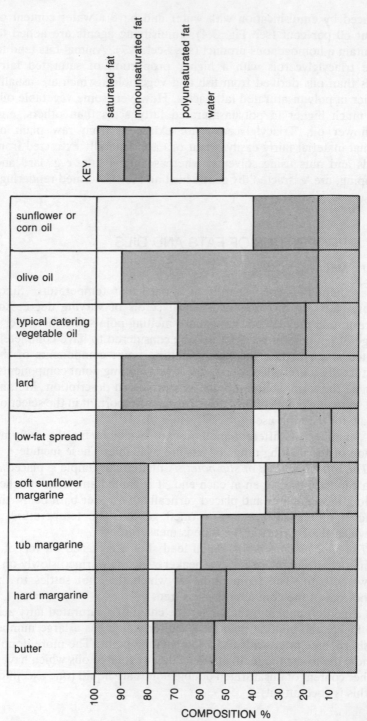

FIG. 3.4 The % composition of a range of fats and oils

Plasticity

A property of fats important to some of their applications in catering (see Sect. 3.5) is that of plasticity, which is related to the melting and slip points. The plasticity of any product, is that property which enables it to change shape under pressure and to maintain that shape when the pressure is removed. Fats, in varying degrees, depending upon temperature, are plastic and thus they have use as spreads to coat the surface of cereal products and improve their palatability (e.g. bread and butter).

The plasticity of a fat depends on the fact that it is composed of a mixture of triacylglycerols, each with its own melting point. This means that for a block of fat at any given temperature some of the triacylglycerols will be liquid and some will be crystalline solids. The range of temperatures over which the fat is plastic is known as its 'plastic range'. Fats containing mixtures of triacylglycerols with a large range of melting points will be plastic over a wider temperature range. Thus animal fats tend to be 'hard' fats with a narrow plastic range because they have little or no polyunsaturated fatty acids (PUFA) and fewer short-chain fatty acids. Butter is an exception and has a relatively low slip point compared with other animal fats. Even so, butter is relatively difficult to spread straight from the refrigerator; its spreading properties can be improved by warming which results in melting a greater proportion of the solid triacylglycerols. Most modern margarines will spread straight from the refrigerator because in their manufacture the ratio of solid-to-liquid triacylglycerols has been carefully controlled to ensure that it will have a wide plastic range.

Other than in relation to shortening and creaming (see Sect. 3.5), it is important to choose a fat with the correct plastic range (i.e. a mixture of triacylglycerols with a wide range of melting points). Fats with too many low-melting point triacylglycerols will be too soft and may be difficult to store during the summer, since at higher temperatures the triacylglycerols are mostly liquid. Selection of a fat with too many high-melting point triacylglycerols if incorporated into food products causes 'palate cling', due to the fact that the melting point of too great a proportion of the triacylglycerols is above 37 °C-body temperature- and thus will solidify on the roof of the mouth causing a greasy sensation. Furthermore, it is likely that the flavour of the food eaten will tend to stay in the mouth, as many volatile flavour molecules are fat-soluble, e.g. retained onion taste from Cornish pasties made with a relatively hard fat.

Smoke and flash points

Continued heating of a fat or oil above its melting point results in the liquid reaching the 'smoke point'. This is defined as the temperature at which a thin continuous stream of bluish smoke appears from the top of the oil which is being heated in an open dish. The smoke point of lard is about 185 °C. Smoke point is reduced by:

(i) increase in the concentration of free fatty acids due to the development of hydrolytic rancidity (see Sect. 3.4.2),
(ii) repeated heating in the presence of food particles. Fats and oils should be replaced regularly and strained frequently to remove food particles.

A good frying agent will have less than 0.4 per cent monoglycerides and less than 0.05 per cent free fatty acids, a smoke point of 218 °C or higher, i.e. 20 °C above the maximum frying temperatures normally used. A knowledge of smoke points is obviously of importance in the safe and efficient use of oils in deep-fat frying. Heat will also cause the decomposition of glycerol to acrolein (see Fig. 3.5), a substance with a characteristic strong irritating smell.

The 'flash point' of an oil is the temperature at which the mixtures of vapour given off from an oil during heating will ignite. For refined olive oil the smoke point is 227 °C and the flash point 326 °C, for corn oil the smoke and flash points are 199 °C and 321 °C, respectively. Thus excessive heating of a fat or oil above its smoke point could result in the flash point being reached and be a fire hazard.

3.4.2   RANCIDITY

'Rancidity' is the term used to describe spoilage or deterioration of a fat or an oil, for example the development of 'off' smells or odours during storage (see Fig. 3.5). The development of rancidity in a fat or oil may be due to incorrect processing and/or storage or too long a period of storage. Rancidity can be classified into three types:

(a) Hydrolytic rancidity.
(b) Oxidative rancidity.
(c) Absorption rancidity.

Edible fats should be used in strict rotation and stored with care to maximise quality. The use of rancid fats in the production of a food item will obviously affect its organoleptic properties (see Sect. 11.1).

Hydrolytic rancidity
Hydrolytic rancidity occurs as a result of hydrolysis of a fat to glycerol and free fatty acid molecules (see Fig. 3.5). Hydrolytic

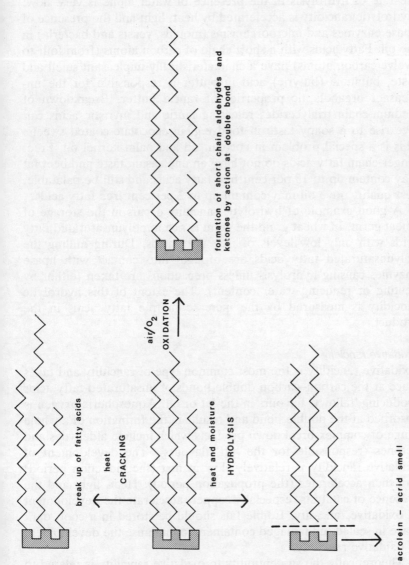

formation of short chain aldehydes and ketones by action at double bond

air/O₂

OXIDATION

heat
CRACKING

break up of fatty acids

heat and moisture
HYDROLYSIS

acrolein – acrid smell

FIG. 3.5 The chemical changes in a triglyceride molecule during the development of rancidity

rancidity can occur in both saturated and unsaturated fats. Water must be present in the fat for hydrolytic rancidity to take place but the rate of hydrolysis in the presence of water alone is very slow. Hydrolytic rancidity is accelerated by heat, light and the presence of lipase enzymes and microorganisms (moulds, yeasts and bacteria) in the oil. Fatty acids with a short chain of carbon atoms (from four to twelve carbon atoms) have a characteristically unpleasant smell and taste, butanoic (butyric) acid in butter is responsible for the unpleasant organoleptic properties of rancid butter. Breakdown of medium-chain triglycerides releasing lauric and myristic acids can give rise to a soapy taste in food e.g. in chocolate-coated sweets. This is a special problem in coconut oil and palm kernel oil. Free, longer-chain fatty acids do not have an unpleasant taste and beef fat may contain up to 15 per cent free fatty acids and still be palatable, best quality olive oil may contain up to 2 per cent free fatty acids.

A good example of hydrolytic rancidity occurs in the storage of wheat germ. In wheat grain the germ is rich in polyunsaturated fatty acids with only low levels of free fatty acids. During milling the polyunsaturated fatty acids are brought into contact with lipase enzymes causing hydrolysis unless precautions are taken (either by heating or reducing water content). The extent of this hydrolytic rancidity is measured by the increase in free fatty acids in the product.

Oxidative rancidity

Oxidative rancidity is the most common type of rancidity and takes place at the carbon–carbon double bonds of unsaturated fatty acids producing 'tallowy' flavours in the fat or oil. Atmospheric oxygen is absorbed at the double bond and results in the formation of a whole range of complex breakdown products which include aldehydes and ketones (responsible for the 'off' flavours). The development of oxidative rancidity is relatively slow at first (the induction period) and then accelerates (the propagation period). Heat, light and the presence of catalysts, especially copper, accelerate the development of oxidative rancidity. Edible fats should be stored in a cool, dark place in sealed, undamaged containers to minimise the development of oxidative rancidity.

Theoretically the susceptibility to oxidative rancidity is related to the number of double bonds – the more double bonds the more susceptible the product. While this is true in practical terms, the presence of natural antioxidants exerts an effect. Thus fish oils are very susceptible, whereas plant oils contain natural antioxidants which, unless denatured, slow down the process of oxidative rancidity. The most common group of natural antioxidants are the tocopherols, e.g. vitamin E.

Oxidative rancidity is a particular problem in the case of foods with a large surface area. For example, potato crisps which have a thin coating of oil remaining on them are particularly susceptible unless protected by an antioxidant. Paradoxically, it appears that some British consumers have become used to a slightly rancid taste in crisps and actually prefer this to the flavour of really fresh crisps. Increasing concern is being expressed about use of some common anti-oxidants, e.g. E320, butylated hydroxyanisole (BHA), and this is not permitted in baby foods. BHA is often used in conjunction with E321 butylated hydroxytoluene (BHT) and E310 propyl gallate (PG).

Absorption rancidity

Odour molecules are volatile substances and are soluble in fat. Strong smells may be absorbed by the fat or oil and so give rise to unpleasant flavours. Paints, varnishes, solvents and solvent-containing products should be stored well away from edible fats and oils, as should strong smelling foods such as onions and garlic.

3.5   USES OF LIPIDS IN CATERING

3.5.1   EMULSIONS AND EMULSIFYING AGENTS

Most food products which contain fats or oils also contain water, e.g. margarine, salad dressings and ice-cream. Fats and oils are not miscible with water and so instead of producing a homogenous solution they form an emulsion. An emulsion is a two-phase liquid system composed of two normally immiscible liquids in which one phase (the disperse phase) is dispersed as tiny droplets in the other (the continuous phase) (see Fig. 3.6).

An oil-in-water (o/w) emulsion has tiny droplets of oil dispersed in a continuous phase of water, e.g. milk, cream, mayonnaise and salad-cream. A water-in-oil (w/o) emulsion has water as the disperse phase and oil as the continuous phase, e.g. butter and margarine.

On standing, emulsions tend to separate into their two phases with the less dense phase rising to the top. Emulsions which separate quickly in this way are called 'temporary'. An emulsion which tends not to separate is described as 'permanent'. Emulsifying agents, or emulsifiers, help to stabilise emulsions making them more permanent and so prolonging shelf-life. Emulsifiers operate on the surface of each droplet of the disperse phase forming a one mole-

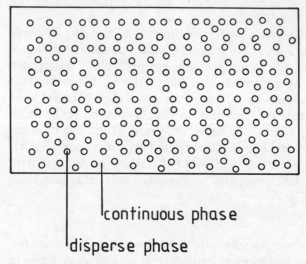

continuous phase

disperse phase

FIG. 3.6 A microscopic view of a section of an emulsion showing the tiny droplets of the disperse phase distributed through the continuous phase

cule thick layer which prevents coalescence of the drops of the disperse phase and maintains separation of the two layers. The molecule of an emulsifying agent consists of two parts, a hydrophilic (water-loving) region and a hydrophobic (water-hating) region. The hydrophilic region is polar and is attracted to water, the hydrophobic region is non-polar and is attracted to the oil. In many emusifiers the hydrophobic region is a long hydrocarbon chain. The molecules arrange themselves at the oil–water interface so that the hydrophilic region is in the water and the hydrophobic region is in the oil.

Important emulsifying agents include:

1. *Proteins.* A protein molecule has polar and non-polar regions which can arrange themselves at the oil–water interface and so form a layer which resists the coalescing of the disperse phase. Proteins act as emulsifiers in milk as well as in ice-cream.

2. *Lecithin from egg yolk* (see Sect. 2.6.2). Lecithin is a phospholipid which is present in egg yolk, butter and vegetable oils. In butter and margarine each water droplet is surrounded by a skin of lecithin molecules. Egg yolk can be used for the preparation of mayonnaise or salad-cream which are oil-in-water emulsions of vegetable oil and water, together with possibly vinegar or lemon juice. The best oil to use is olive oil which is high in oleic acid (a monounsaturated fatty acid) but is expensive. Owing to the presence of lecithin, salad-cream does not separate on standing and is termed a 'permanent emulsion'. This is in contrast to

French and Italian dressings which are only partly stabilised by mustard and tend to separate on standing, thus they are termed 'temporary emulsions'.

3. *Glyceryl monostearate* (GMS) which is used as an emulsifying agent in a number of different food emulsions, e.g. margarine, mayonnaise and ice-cream. Glyceryl monostearate is a monoacylglycerol (see Sect. 3.2.1) (glycerol and one molecule of stearic acid) in which the free hydroxyl groups of the glycerol molecule act as the hydrophilic part of the molecule and the long hydrocarbon chain of the stearic acid molecule acts as the hydrophobic part.

4. Detergents are an important group of emulsifying agents which are used with water in cleaning (see Ch. 8). They operate by producing an emulsion of the soiling material enabling its removal.

3.5.2   FRYING

Lipid products, usually oils, can be used in frying although current healthy eating policies (see Ch. 7) suggest its use should be reduced and the food grilled instead.

The high temperature achieved before oils start to deteriorate (see Sect. 3.4.1) combined with a high thermal capacity means that the fried food is cooked quickly. This gives the food a crisp texture and surface browning. As oils (the exception is olive oil) have little natural taste, the fried food retains its characteristic flavour properties. However, some oil is absorbed by the food (usually about 10–15 per cent) and this increases its energy content.

Most fats and oils can be used in frying though some are better than others. Butter, highly prized by some chefs, is not that satisfactory because it contains 20 per cent water and its component triacylglycerols contain short-chain fatty acids. While these can contribute to flavour they tend to break down rapidly and discolour on heating. Margarine has a similar water content (see Fig. 3.4) but is less susceptible to denaturation.

In order for caterers to get the best out of frying oils they must be looked after. Care should be taken not to overheat them and they should be strained thoroughly and frequently to remove burnt food particles. Oils need complete changing regularly, otherwise their smoke point will be reduced so much that the food is not fried at a sufficiently high temperature and it becomes soggy with a higher energy value. Usually at the same time the fried foods would start to taste unpleasant as a result of retention of oil breakdown products.

3.5.3   CREAMING

The plasticity of a fat is important for determining its creaming properties which can be defined as its ability to incorporate air bubbles when beaten. All fats do not cream equally as well and one with a wide plastic range is best. One disadvantage of using butter in cake making is its narrow plastic range. A drop in temperature of a few degrees makes it too hard to cream and a rise in temperature of a few degrees makes it too soft. Hydrogenated vegetable shortening (cake margarines) maintain desirable plasticity over a wide range of temperatures as well as containing emulsifying agents.

The first stage in cake making involves creaming the fat with sugar. The fat softens and is mixed with sugar which results in a slushy mixture which then traps air making it light and fluffy. Subsequently, eggs are beaten in gradually to form an oil-in-water emulsion stabilised by the lecithin in the egg. Cake margarine or high-ratio fats contain in addition glyceryl monostearate (3–10 per cent) which greatly increases the stability of the emulsion. Owing to the greater emulsifying properties, these fats permit the use of greater concentrations of sugar per unit weight of fat (hence the term 'high ratio').

3.5.4   SHORTENINGS

Cooking fats are used as shortening agents in the production of a variety of foods including biscuits, shortbread, pastry, etc. These products are made from flour which will contribute starch granules and gluten (see Sect. 2.5.1). In the presence of water and heat the starch granules will burst and swell releasing polysaccharide chains (see Sect. 1.3.3). In the presence of fat the released polysaccharides will tend to stick together and form a dense network, thus, for instance, pastry would be tough and difficult to chew. The presence of fat forms a barrier between some of the released polysaccharide chains preventing this from happening. In addition, the fat coats the gluten molecules helping to prevent contact with water molecules. In this way fat 'waterproofs' the flour and limits the development of the gluten, leading to the formation of a shorter gluten network. The resultant pastry is smoother, less tough and more appetising. The fat is said to have 'shortened' the pastry.

In practice the conditions must be carefully controlled in order to make good pastry. Thus an adequate quantity of a fat with a suitable plastic range and slip point must be used. If the fat has too high a slip point and poor spreading power there is a possibility that the starch granules will burst and the released polysaccharide will set into a hard unshortened mass. This happens because the fat triacylglycerols are predominantly solid and immobile. The fat therefore must have sufficient liquid triacylglycerols to be mobile and easily dispersed in tiny pieces which can coat flour granules. Note, the use of a fat with too low a slip point or an oil results in a crumbly greasy pastry since each flour particle is coated and little gluten development takes place. It is for this reason that pastry which requires a lot of handling is made on a cool surface – to counteract the warming effect of kneading which could cause too many triacylglycerols to melt. To overcome these problems manufacturers produce, by means of hydrogenation and other methods, shortenings of the correct plasticity for particular applications in the food industry, e.g. cake margarine, pastry margarine, etc. (see Table 3.2). Hospital caterers may come across medium chain triglyceride (MCT) oils which are extracted from coconut oil and consist mostly of saturated eight and ten carbon atom fatty acids.

3.6   DIGESTION OF LIPIDS

Digestion of lipids takes place in the small intestine (see Fig. 3.7). As chyme passes through from the stomach into the small intestine it is mixed with bile, pancreatic juice and intestinal juice. Bile is produced by the liver and contains bile salts which are emulsifying agents. The emulsification of the fat in the chyme results in the formation of tiny droplets which have an increased surface area for enzyme action. Pancreatic juice contains various enzymes, one of which is a lipase. Lipases hydrolyse the bonds between the glycerol part of the acylglycerols and the fatty acid part, resulting in a complex mixture of monoacylglycerols, free fatty acids and glycerol. The breakdown products group themselves into micelles which can pass into the lining of the small intestine. Any lipid material which is not digested remains in the lumen and excessive amounts result in a condition called 'steatorrhoea' in which the stools are fatty, bulky and very light in colour. MCT oils are hydrolysed more easily by pancreatic lipase than other fats and once absorbed pass straight to the liver. They are used to treat patients with steatorrhoea as they are usually absorbed much better than other fats.

The fate awaiting the monoacylglycerols and free fatty acids in the cells lining the lumen depends upon the length of the carbon backbone of the fatty acid. Medium- and short-chain fatty acids pass on directly into the blood capillaries in the villus and are transported to the liver via the hepatic portal vein. The long-chain fatty acids are resynthesised into triacylglycerols and become coated with protein,

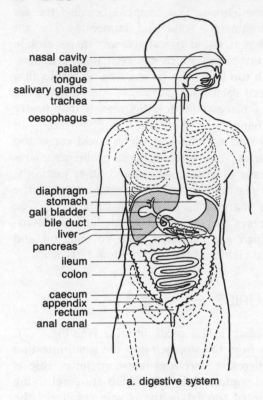

nasal cavity
palate
tongue
salivary glands
trachea
oesophagus

diaphragm
stomach
gall bladder
bile duct
liver
pancreas
ileum
colon

caecum
appendix
rectum
anal canal

a. digestive system

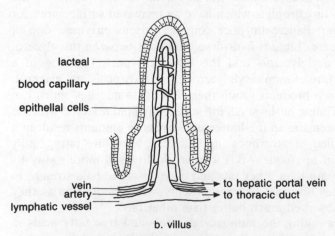

lacteal
blood capillary
epithellal cells

vein ——→ to hepatic portal vein
artery ——→ to thoracic duct
lymphatic vessel

b. villus

FIG. 3.7 Fats are absorbed via the villi of the ileum either directly into the bloodstream or indirectly via the lymphatic system (a) digestive system (b) villus (e) venous drainage from gut (d) lymphatic drainage from gut

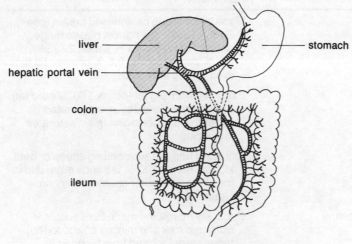

c. venous drainage from gut

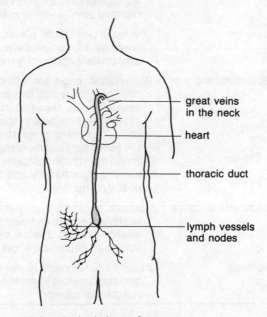

d. lymphatic drainage from gut

TABLE 3.2 Fats used in catering

Fat	Comments
Butter	Made by churning pasteurised cream (see Sect. 11.6.3); has narrow plastic range; approx. 81 % fat, 16 % water, 2 % salt, 0.5 % carbohydrate, 0.5 % protein; fat high in saturated fatty acids
Lard	Extracted from pig fat (nearly 100 % pure fat); use being replaced by hydrogenated vegetable shortenings; high in saturated fatty acids
Suet	Extracted from fat surrounding sheep or beef kidney; nearly 100 % fat; finds more use in the UK than in other countries; high in saturated fat
Hard margarine	Originally margarine made from suet, skimmed milk and minced cow's udder!; today manufactured from blended hydrogenated vegetable oils; about 80 % fat; high in saturated fatty acids; relatively high slip point; used for making pastry
Cake margarine	Lower slip point, good plastic range, good creaming properties; lower saturated fatty acid content than pastry margarine
Soft-spread margarine (in tubs)	Wide plastic range, spreads straight from refridgerator; typical composition 80 % fat; vegetable oils, skimmed milk, salt, non-fat milk solids, emulsifiers, starch, vitamins, colourings, flavourings; since about 1982 UK public spreads more margarine on its bread than butter; contains more polyunsaturated fatty acid than cake or pastry margarine
Polyunsaturated margarine	Contains about 45 % polyunsaturated fatty acids; advertised as being healthier in relation to heart disease; usually based on sunflower or corn oil; about 80 % fat
Low-fat spreads	About 40 % fat; much higher moisture content therefore lower in calories; not suitable for cooking

in which form they are termed 'chylomicrons'. The chylomicrons pass into the lacteals in the villus. The lacteals pass the chylomicrons to the thoracic duct and so to the great veins of the neck where they enter the bloodstream. This process is illustrated in Fig. 3.7.

3.7   USES OF LIPIDS IN THE BODY

The main functions of lipids in the body are as follows:
1. To provide essential fatty acids for cell structure and function. Adult humans need between 2 and 10 g of linoleic acid per day. Much of these essential fatty acids are utilised for the production of cell membranes. Lack of essential fatty acids in the diet can result in skin problems and eczema.
2. To act as intermediates for the synthesis of hormone-like substances involved in human metabolism.
3. To act as a vehicle for the fat-soluble vitamins in food and across the wall of the gut. Fat-soluble vitamins dissolve in the fat in food and are carried across the wall of the gut into the bloodstream for distribution and utilisation in the body.
4. To act as a source of energy. On average 20 per cent of the British diet is made up of fat which due to its high energy content provides about 40 per cent of our energy intake – remember fat is a concentrated energy source and will provide 37 kJ/g (9 kcal/g) whereas carbohydrate and protein provide about 17 kJ/g (4 kcal/g). Current healthy eating policies (see Ch. 7) stress the importance of reducing the contribution of fat as a percentage of the total energy intake. Ideally fat should not contribute more than thirty five per cent of the energy intake of the diet.
5. To act as an energy store in the body. Fat is a very concentrated source of energy and is the most efficient medium for storing energy in the body. Fat deposits can be produced from carbohydrate, protein or fat intakes in excess of energy requirements and stored under the skin and around organs in 'adipose' tissue. The bodies of normal persons may contain between 15 and 25 per cent fat, in obese persons this figure may be over 40 per cent.

3.8   TESTS FOR LIPIDS

A small quantity of the test food is rubbed on to a piece of filter paper which becomes translucent. The grease spot will wash out with acetone but not with water. A liquid sample can be tested by adding a small quantity of the sample to an equal volume of water, adding a little Sudan III (an oil-soluble, water insoluble dye) and shaking. On separation, the oil droplets will have taken up the red colour of the dye.

QUESTIONS

1. (a) What is the difference between a fat and an oil?
   (b) Describe the structure of a triacylglycerol (triglyceride).
   (c) What is meant by the term 'polyunsaturated'?
   (d) Why are cis-polyunsaturated fatty acids important to health?
   (e) Name two foods that are rich in cis-unsaturated fatty acids.
2. (a) What is meant by the term 'plasticity' of a fat?
   (b) Why is important to select fats of the correct plastic range in catering for each of the following applications: (i) creaming, (ii) shortening?
3. (a) What is meant by the terms 'smoke point' and 'flash point' of a fat or oil?
   (b) Why is it important to strain oils used for frying?
4. (a) What is an 'emulsion'?
   (b) How do emulsifying agents work to stabilise emulsions?
   (c) Name two food products which are emulsions. For each product list; (i) the nature of the disperse phase; (ii) the nature of the continuous phase; (iii) the emulsifying agent.

METABOLISM AND ENERGY

4.1   INTRODUCTION

Humans need energy in order to work, not just the more obvious types of activity such as preparing and serving food, but also other forms of mechanical effort such as walking, talking, lifting objects and playing physical games. Metabolic work is performed in our bodies when we digest foods and the products of digestion are used for the growth and repair of tissues. In order to carry out all these forms of work we must provide our bodies with energy. The body obtains energy by the oxidation of fuel nutrients from foods, especially carbohydrates and fats, and to a lesser extent protein and alcohol. The release of energy from nutrients is termed 'respiration'. The significance of respiration in the continuing performance of the body's processes (see Sect. 10.2), namely, life, is underlined by the speed with which death ensues when oxygen supplies are cut off, for example, after drowning or the dramatic effect, within minutes, of the poison cyanide on the body's tissues (cyanide inhibits the action of respiratory enzymes and so prevents energy production).

4.2   METABOLISM

'Metabolism' is the general term used to describe all the chemical reactions that occur in the cells of living things. The study of metabolic reactions is called 'biochemistry'. Each biochemical change is controlled by a specific protein called an 'enzyme'. A typical mammalian cell contains about 3000 different enzymes, each controlling one particular type of chemical change. Complex chemical reactions represent large steps but are achieved as a result of a series of many smaller steps, which combined together give the desired chemical change. The series of small steps together constitute an organised metabolic system called a 'metabolic pathway'. The cell with its many metabolic pathways is like a factory containing many production lines.

Metabolic reactions can be divided into two groups:
(a) Anabolic reactions.
(b) Catabolic reactions.

Anabolism includes all the chemical changes concerned with the manufacture of the building blocks required for growth, defence and repair of cells, i.e. synthetic reactions. Anabolic reactions require energy which is provided by catabolic reactions.

Catabolism describes degradative (or breakdown) reactions, including digestion, as well as energy-producing reactions. The substrates for catabolic reactions can be derived from the materials brought to the cell through the bloodstream, i.e. nutrients, or if no new materials are provided then those making up the cell itself are used. Exogenous catabolism refers to the breakdown of compounds arriving at the cell; endogenous catabolism concerns the breakdown of cellular components and only occurs during periods when energy intake is not as great as energy expenditure.

4.3   ENERGY IN CELLS

Energy is produced in cells according to the requirements of the body, by the catabolism of carbohydrates and fats. Proteins can also be broken down to produce energy but this is not desirable except in cases where the protein intake is excessive and enough protein is available for the growth and repair of tissues. If intakes are close to the amounts required for growth and repair, and insufficient carbo-hydrates and fats are available for breakdown, then protein will be diverted from its primary function and used instead for energy production, resulting in protein deficiency. Carbohydrates and fats are thus said to be 'protein-sparing'. The chemical energy we produce is in the form of energy-rich compounds, e.g. adenosine triphosphate (ATP), which are then used as required for performing mechanical work, to maintain the tissues of the body and for growth. Heat is a by-product of these reactions since conversion from chemical energy to mechanical energy is only about 15–20 per cent efficient, the rest being lost as heat energy. This stimulates the production of sweat which cools the body down.

In the typical British diet 40 per cent of our energy is derived from fats, 20 per cent carbohydrates, 6 per cent from alcohol, that is 66 per cent of the diet provides energy, leaving 34 per cent of the diet for all other requirements.

4.4   UNITS OF ENERGY AND THE ENERGY VALUES OF FOOD

The most common unit used for heat energy is the calorie which is the amount of heat energy required to raise the temperature of one gram of water by one degree Centigrade. One calorie (cal) is equivalent to 4.184 joules (J). The Joule is the Systeme Internationale (SI) unit and 1000 Joules = 1 kilojoule (kJ). The calorie is a very small unit in comparison to human energy requirements and therefore the Calorie (kilocalorie) is a more suitably sized unit.

$$
\begin{aligned}
1 \text{ Calorie} &= 1 \text{ kcal (kilocalorie)} \\
&= 1000 \text{ cal} \\
&= 4184 \text{ J} \\
&= 4.184 \text{ kJ (kilojoules)} \\
1 \text{ kcal} &= 4.184 \text{ kJ} \\
1 \text{ kJ} &= 0.239 \text{ kcal} \\
1 \text{ MJ (megajoule)} &= 10^6 \text{ J}
\end{aligned}
$$

For ease of conversion that 4.184 is rounded up to 4.2. **Thus, to convert kilocalories to kilojoules, multiply the value for kilocalories by 4.2; to convert kilojoules to kilocalories, divide the value for kilojoules by 4.2.**

The amount of energy released by the catabolism of various food chemicals is not the same (see Table 4.1).

TABLE 4.1 Energy nutrients

Nutrient	Energy provided by the catabolism of 1 g of nutrient	
	(kJ)	(kcal)
Fat	37	9
Protein	17	4
Carbohydrate	16	4
Alcohol	29	7

Knowledge of the level of each of these nutrients in individual foods allows calculation of the energy which would be obtained by eating a particular quantity of that food. For example, 100 g of fried lamb's liver provides 3.9 g of carbohydrate, 20.7 g of protein and 10.9 g of fat. Using conversion factors as shown in Table 4.1 the energy content of a 50 g portion of lamb's liver can be calculated.

$$\text{energy content} = \text{carbohydrate energy} + \text{protein energy} + \text{fat energy}$$

$$\text{100 g portion} = (3.9 \times 16) + (20.7 \times 17) + (10.9 \times 37)$$
$$= 817.6 \text{ kJ}$$

$$\text{50 g portion} = \frac{(817.6 \times 50)}{100}$$

$$= 418.8 \text{ kJ}$$
$$\text{or} \qquad 97.7 \text{ kcal}$$

Note that foods with high water content tend to be low in calories and foods with high fat contents tend to be high in calories. The fat, carbohydrate and protein content of various foods and the calculated energy provision are shown in Table 4.2.

4.5   ENERGY REQUIREMENTS

4.5.1   BASAL METABOLIC RATE (BMR)

We obviously need energy to move around in order to accomplish the many tasks that make up our day's routine, e.g. working, engaging in sports, even just sitting and watching television. We also need energy to keep up the activity of the various organs of the body, (e.g. brain, liver and kidney), to circulate blood, to breathe and to maintain a steady body temperature of 37 °C. This is called 'basal metabolism', i.e. the minimum level of metabolism necessary for life. The amount of energy needed for these processes is called the basal metabolic rate (BMR).

Energy consumption can be determined by using a respirometer which measures the amount of oxygen used. Oxygen is required for catabolism and can be directly related to the amount of energy produced, and therefore used, by the body. Every litre of oxygen used is equivalent to 20.26 kJ (4.825 kcal). In order to measure an individual's basal metabolic rate, the subject must be lying at rest, (but not asleep!), and wear light clothing in a comfortably warm room, at least 12 hr after the last meal. The rate of energy expenditure is expressed per unit of body surface area – joules per second per square metre ($J s^{-1} m^{-2}$), i.e. watts per square metre ($W m^{-2}$).

Figure 4.1 shows the percentage of the food energy used up for basal metabolism.

4.5.2   FACTORS AFFECTING BASAL METABOLIC RATE

The main factors that affect basal metabolic rate are:
1. *Body weight*. Generally a larger person will have a greater BMR

TABLE 4.2 Carbohydrate, protein and fat content of various foods and their calculated energy provision

Food	Carbohydrate			Protein			Fat			Total energy (kJ/100 g)
	(g/100 g)	(kJ)	(% energy)	(g/100 g)	(kJ)	(% energy)	(g/100 g)	(kJ)	(% energy)	
Beef (roast, topside)	0	0	0	26.6	452.2	50.5	12.0	444.0	49.5	896.2
Plaice (fried in crumb)	8.6	137.6	14.5	18.0	306.0	32.2	13.7	506.9	53.3	950.5
Egg (boiled)	trace	—	—	12.3	209.1	34.1	10.9	403.3	65.8	612.4
Butter	trace	—	—	0.4	6.8	0.2	82.0	3034.0	99.8	3040.8
Sugar (white)	105.0	1680.0	100.0	trace	—	—	0	0	0	1680.0
Bread (white)	49.7	795.2	80.3	7.8	132.6	13.4	1.7	62.9	6.3	990.7
Cheese (Cheddar)	trace	—	—	26.0	442.0	26.3	133.5	1239.5	73.7	1681.5
Potato (boiled)	19.7	315.2	92.0	1.4	23.8	7.1	0.1	3.2	0.9	342.7

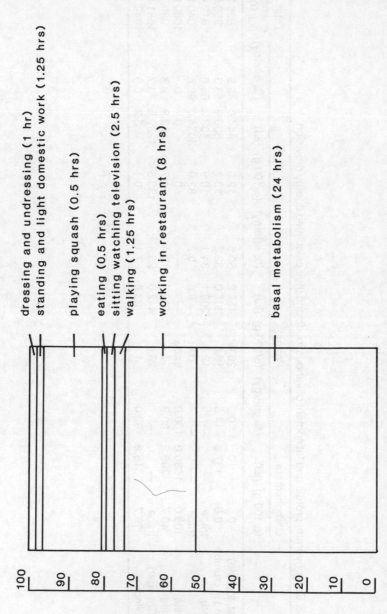

FIG. 4.1 Approximate energy expenditure for a male waiter (11.6 MJ/day (2800 kcal/day))

than a small person. However, it is not total body weight which is important but lean body weight, i.e. weight – fat weight, owing to the fact that fat tissue requires little energy for maintenance. Thus, a smaller well muscled person could have a higher BMR than a larger, fatter person.

2. *Sex*. Metabolic rate is higher in men than in women of the same height and weight because women have a greater proportion of body fat.

3. *Age*. Children should have a lower BMR than adults because their lean body size is usually smaller, but *proportionally* their BMR is higher because the cells are actively engaged in growth, i.e. there is a higher BMR per kilogram lean body weight. BMR falls throughout life.

4. *Level of hormones*. The chief substances that regulate BMR are the thyroid hormones, e.g. thyroxine (see Sect. 6.3.1). The level of thyroxine in the blood can be used as an index of BMR. Individuals whose thyroid glands secrete high levels of thyroxine have a high BMR and tend to lose weight. Low levels of thyroxine result in a low BMR and a tendency to increase weight. An overactive thyroid can increase BMR by up to 20 per cent and cause a person to be underweight and active, an underactive thyroid can decrease BMR by up to 20 per cent, resulting in overweight and slowness.

Adrenalin is secreted from the adrenal glands when we are frightened and increases BMR making us more able to respond – the so called 'fight or flight reflex'. Emotional stress increases adrenalin output and can cause us to increase basal metabolic rate.

4.5.3 ENERGY EXPENDITURE AND ACTIVITY

When we sit up or stand up we use about 20 and 30 per cent more energy, respectively, than we would if we were lying down. When we walk around the amount of energy we use depends on our weight and the speed at which we move. Our daily expenditure of energy in the form of activity consists of both work activities and leisure activities.

Table 4.3 shows the energy consumed in carrying out various activities.

4.5.4 METABOLISM OF FOOD

The eating of food increases the metabolic rate, since energy is

TABLE 4.3 Energy consumed in carrying out various work and leisure activities

Activity	Energy expenditure (kJ/min)	(kcal/min)
Resting		
Men	4.6	1.1
Women	3.8	0.9
Very light work	4–8	1–2
(e.g. sitting, reception work, accounting)		
Light work	8–12	2–3
(e.g. walking, dusting, setting a table, washing dishes)		
Moderate work	12–21	3–6
(e.g. bed making, vacuuming, kneeling to clean floors)		
Heavy work	28–60	7–15
(e.g. chopping wood)		
Leisure Activities		
(e.g. playing cards, knitting, watching television)	4–8	1–2
(e.g. tennis, cycling, football, running)	21–35	6–9
(e.g. squash)	60	15

required for secretion of digestive juices, the absorption of nutrients and their utilisation in the body. This effect is called the 'thermic effect' of food. On normal diets the increase is equivalent to about 10 per cent over a 24 hr period.

4.5.5   GROWTH AND REPAIR OF TISSUES

Protein synthesis for the growth and repair of tissues requires energy input. Energy requirements for growth are obviously high in children particularly through periods of rapid growth, e.g. during the teenage years. After growth is completed protein synthesis still takes place for the maintenance of the body cells and the synthesis of enzymes for metabolic reactions.

4.5.6   ENERGY REQUIREMENTS IN HUMANS

The energy requirement per day is therefore the sum of the energy required for:
  (a) Basal metabolism.
  (b) Daily activities (work and leisure occupations).

TABLE 4.4 Recommended daily amounts of energy for various ages and activities and conditions

Age	Activity or condition	Energy intake			
		Male		Female	
		MJ	(kcal)	MJ	(kcal)
1		5.0	1200	4.5	1100
2		5.75	1400	5.5	1300
3–4		6.5	1560	6.25	1500
5–6		7.25	1740	7.0	1680
7–8		8.25	1980	8.0	1900
9–11		9.5	2280	8.5	2050
12–14		11.0	2640	9.0	2150
15–17		12.0	2880	9.0	2150
18–34	Sedentary	10.5	2510	—	
	Moderately active	12.0	2900	—	
	Very active	14.0	3350	—	
35–64	Sedentary	10.0	2400	—	
	Moderately active	11.5	2750	—	
	Very active	14.0	3350	—	
65–74	Sedentary	10.0	2400	—	
Over 75	Sedentary	9.0	2150	7.0	1680
18–54	Most occupations	—		9.0	2150
	Very active	—		10.5	2500
	Pregnant	—		10.0	2400
	Lactating	—		11.5	2750

(c) Metabolism of food.

(d) Growth and repair of tissues.

The recommended energy intakes of different ages and activities of persons are shown in Table 4.4. Individuals engaged in sporting activities or other energy-demanding occupations will obviously need more energy.

Exercise not only uses up energy in its own right but also increases the BMR. Aerobic exercise (i.e. that using up oxygen) increases the metabolic rate by up to 30 per cent initially, but even after 24 hr the BMR may be 10 per cent higher. Thus exercise is recommended for individuals trying to slim and the number of those engaged in aerobic exercise, brisk walking, jogging, swimming, cycling, etc., has increased in recent years. To be beneficial such exercise should last a minimum of 20 min and be performed at least three times a week.

During crisis situations like starvation the body tries to conserve energy by reducing the BMR. Similar circumstances apply when people are dieting, the body reduces its BMR making it harder to lose weight. The trick in slimming is to cut energy intake and, by exercise, boost energy output.

4.6   ENERGY BALANCE

To maintain constant body weight there must be sufficient energy provided by the nutrients of the diet so that energy intake equals energy expenditure. If energy expenditure is greater than energy intake than there will be a diversion of protein from growth and repair of the body and a breakdown of the fat tissue to maintain requirements. Loss of weight will ensue and if allowed to continue unchecked could be harmful. This occurs during starvation and anorexia nervosa. If energy intake exceeds energy expenditure then there will be a storing of energy in the body in the form of fat which is an extremely concentrated form of energy (37 kJ/g). Fat is deposited underneath the skin and around the body organs and in excess is a health risk as well as being unsightly. At least this is true in Western societies. In certain cultures excess body fat is considered to be a sign of great beauty. Excess body weight is one of the major nutritional problems in Western society. One recent survey showed 39 per cent of British males and 32 per cent of British females to be overweight, and 6 per cent of males and 8 per cent of females to be obese. To be overweight a person must be over 10 per cent above their ideal body weight for height, obese persons are over 20 per cent above ideal body weight for height.

There are a number of health risks associated with excess body weight. Excessive strain on the skeletal system can lead to problems with the bones and joints, causing arthritis, especially in females. Blood pressure is increased in overweight persons which increases the risk of susceptibility to cardiovascular disease and associated problems. Obese persons have a shorter life expectancy than their counterparts of normal body weight and should seek to reduce to their desired weight for height range in order to ensure that they avoid these problems. A dietitian's or doctor's advice should be sought before any form of weight reduction regime is commenced.

When energy intake equals energy expenditure the body is said to be in energy balance and it is desirable to achieve this throughout adult life (see Fig. 4.2).

For quite a large number of people this does not take place but the causes of overweight can vary:

1. *Heredity*. To a certain extent body type and structure tend to be inherited. Thus, there is a tendency for overweight persons to

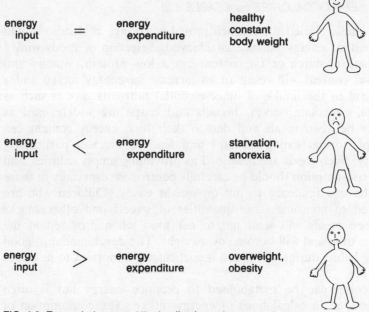

energy input	=	energy expenditure	healthy constant body weight
energy input	<	energy expenditure	starvation, anorexia
energy input	>	energy expenditure	overweight, obesity

FIG. 4.2 Energy balance and the implications of energy imbalance

have overweight children, although this may be because they share the same diet.

2. *Reduced physical activity.* Young people tend to adopt set dietary patterns and, when combined with their physical activity, are in energy balance. As they get older although their diet stays the same, their physical activity and thus their energy expenditure tends to decrease. As a result they put on weight and suffer from 'middle-age spread'. This is classically seen in keen footballers and rugby players who train hard but drink considerable quantities of beer. As they get older they stop engaging in sport but continue to drink the beer!

3. *Bad eating habits.* In normal circumstances, most people eat more than they should and this is particularly significant if they indulge in the wrong types of food. Often these bad eating habits start early in life when children are given sweet things as treats (see Sect. 4.6.1 below).

4. *Psychological problems.* Food acts as a comforter when people are bored or depressed.

5. *Endocrine problems.* Sometimes (not often) an individual may have hormonal problems resulting in their being overweight (see Sect. 4.5.2).

4.6.1   EMPTY CALORIES (see TABLE 1.3)

Following a varied diet, which provides a range of foods, should ensure that energy balance is achieved. Selection of foods with a high sugar, starch or fat content but a low protein, vitamin and mineral content will result in an increase in energy intake and a decrease in the intake of other essential nutrients. Foods such as sweets, chocolate, cakes, biscuits and crisps are widely used as snacks between meals and due to their high energy content can disrupt normal eating patterns and lead to disease, particularly obesity. Such foods are described as providing 'empty calories' and their consumption should be carefully controlled, especially in those who have a tendency to put on weight easily. Children who are allowed to consume large quantities of sweets and other snacks between meals will tend not to eat food when provided at the proper time and will become overweight. The development of good eating habits during childhood is particularly important to health in later life.

Alcohol can be metabolised to produce energy but is often disregarded in calculations of energy intake. The consumption of large amounts of alcohol will lead to increases in bodyweight as well as other physiological and social problems (e.g. cirrhosis of the liver, alcoholism and drunken driving). Table 4.5 shows the alcohol content of a number of different drinks and the corresponding energy provision.

TABLE 4.5 Alcohol content of alcoholic beverages

Alcoholic beverage	Alcohol content (g/100 cm^3)	Energy value (kJ/100 cm^3)
Bitter	3.1	132
Lager	3.2	120
Cider, dry	3.8	152
Cider, sweet	3.7	176
Wine, red	9.5	284
Wine, rosé	8.7	294
Wine, dry white	9.1	275
Wine, sweet white	10.2	394
Port	15.9	655
Sherry, dry	15.7	481
Spirits (40% by volume)	31.7	919

4.6.2   ARE YOU OVERWEIGHT?

There are various ways to check if you are overweight. One fairly simple but crude method involves looking at height–weight tables or charts. These should take into account size of frame. Another way is to calculate the body mass index (BMI) using the following formula:

$$BMI = \frac{\text{weight in kg}}{(\text{height in m})^2}$$

Ideally your BMI should be below 25. A person who has a BMI of over 30 is classed as obese.

A full medical examination is needed to make a proper assessment before corrective measures are taken, and it is essential that a doctor is consulted before embarking on a slimming regime.

4.6.3 HOW MUCH FAT CAN YOU EAT?

From Table 4.4 you can find your recommended energy intake for your age, activity and sex. For a 28 year old hotel manager recommended intake of energy (male, 18–34 years, sedentary life style) would be 2510 kcals. Current nutritional advice suggests a maximum of 35 per cent of energy should come from fat in the diet, i.e. 35 per cent of 2510 kcals = 878.5 kcals. Each gram of fat supplies 9 kcals, therefore a maximum of 98 g of fat per day can be eaten. You can estimate your fat intake from each component in your diet by reference to portion sizes and food composition tables (e.g. see Table 4.2) or from the labels of processed foods.

QUESTIONS

1. Use the conversion factors given in the chapter to calculate the values required to complete the following table:

	kcal/100 g	kJ/100 g
Butter	740	
Mashed potato		499
Roast chicken	148	
Boiled egg		612

2. Explain the meaning of each of the following terms:
   (a) metabolism;
   (b) 'aerobics';
   (c) empty calories.
3. List four food components which can be catabolised (broken down) to produce energy. State the energy obtained per gram of each food component.
4. (a) What is meant by basal metabolic rate?
   (b) Describe how basal metabolism is measured.
   (c) List the factors which affect basal metabolism.

5

VITAMINS

5.1 INTRODUCTION

As well as the major organic nutrients required by the body, i.e.
carbohydrates, proteins and fats, a number of minor ones are
needed in minute amounts to maintain normal health. Collectively,
these widely different organic substances are grouped together as
'vitamins' and must be provided by the diet since they cannot be
synthesised by the body. A balanced diet (see Sect. 7.2), selected
from a range of foods, will provide all the vitamins required by the
body without resort to vitamin supplementation such as tablets,
capsules, etc. Vitamin supplementation should, therefore, only be
necessary when there is an increased demand for vitamins, e.g.
when there is an impairment in absorption, during recovery from
illness and possibly during pregnancy and lactation.

Chemically vitamins are very different (see Fig. 5.1). Each
vitamin is required for a specific metabolic process, many acting as
coenzymes, i.e. factors which are required by an enzyme for its
activity. Dietary deficiency of a vitamin means that this process
cannot be carried out, the tissue levels of the particular vitamin will
drop (a state known as 'hypovitaminosis',) and a specific deficiency
disease results. Deficiency diseases can be treated by administration
of the particular vitamin via the diet or by supplementation. For
example, ascorbic acid (vitamin C) is required by the body for the
production of collagen, the protein of connective tissue (see Sect.
2.5.1). The body is unable to store vitamin C which therefore needs
to be taken daily. Deficiency of vitamin C in the diet leads to a drop
in the tissue levels – hypovitaminosis C – and will eventually mean
that collagen cannot be produced and maintenance of the body's
connective tissue will be impaired leading to the vitamin C deficiency
disease 'scurvy' which can be treated only by administration of
vitamin C.

The intake of a vitamin is determined by the amount of the
vitamin in a particular food and the amount of the food consumed.

Intake = (amount of vitamin in food) × (amount of food eaten)

Vitamins are usually considered in two categories which reflect their solubility:
(a) Fat-soluble vitamins – A, D, E and K.
(b) Water-soluble vitamins – B complex and C.

The recommended daily allowances, dietary sources and deficiency diseases are summarised in Table 5.1.

5.2   FAT-SOLUBLE VITAMINS

The fat-soluble vitamins are associated with foods containing fats. Food fats act as a vehicle for the absorption of fat-soluble vitamins from the gut into the bloodstream. Fat-soluble vitamins can be stored in the body, primarily in the liver, and so blood concentrations of these vitamins can be maintained until the tissue stores are depleted, thus deficiencies of fat-soluble vitamins take longer to develop than those of water-soluble vitamins, e.g. in previously well nourished persons the time taken to produce vitamin A deficiency may be as long as 2 years. Accumulation of very high levels of vitamins in the body is known as 'hypervitaminosis' and can lead to toxicity problems, e.g. hypervitaminosis A.

5.2.1   RETINOL (VITAMIN A)

The chemical name of vitamin A is 'retinol'. It is only found in animal foods, but many fruits and vegetables, e.g. tomatoes and carrots as well as darker green leafy vegetables, contain carotenes, a group of orange and yellow pigments. Carotenes can be converted to retinol in the body and thus have vitamin A activity. The vitamin A content of a diet is the sum of the retinol, *per se*, and the retinol which can be produced from the carotenoid pigments supplied in the diet. The recommended daily intake of vitamin A in Britain is 750 µg of retinol equivalents (1 retinol equivalent = 1 µg retinol or 6 µg of β-carotene or 12 µg of other biologically active carotenoids) increasing to 1200 µg during lactation.

Retinol is used in the body for the production of visual purple (rhodopsin) which is the light-sensitive pigment in the receptors of the retina of the eye responsible for distinguishing light from dark. At night when lighting conditions are so dim that we cannot see colours, this pigment is particularly important.

name	structure
retinol	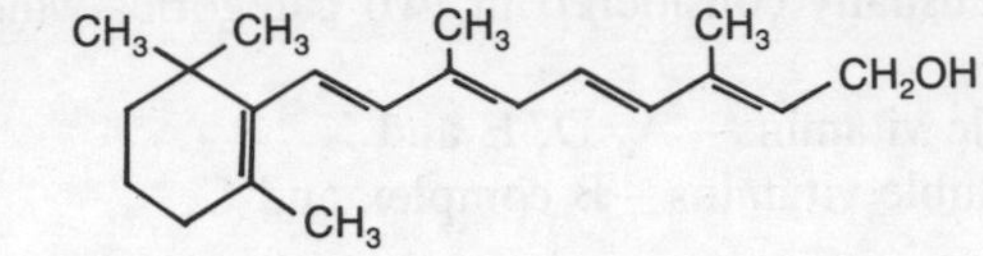
thiamin	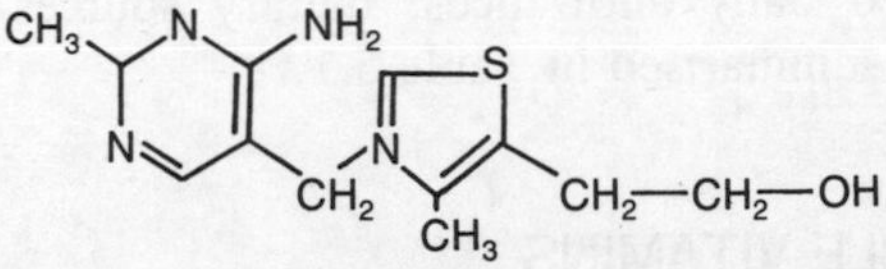
riboflavin	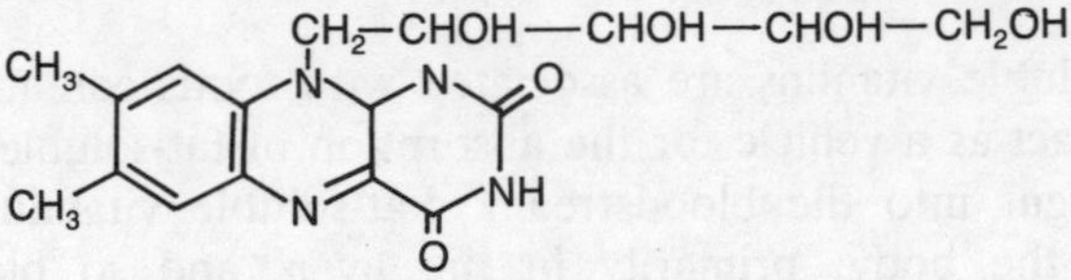
nicotinic acid	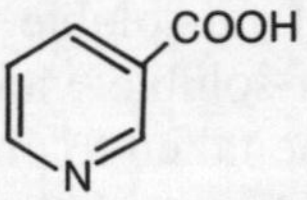
pantothenic acid	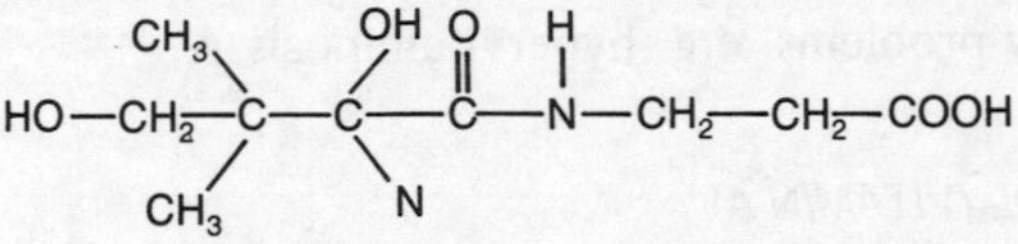
pyridoxine	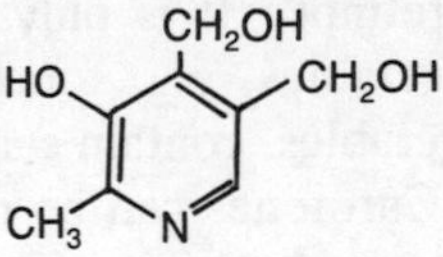
folic acid	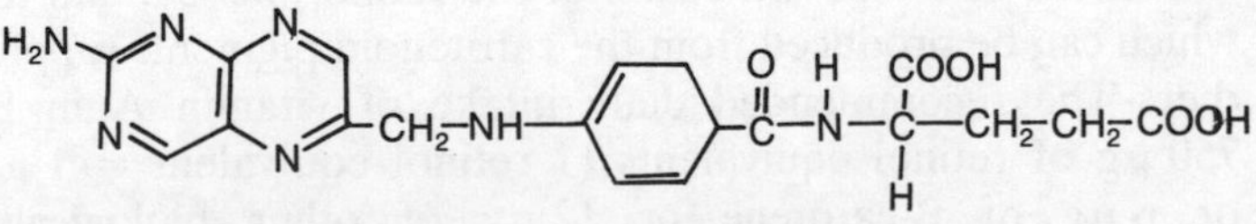

FIG. 5.1 Chemical structure for vitamins

name	structure

cyanocobalamin

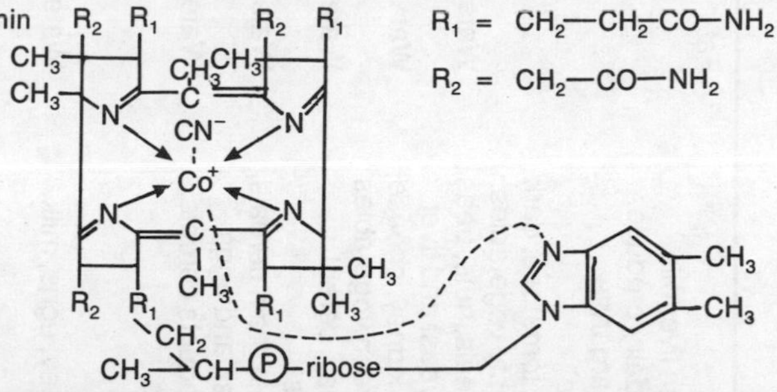

$R_1 = CH_2-CH_2-CO-NH_2$

$R_2 = CH_2-CO-NH_2$

$CH_3-CH(-\overset{}{P})-ribose$

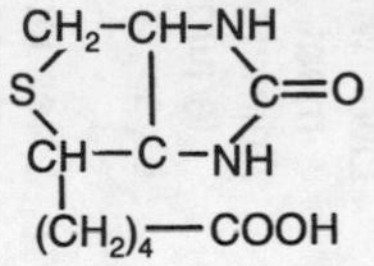

biotin

$(CH_2)_4-COOH$

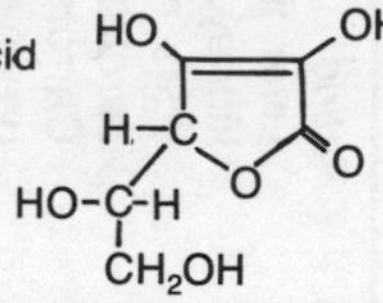

ascorbic acid

CH_2OH

cholecalciferol

HO

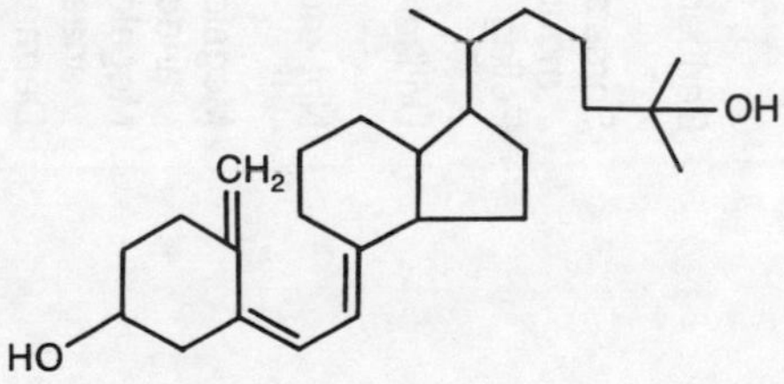

alpha tocopherol

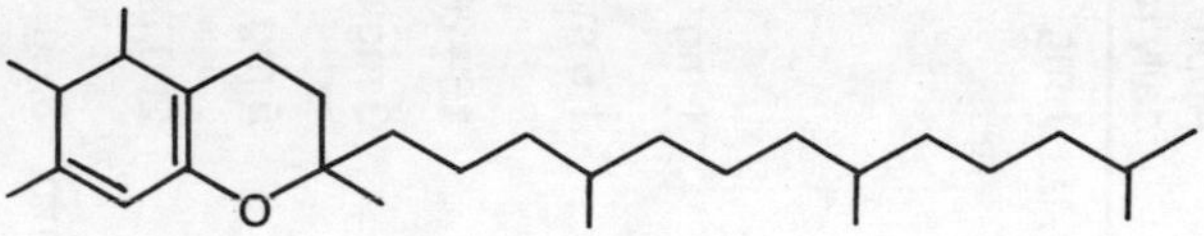

menadione

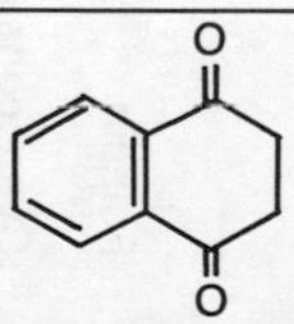

TABLE 5.1 The Vitamins

Vitamin	Alternative name	Approximate adult daily requirement	Deficiency disease	Principal dietary sources	Solubility
A	Retinol	1 mg	Night blindness	*Retinol·* Liver, fish liver oils, kidney, dairy produce, eggs, margarine *β-carotene* Carrots, tomatoes, dark green leafy vegetables	Fat
B_1	Thiamin	1 mg	Beriberi	Whole cereals, nuts, peas, beans, yeast and liver	Water
B_2	Riboflavin	1.5 mg	Sores around mouth	Milk, liver, kidney, cheese, eggs, green vegetables	Water
B_3	Niacin Nicotinamide	15–20 mg	Pellagra	Liver, kidney, cereal products	Water
B_6	Pyridoxine	3 mg	Unlikely	Liver, whole grain cereals, meat, fish and eggs	Water
Pantothenic acid	—	5 mg	Not known	Animal products cereals, legumes	Water
Folic acid	Folacin	200 μg	Megaloblastic anaemia	Liver	
B_{12}	Cyanocobalamin	3 μg	Megaloblastic anaemia	Liver, kidney, eggs, milk, cheese	Water
Biotin	—	100 μg	Dermatitis	Offal, egg yolk, dairy products, cereal, fish, fruit	Water

C	Ascorbic	30 mg	Scurvy	Blackcurrants, potatoes, cabbage and Brussels sprouts, citrus fruits	Water
D	Calciferol	3 µg	Rickets in children, osteomalacia in adults	Fish liver oils, fatty fish, fortified margarine, eggs, liver	Fat
E	Tocopherol	—	Not known	Vegetable oils, cereals, eggs	Fat
K	—	100 µg	Unlikely	Vegetable foods	Fat

Retinol deficiency leads to 'night-blindness'. Vitamin A deficiency is not common in Britain but occurs frequently in under-developed countries. It is important for normal growth of children, particularly for teeth and bones and also results in changes in epithelial tissues leading to the hardening and drying out of the mucous membranes in the mouth, nose and respiratory passages. Long-term deficiency results in dry and scaly skin and in the eye condition called 'xeropthalmia' which eventually leads to total blindness.

The most important animal sources of vitamin A are liver, milk, cheese, butter, and eggs. Margarine is fortified by the addition of carotene or retinol so that the levels of vitamin A are similar to those provided by butter. Both green and yellow vegetables are good sources of carotenes.

Owing to the fat-solubility and storage in the body of vitamin A long-term large doses of vitamin A can accumulate and are toxic. Hypervitaminosis A (see Sect. 5.2) can lead to irritability, swellings over the long bones (in the arms and legs) and dry itchy skin in children, and nausea, headache and diarrhoea in adults. These symptoms can be relieved by discontinuing vitamin A supplementation. Some animal livers can accumulate very high levels of vitamin A and prospective Arctic explorers should avoid eating polar bear livers for this reason! There have been several reported cases of individuals eating vast amounts of carrots which contain high levels of β-carotene. The orange pigment dissolves in body fats and the skin itself will become deep orange in colour. Discontinuation of the carrot-based diet will allow the person to resume a more normal hue.

5.2.2 VITAMIN D

Vitamin D has two important active forms, vitamin D_2 (ergocalciferol) which is provided by the diet, and vitamin D_3 (cholecalciferol) which can be produced in the skin from suitable compounds by the action of ultra-violet light in sunlight. Vitamin D does not therefore have to be provided by the diet if exposure to sunlight is sufficient. Sunlight is the most important source of vitamin D for most people and for this reason vitamin D is sometimes known as the 'sunshine' vitamin.

Vitamin D is needed for the synthesis of a hormone which is essential for the absorption of calcium and phosphorus from the gut and their deposition in bones and teeth. In children, vitamin D deficiency can lead to rickets, in adults the corresponding deficiency disease is called 'osteomalacia' in which bones become softer and more porous. Calcium and phosphorus deficiency can also lead to these conditions (see Sect. 6.2.1). In Britain, vitamin D deficiency is rarely seen in adults except during pregnancy and lactation, and in old age when the active form of vitamin D is less easily produced. One clearly identifiable high-risk group are Asian women in purdah who for religious reasons must keep their bodies completely covered when out-of-doors and, moreover, often consume diets low in vitamin D. Darker skins afford more protection from overproduction of vitamin D in regions nearer the equator where exposure to ultra-violet light is greater, but are a disadvantage in most European countries. Recommended daily intakes of vitamin D in Britain reflect the importance of sunlight, supplementation is not usually necessary during the summer but children and adolescents who have an increased requirement for vitamin D should receive 10 g per day during the winter. Housebound adults, and pregnant and lactating women should also receive 10 g per day.

Few foods are good sources of vitamin D, though it is nearly always associated with animal fats. Oily fish is probably the best source but eggs, butter, liver and cheese are important sources. Margarine is an important source, not that it naturally contains a high level of the vitamin but because the product has, by law, to be fortified with vitamin D for retail sale. Caterers should note, however, that this law does not apply to margarine produced specifically for catering purposes.

Hypervitaminosis D leads to high blood calcium concentrations and the deposition of calcium in soft tissues, particularly the kidneys, and can result in kidney damage.

5.2.3   VITAMIN E

Vitamin E is a misnomer in human nutrition since a vitamin is defined as an organic substance required in minute amounts to avoid the development of a specific deficiency disease. The true role of vitamin E is not fully known but is thought to involve the antioxidant character of the compound. Vitamin E and other tocopherols are common natural antioxidants in lipid materials (see Sect. 3.4.2). Although vitamin E deficiency can be demonstrated in rats, the same does not apply to humans. Deficiency would be most unlikely to affect humans as vitamin E occurs widely in foods. Vegetable oils, cereal products and eggs are the richest sources of vitamin E.

A number of scientifically indefensible claims are associated with vitamin E and many food faddists take enormous doses of it to prevent heart disease, old age and skin problems, as well as attempting to increase sexual potency. There is, however, no evidence that these large doses of vitamin E are toxic.

5.2.4   VITAMIN K

Vitamin K is an essential component of the very complex blood clotting mechanism. It occurs widely in fresh green leafy vegetables such as broccoli and spinach. Moreover, our symbiotic intestinal bacteria synthesise vitamin K which we can then absorb. Deficiency is only likely to develop in persons with fewer gut bacteria than normal, such as those undergoing long-term treatment with antibiotics or who have had sections of their intestines removed.

5.3   WATER-SOLUBLE VITAMINS

The water-soluble vitamins include the vitamin B complex and vitamin C. They are not stored in the body and surplus or excess pass out in the urine. Thus water-soluble vitamin deficiencies appear more rapidly than deficiencies of the fat-soluble vitamins and toxic effects are much less likely to be observed.

5.3.1   VITAMIN B COMPLEX

The B vitamins which are known to be required by humans consist of eight different chemical substances. Their similarities include:
 (a) Solubility in water.
 (b) Nitrogen as part of the molecules.
 (c) A presence in large quantities in liver.
 (d) Roles as major coenzymes in body cells.
 (e) Generally they are found in similar foods.
 B vitamins are required for growth, reproduction and correct functioning of the nervous system.

5.3.2   THIAMIN (VITAMIN B₁)

Thiamin was the first of the B complex vitamins to be obtained in a pure form, hence its name Vitamin B_1. It is essential for one of the steps in the breakdown of carbohydrate to produce energy, thus a thiamin-deficient diet will result in an inability to obtain energy from carbohydrate. Carbohydrate-rich diets lead more quickly to thiamin deficiency than fat-rich diets, as thiamin is not needed for the release of energy from fat. Thiamin deficiency is characterised by loss of appetite, anxiety, irritability and lack of energy, and eventually a deficiency disease called 'beriberi'. The recommended daily intake of thiamin is related to the carbohydrate content of the diet and lies between 0.7 and 1.3 mg depending mainly on the individual's level of activity, energy expenditure and thus energy requirement. Younger, more active men, with high energy expenditure, require higher intakes (see Table 4.4).

All plant and animal sources contain some thiamin but cereal germs, nuts, peas, beans and other pulses, yeast and liver are the richest sources. Low-extraction (white) flours (i.e. flours where the proportion of whole grain that is used to make the flour is low and a large proportion of the original grain is discarded as bran) are fortified in Britain by the addition of thiamin to bring the level of the vitamin in the flour to 0.24 mg/100 g, the same as one would expect to find in wholemeal flour.

5.3.3 RIBOFLAVIN (VITAMIN B_2)

Riboflavin (vitamin B_2) is a component of two coenzymes involved in oxidation–reduction reactions which are of great importance in the release of energy from foods. Dietary deficiency of riboflavin results in the eruption of sores around the mouth and nose but, surprisingly, does not lead to a more serious deficiency disease.

Unlike the other B vitamins, the level of riboflavin is relatively high in dairy produce and low in cereal grains. The best sources of riboflavin are milk (which is the most important single source in the British diet), liver, eggs, green vegetables, yeast extracts and meat extracts. Exposure of riboflavin to ultra-violet light results in large losses of the vitamin, and for this reason milk should not be left for long periods on doorsteps. One pint of fresh milk provides about half the daily riboflavin requirement but two hours exposure of milk to sunlight in a glass bottle can result in loss of between 50 and 70 per cent of the riboflavin. The use of opaque cartons does help to minimise this problem. The recommended daily intake of riboflavin is 1.6 mg for men and 1.3 mg for women, rising to 1.6 mg and 1.8 mg during pregnancy and lactation, respectively.

5.3.4 NICOTINIC ACID (VITAMIN B_3)

Nicotinic acid and nicotinamide are two forms of the same vitamin which is known as 'niacin' in America. Nicotinamide is, again, a component of two coenzymes which are involved with the release of energy from foods. The amino acid tryptophan can be converted to nicotinamide in the body and 60 mg of tryptophan can replace 1 mg of dietary nicotinamide (see Table 2.2 and Fig 5.1). Dietary deficiency of nicotinamide which is not replaced by tryptophan leads to pellagra (Italian; *pelle* means skin and *agra*, rough) a disease which affects the skin, gut and nervous system causing dermatitis, diarrhoea, depression and sometimes dementia, and eventually death. Milk and eggs are not good sources of nicotinamide yet they can both be used for the cure of pellagra since they are rich in tryptophan. Pellagra is very common in countries where the staple cereal is maize because the nicotinic acid is present in a bound form and is not available to the body. In Mexico, where maize is eaten in the form of tortillas, preparation involves treatment of the maize with lime which releases the nicotinic acid from its bound form.

In Britain the main food sources of nicotinic acid in the diet are meat and meat products, bread and flour, fortified breakfast cereals, vegetables, and milk. The recommended daily intake of nicotinic acid (or its equivalent in terms of tryptophan) should be 18 mg for men and 15 mg for women, increasing to 18 and 21 mg during pregnancy and lactation, respectively, when the demands are higher.

5.3.5   PYRIDOXINE (VITAMIN B₆)

Vitamin B_6 occurs as three closely related substances – pyridoxine, pyridoxal and pyridoxamine. Vitamin B_6 is used for the production of pyridoxal phosphate, a coenzyme for over sixty different enzyme systems. Vitamin B_6 is involved in the metabolism of all the amino acids and in the production of haemoglobin for red blood cells.

Pyridoxine is widely distributed in plant and animal foods. Liver, whole grain cereals, peanuts and bananas are particularly good sources. Owing to the widespread occurrence of vitamin B_6, a deficiency is unlikely to occur except in certain groups. Pyridoxine has been prescribed for alleviating symptoms of premenstrual tension and seems successful in about 30 per cent of cases. Also, pyridoxine sometimes helps depression developed by a minority of contraceptive pill takers. However, one report suggests that excessive intakes may cause numbness in the limbs. In Britain there is no set recommended daily intake for pyridoxine.

5.3.6   PANTOTHENIC ACID

Pantothenic acid is needed for the release of energy from fats and carbohydrates. Animal products, cereals and legumes are rich sources of pantothenic acid but it is so widely distributed in foods that dietary deficiency is unlikely to occur and thus no recommended daily intake is set in Britain.

5.3.7 FOLIC ACID

Folic acid (folate) is required for the production of red blood cells and deficiency of folic acid leads to a form of anaemia known as 'megaloblastic anaemia', a particular problem during pregnancy. The recommended daily intake of folate for adults is 300 μg, rising to 500 μg during pregnancy and 400 μg during lactation. Green vegetables, liver and kidney, whole cereals, nuts and legumes are good sources of folic acid.

5.3.8 CYANOCOBALAMIN (VITAMIN B_{12})

Vitamin B_{12} is unique among the vitamins because it only occurs in animal tissues and yeasts and is not found at all in plants. Vitamin B_{12} is involved in maintenance of folic acid levels and the nervous system. Deficiency results in the same symptoms as folate deficiency, as B_{12} maintains folate levels and therefore can be cured by treatment with either vitamin B_{12} or with folic acid. Degradative changes which can occur in the nervous system due to B_{12} deficiency however can only be treated with vitamin B_{12}. Apart from certain persons who have an inherited inability to absorb vitamin B_{12} from the gut (a condition called 'pernicious anaemia') the only people likely to suffer B_{12} deficiency are vegans – persons who consume no foods of animal origin and do not supplement their diet with vitamin B_{12}-rich extracts, such as yeast. Although liver is the richest source of vitamin B_{12}, useful amounts occur in milk and cheese, eggs, meat and fish.

5.3.9 BIOTIN

Biotin is essential for the release of energy from dietary fats. Gut bacteria produce biotin which can then be absorbed and utilised by the human host. Although offal and egg yolk are rich sources of biotin, dairy products, cereals, fish, fruit and vegetables also provide useful amounts. Again no recommended daily intake of biotin is set in Britain. The only reported cases of biotin deficiency have appeared in persons who have consumed large amounts of raw egg over a long period of time and as a result usually suffer from severe dermatitis. One such case is illustrated by a man whose diet consisted mainly of six dozen raw eggs and 56 pints of red wine per week. Raw egg white contains a substance called 'avidin' (see Table 2.1) which combines with biotin making it unavailable to the body.

5.3.10 ASCORBIC ACID (VITAMIN C)

Long-term shortage of vitamin C is one of the earliest recorded deficiency diseases, and eighteenth century sailors frequently died of scurvy. It was discovered that fresh fruits cured the disease, especially citrus fruits (oranges, lemons and limes). Lime extracts were used by the British Navy to avoid scurvy, hence the name 'limeys'. As mentioned earlier in the chapter, ascorbic acid is required for the production of collagen in the body and a dietary deficiency of vitamin C leads to breakdown of the body's connective tissues, and eventually scurvy. Scurvy is rarely seen today except in old persons whose diet may be limited because of chewing difficulties, and the acidity of many of the foods which are good sources of the vitamin and possibly the cost of vitamin C-rich foods. Poor wound healing and the development of pressure sores in long term hospital geriatric patients is attributed to low vitamin C content of institutionalised cooking due to poor menu planning combined with long preparation, cooking and serving times (see Sect. 13.3.3). Vitamin C is also important in the absorption of iron (see Sect. 6.2.7).

Vitamin C is another of the vitamins which has caught the attention of the food faddists and a number of extra-antiscorbutic roles (roles other than in the prevention of scurvy) have been ascribed to it. Vitamin C megatherapy – the intake of vast amounts of vitamin C, e.g. doses of 1 g and more per day – is often recommended as a way of avoiding a variety of complaints including the common cold, headaches, heart disease, schizophrenia and cancer. Scientific substantiation of these claims is difficult since for every report proving a particular extra-antiscorbutic claim there is another giving contradictory evidence. Large doses of vitamin C appear in the urine within several hours and so are not retained by the body. Rebound scurvy may occur in persons who have received large doses of vitamin C and then return to more reasonable intakes. This disease may also be seen in new-born babies whose mothers have taken very large doses of the vitamin during pregnancy.

The recommended daily intake of vitamin C currently in the United Kingdom is 30 mg for adults increasing to 60 mg during pregnancy and lactation although there are suggestions that these should be increased. Important food sources of ascorbic acid are nearly all of plant origin, and include fresh fruits and vegetables such as citrus fruits, cabbage, Brussels sprouts, green peppers, tomatoes and blackcurrants. The only animal food with appreciable amounts of vitamin C is liver.

Potatoes are not a rich source of vitamin C, yet they represent one of the major providers of the vitamin in the British diet because of the large amounts consumed. The vitamin C content of main-crop potatoes stored over the winter will decrease as the months go by. The vitamin C content is usually about 30 mg/100 g in freshly dug main-crop potatoes, after storage for 2 and 6 months this level will have dropped to about 20 and 10 mg/100 g, respectively.

5.4 VITAMIN LOSSES DURING FOOD STORAGE, PREPARATION AND COOKING

Water-soluble vitamins, especially vitamin C, are more subject to losses during cooking than fat-soluble vitamins because:
1. They tend to be more susceptible to breakdown by heat than the fat-soluble vitamins, this breakdown may be accelerated if heating is carried out in alkaline conditions, e.g. during the boiling of vegetables with added sodium bicarbonate. Stability of chlorophyll is improved in alkaline conditions and some older people add sodium bicarbonate to their vegetables to keep their attractive bright green colour. Ascorbic acid, thiamin, riboflavin and pyridoxine are heat-labile (heat-sensitive), particularly under alkaline conditions.
2. They are readily leached from foods during storage in water or boiling. For the heat-stable, water-soluble vitamins, leaching from foods probably represents the major method of loss. Catering practice of peeling potatoes, chipping and storing under water until use, almost completely depletes their vitamin C content.
3. Some of the vitamins are particularly susceptible to oxidation during preparation. The more finely diced the food, the greater the surface area exposed and the greater the rate of oxidation. Vitamin C is probably the vitamin most sensitive to oxidation but dried diced dehydrated products, e.g. carrots, can lose their carotenes by oxidation and thus their potential vitamin A activity is destroyed.

Of all the vitamins, probably the most susceptible to breakdown during food storage, preparation and cooking is vitamin C. Storage of vegetables before use although unavoidable can reduce the vitamin C content. Correct storage will minimise vitamin C losses. Vitamin C is very easily oxidised by atmospheric oxygen and by the action of an enzyme – ascorbic acid oxidase – which is present in plant tissues. Dicing and slicing of fruits and vegetables removes the natural compartmentalisation within the food which normally prevents the meeting of enzyme and substrate. The time taken for the preparation of foods should be kept as short as possible to minimise these losses. Boiling water drives off oxygen, thus in cooking placing foods directly into boiling water inactivates enzymes and reduces vitamin C losses. Blanching of vegetable foods prior to freezing can help maintain the ascorbic acid content of frozen foods.

Different systems of cook-chill catering (see Sect. 13.5.1) are widely in operation but losses of vitamin C in vegetables have been found of the order of 6% per day during chilled storage, which will often be less than during periods of warm holding found in traditional cook-serve catering.

In order to maximise the vitamin content, caterers should follow a few simple rules:

1. Prepare foods as close as possible to the time of consumption to avoid lengthy periods for prepared food to undergo enzymic action and atmospheric oxidation.
2. Cook or store foods in acidic rather than alkaline conditions, e.g. by the addition of lemon juice to cooking water or to fruit salads.
3. Do not use sodium bicarbonate during cooking to preserve the bright green colour of the chlorophyll in green vegetables.
4. Minimise the volume of water used for the boiling of vegetables.
5. Utilise the cooking water from vegetables in the preparation of gravies and sauces to return water-soluble vitamins leached from foods to the meal.
6. Keep cooking times as short as possible.
7. Plating and serving times for meals should be as short as possible. Warm-holding improves microbiological quality (see Sect. 13.3.4) but adversely affects nutritional quality. This is of particular importance in hospital catering where long delays between food preparation and point of service have been a problem.
8. Size, e.g. dicing and slicing, is important in determining vitamin losses and decreasing the size of the piece of the food increases the surface area-to-mass ratio and so increases the possibility of oxidation. Foods should be cut rather that torn, grating should be avoided.

QUESTIONS

1. (a) What are vitamins?
   (b) Name the two groups into which vitamins are divided and list the components of each group.
   (c) Why should it not be necessary, under normal circumstances, to take vitamin supplements?
   (d) Under what circumstances may it be necessary to take vitamin supplements?
2. (a) Carrots contain no retinol yet they are a useful dietary source of vitamin A. Explain this statement.
   (b) For what biological role is vitamin A required?
   (c) What symptoms are associated with vitamin A deficiency?
   (d) Why is vitamin D sometimes known as the 'sunshine vitamin'?
3. (a) What is the alternative name for vitamin C?
   (b) Name the deficiency disease associated with vitamin C.
   (c) What is meant by the term 'megatherapy'?
   (d) Blackcurrants contain about 200 mg ascorbic acid per 100 g and potatoes contain only about 20 mg ascorbic acid per 100 g yet potatoes are a much more important source of ascorbic acid in the British diet. Explain this statement.
4. Explain each of the following statements:
   (a) Cooking green vegetables with added sodium bicarbonate so that they keep their attractive green colour reduces their nutritional value.
   (b) The vitamin content of finely diced vegetables is lowered.
   (c) Potatoes should not be peeled, chipped and stored under water prior to use.
   (d) The volume of water used for cooking of vegetables should be minimised.
   (e) Plating and serving times for meals should be kept as short as possible.

6

MINERALS

6.1   INTRODUCTION

Minerals are essential inorganic elements derived from foods and are utilised within the body for three main functions:
1. As inorganic constituents of bones and teeth, e.g. calcium, phosphorus and magnesium.
2. As soluble salts, or electrolytes, to control the composition of body fluids and cells, e.g. sodium and chlorine in blood, potassium, phosphorus and magnesium in cells.
3. As components of enzymes and other proteins, e.g. iron, zinc, magnesium.

In contrast to the other nutrient and food chemical groups already considered, i.e. carbohydrates, proteins, fats and vitamins, all of which are organic nutrients, the minerals are a group of elements which are taken in as inorganic substances, e.g. sodium chloride. Some elements, for example, carbon, hydrogen, nitrogen, sulphur and cobalt, can only be utilised by the body when ingested in organic form, e.g. cobalt in preformed vitamin B_{12}. Oxygen is present in a number of essential organic nutrients but is also taken in as inorganic oxygen, via the lungs, and utilised in the body for the oxidation of foodstuffs and the release of energy (see Ch. 4). Water is an inorganic compound which is essential for maintaining the correct concentration of the body tissues.

The minerals can be divided into two groups depending upon the level required by the human body:
(a) Major minerals or macrominerals.
(b) Trace elements. The inorganic salts and the electrolytes are classified as major minerals. Those minerals required only in small amounts as components of enzymes, proteins and other compounds are usually classified as 'trace elements'.

Iron is more difficult to classify as it falls between the two groups. The body requires iron for the production of haemoglobin but the whole body iron content is only about 4 g which is enough to make a 2 in nail. In this chapter iron will be included in the major

TABLE 6.1 Approximate mineral composition of an adult man

Mineral	Composition (g)
(a) Major minerals	
Calcium	1050
Phosphurus	700
Potassium	245
Sulphur	175
Chlorine	105
Sodium	105
Magnesium	50
Iron	2.8
(b) Trace elements (present at less than 0.005 % of whole bodyweight)	
Manganese	0.21
Iodine	0.03
Copper	0.10
Fluorine	Trace
Zinc	Trace
Cobalt	Trace
Molybdenum	Trace
Selenium	Trace

minerals. A typical 70 kg male contains about 4 kg of minerals, the breakdown of which is shown in Table 6.1.

It is important to remember that the amount of a mineral provided by a food is a function of the amount ingested, the level of the mineral in the food, *and also* its availability in the food, e.g. spinach contains large amounts of calcium and iron which are made unavailable by high levels of oxalic acid. Phytic acid reduces the availability of many minerals from whole grain cereal products. Interrelationships with other nutrients can also affect the absorption of minerals, e.g. eating vitamin C rich foods in combination with iron-rich foods (see Sect. 6.2.7).

6.2 MAJOR MINERALS

6.2.1 CALCIUM (Ca)

Calcium is a metallic element and the most abundant mineral in the body. Ninety-nine per cent of the body's 1000–1500 g of calcium is contained within the bones and teeth as tiny crystals of calcium phosphate (hydroxyapatite), $C_{10} (PO_4)_6 (OH)_2$. The deposits of calcium are static in teeth, but in bone there is a continual turnover, with calcium being deposited and then mobilised and redeposited. Thus the shape of our bones is being continually modified throughout our lives. This mobilisation of calcium from the bones enables them to act as a reserve supply which can be used to maintain the remaining 1 per cent of the calcium in the body, which is necessary for the contraction of muscles, for nerve function, as a component of various proteins and in blood clotting. It is also used as a 'messenger' for release of compounds from cells.

Vitamin D (see Sect. 5.2.2) is essential for the absorption of calcium from the gut and utilisation within the body. If the vitamin D concentration in the body (i.e. vitamin D status) is low, then calcium is not absorbed and it passes from the body in the faeces. Normally the body absorbs 20–40 per cent of the dietary calcium, the remaining 60–80 per cent passing unabsorbed from the body. The body responds to the calcium content of the diet and absorption is more efficient when dietary calcium content is lower, and vice versa. Absorption of calcium is decreased when the diet contains large amounts of dicarboxylic acids which complex with calcium and other minerals forming insoluble salts. Examples include phytic acid, from whole cereals, and oxalic acid, e.g. from rhubarb. Much of the calcium in spinach is unavailable due to high oxalic acid levels.

The recommended daily allowance of calcium is 500 mg/day, rising to 1200 mg during pregnancy and lactation. The deficiency disease of calcium is rickets in children and osteomalacia in adults. Rickets and osteomalacia appear to be on the increase in the United Kingdom and deficiency is likely to be caused by low vitamin D status rather than dietary deficiency of calcium. Major sources of calcium in the diet are milk, cheese, bread, flour and green vegetables. Bones of some small fish, such as sardines and whitebait which are eaten whole, are also good sources of calcium. Hard water is an additional source for some people in certain hard water areas. Calcium carbonate (creta) is added to flours in Britain so that the level of calcium carbonate is 230–390 mg per 100 g.

6.2.2 PHOSPHORUS (P)

Phosphorus is a non-metallic element and is the second most common mineral in the body (see Table 6.1). The bones and teeth contain 80 per cent of the phosphorus, the remaining 20 per cent is in the blood and tissues. It has many functions in the body, acting as a pH buffer and is an important component of nucleic acids, i.e.

deoxyribosenucleic acid (DNA) and ribosenucleic acid (RNA). Phosphorus also occurs in the phospholipids (see Table 2.1), e.g. lecithin (see Sect. 2.6.2). It is important in the structure of the energy-rich compounds (e.g. ATP) produced in the body during catabolism (see Sect. 4.2).

Phosphorus occurs widely in foods and its distribution follows that of protein, so that if the provision of protein is sufficient so also is that of phosphorus. Protein-rich foods (meat, fish and poultry, milk and cheese, nuts, legumes, and whole grains) are important sources. A deficiency of phosphorus is unknown in humans.

6.2.3 MAGNESIUM (Mg)

Magnesium is a metallic element. Over half of the body's 20–30 g of magnesium is present in the bones and teeth, the rest is found in soft tissue cells, especially liver and muscle. Magnesium is essential in cells for the production and utilisation of energy, for the regulation of body temperature, for muscle contraction and for protein synthesis.

Magnesium deficiency is rare, provided the diet is based on a wide range of foods, but is seen in chronic alcoholics where it results in nervous and muscular irritability, behavioural disturbances, depression and delirium. Magnesium occurs widely in foods, especially vegetable foods. Chlorophyll (the green photosynthetic pigment of plants) contains magnesium. Meat, whole grains, nuts, beans and leafy vegetables are important sources.

6.2.4 SODIUM (Na)

The total amount of sodium in the human body is about 90 g, of which about 50 per cent is in the blood and other extracellular fluids, 38 per cent is in bone and 12 per cent is in the cells. The concentration of sodium is low inside cells and high outside cells. Sodium is a key element in the regulation of body water and pH. Energy is used to pump sodium across cell membranes out of cells and, due to the osmotic effect, water is also pulled across the membrane thus controlling the concentration of substances inside the cell. Sodium is also important in the conduction of nerve impulses. Most excess sodium is removed from the body via the urine. If sweating is profuse, e.g. during hot weather, after strenuous exercise or when working in some catering areas, such as a hot kitchen, sodium losses can be very large and there may be a need for higher salt intakes than normal.

Deficiency of sodium results in muscular weakness and cramps.

Sodium is supplied by many chemicals commonly used during food processing. Sodium chloride (common or table salt) is used widely as a flavouring agent and preservative. Sodium hydrogen carbonate (sodium bicarbonate or baking soda) is used as a raising agent in baking, and monosodium glutamate (MSG) is used extensively in cooking as a flavour enhancer for meat products. Sodium nitrate and nitrite are added to cured meat products, e.g. bacon, ham and luncheon meats. Cheese, milk, shellfish, bacon and other processed meats, and salted butter are good sources of sodium. Bread is an important source due to the relatively large amounts consumed by many people. Fresh fruit, vegetables and unprocessed meats are low in sodium.

Sodium intakes have to be restricted in certain kidney diseases or where there is a marked water retention in tissues, i.e. oedema. Premenstrual tension is often associated with water retention just before menstruation takes place, and low-sodium diets may be used to relieve these symptoms. More generally, high blood pressure is associated with high salt intakes and current nutritional advice strongly stresses the reduction of sodium intakes by up to 30 per cent. The use of salt in cooking and at the table greatly increases sodium intakes. The increasing importance of processed foods in the British diet can make it difficult for some people to control their sodium intakes. Salted crisps, peanuts and other snack products have large amounts of salt added. The salf content of some common foods are shown in Table 6.2. Potassium chloride, although having a slightly bitter taste, is commercially available as a. substitute for

TABLE 6.2 Salt content of some common foods

Food	Approximate Salt content (%)
Bovril	11.6
Marmite	11.1
Bacon	5.8
Salami	4.3
Black pudding	3.0
Cooked ham	2.9
Sausages	2.6
Cooked tongue	2.5
Kippers	2.4
Cheddar cheese	1.7
Bread	1.4
Baked beans	1.3
Butter	0–3 g

sodium chloride to reduce sodium intakes. Saltiness is an acquired taste and is disliked by some very young children. For individuals conscious of their salt intake the following hints may be useful:

1. Use only a little salt in cooking. Try using herbs for flavouring instead.
2. Do not add salt at the table prior to tasting.
3. When planning meals or snacks choose foods with a lower salt content. Note the values for processed foods.
4. Never add salt to foods being introduced to children.
5. Remember, low-salt foods may taste a little different but this does not necessarily mean that they are less appetising.

6.2.5   POTASSIUM (K)

Potassium is a metallic element of which about 245 g is present in the human body. Most of the potassium in the body is present in the cells, and potassium levels can be used as an indication of the lean tissue in the body. Very small amounts of the mineral are carried in the blood or stored in the bones. It acts with sodium to maintain the concentration of cellular fluids and to conduct nerve impulses.

Potassium deficiency results in muscle weakness and paralysis. The muscles of the gut can be affected, causing distension with gas, as well as those of the heart, leading to death. Excessive intake results in very similar effects to those of deficiency. Most common foods contain moderate amounts of potassium. Unprocessed meats, milk, fruits and vegetables are good sources. Potassium chloride is not used as a processing aid by food manufacturers and therefore potassium intakes are more easily controlled. Potassium chloride is used as a sodium salt substitute and thus increases potassium intakes while reducing sodium intakes.

6.2.6   CHLORINE (Cl)

Chlorine combined with sodium plays an important part in nerve cells for the conduction of nerve impulses, and in controlling the pH of blood and tissue fluids at between 7.35 and 7.45. Chlorine has a major solo role in the production of hydrochloric acid for gastric juice, which is necessary to activate pepsinogen in the stomach (see Sect. 2.8), for the proper absorption of vitamin B_{12} (see Sect. 5.3.8) and iron (see Sect. 6.2.7), and to suppress the growth of micro-organisms in the stomach. Excretion of chlorine in urine and sweat closely follows that of sodium and it is only through vomiting that losses of chlorine without corresponding losses of sodium will occur.

Chlorine occurs in sodium chloride and potassium chloride (used as a salt substitute). The distribution of chlorine in foods closely follows sodium distribution.

6.2.7   IRON (Fe)

There is a total of about 4 g of iron in the body. About 60–70 per cent of this iron is found in haemoglobin and the related myoglobin (see Fig. 2.4). Haemoglobin reacts with oxygen to form oxyhaemoglobin in which form oxygen is carried in the blood from the lungs to the various cells of the body. Here it is released and utilised for the oxidation of glucose and other substrates in the production of energy (see Sect. 4.3). The life span of a red blood cell is about 3 to 4 months after which the cells are destroyed – fortunately the iron in the cells is recycled and used again for the production of further red blood cells. Iron is also required for the activity of certain enzymes involved in energy production, about 10 per cent of the body pool of iron is used in this way. The remaining 20–30 per cent of iron is stored in the liver as a complex salt called 'ferritin'.

The efficiency of iron absorption from the gut is about 10 per cent and thus to replace the 1 mg lost in the urine every day the recommended daily allowance is 10 mg of iron for an adult male and women past child-bearing age. Blood losses during menstruation increase iron requirements and the recommended daily allowance is 12 mg for women of child-bearing age, 13 mg during pregnancy and 15 mg during lactation. Haem iron (found in haemoglobin and myoglobin provided by animal foods) is about five times more easily absorbed than non-haem iron. Vitamin C (see Sect. 5.3.10) in foods helps to reduce non-haem iron from the iron III (Fe^{3+}) state to the iron II (Fe^{2+}) state, and also maintains it in the reduced state in which it is more readily absorbed across the wall of the gut. Combining vitamin C-rich foods with iron-rich foods thus helps the efficiency of iron absorption. Iron absorption is hindered by phosphoprotein in egg, tannins in tea and coffee, and non-haem iron absorption is also reduced by phytates in unrefined cereals. Iron deficiency is the commonest mineral deficiency in Britain and results in iron-deficiency anaemia, the symptoms of which are paleness of the skin, weakness and shortness of breath. Iron-deficiency anaemia is caused by a low dietary provision of iron or impaired iron absorption and results in reduction of haemoglobin synthesis and the number of red blood cells. Iron deficiency is particularly common in women owing to increased blood losses during menstruation. Good dietary sources of iron are meat, which on average provides 25 per cent of the intake (especially liver and kidney), egg yolk, bread, flour and other cereal products, potatoes and vegetables. Iron is found in cereals, but due to refining about 50 per cent may be lost. To counter these losses, iron is added to flour to bring the content up to 1.65 mg/100 g. Breakfast cereals and some baby foods are similarly fortified.

An accumulation of excess iron in the body results in a condition called 'siderosis' which may be caused by an excessive dietary intake of the mineral. Siderosis is common among the Bantu tribe of South Africa who use iron cooking and brewing vessels. The ingestion of large amounts of iron-rich beer by these people can result in daily iron intakes of about 100 mg. Wines, especially cheap ones, can also be a very rich source of iron thus siderosis can be prevalent amongst chronic alcoholics who drink excessive amounts.

6.3   TRACE ELEMENTS

6.3.1   IODINE (I)

The body pool of iodine is 15–30 mg, of which about 60 per cent is concentrated in the thyroid gland and the remaining 40 per cent occurs mostly in the bloodstream. Iodine is stored in the thyroid gland and is used by the body for only one purpose, i.e. for the production of the thyroid hormones thyroxine and triiodothyronine. Thyroid hormones are the most important factors in controlling the basal metabolic rate (see Sect. 4.5.2).

Iodine deficiency results in simple goitre (a visible swelling in the front of the neck) and can be cured by increasing iodine intakes, e.g. by the use of iodised table salt. Small amounts of iodine may be provided by drinking water and in areas of the country where the iodine content of the water is low the iodine content of the food products grown in the area will also be low. In world-wide terms, goitre is the commonest mineral deficiency disease. In Britain, Derbyshire is a notorious goitre area and the problem is known in this region as 'Derbyshire neck'. Fish and other seafoods are the richest food sources of iodine available but cereals, vegetables and milk also provide iodine.

Excessive consumption of foods which contain natural antithyroid compounds, called 'goitrogens', over a long period of time can also result in the development of goitre, e.g. turnips and cabbage. **Normal** British intakes of these vegetables will not lead to this disease. Excessive intakes of iodine due to long-term treatment with iodine compounds or dried seaweed extracts can cause toxicity problems.

6.3.2 FLUORINE (F)

Fluorine is readily absorbed from the intestine and is contained mainly in the bones and teeth. Its only clear role is as a structural component of teeth which helps their resistance to dental caries (tooth decay). It was first noted that in areas where the fluorine content of the water was high, the teeth of the inhabitants developed brown mottling in the enamel. Later it appeared that although the mottling was disfiguring, no harmful effects were caused and in fact the children's teeth in these areas were more resistant to tooth decay. It is possible that fluorine also strengthens bones and reduces demineralisation in the same way. Levels of fluorine in water above 2 mg/litre result in mottling of the tooth enamel, at about 1 mg/litre no mottling is observed but the incidence of dental caries is markedly reduced. The fluorine content of water supplies in some regions of Britain is adjusted in an attempt to minimise tooth decay. Fluoridation of water supplies is, however, a very emotive subject and produces strong public reaction!

Fluorine is provided by most animal and plant foods but seafoods and tea are among the richest sources. There is no deficiency disease associated with a lack of fluorine in the diet apart from the association between dental caries and low fluoride intakes. Very high intakes of fluorine are toxic and result in deformed teeth and bones.

6.3.3 ZINC (Zn)

Zinc is a metallic trace element acting as a component of enzyme systems involved in diverse physiological roles, including carbon dioxide transport in the blood, carbohydrate metabolism and the production of hormones which control the female menstrual cycle. Human zinc deficiency was first recognized in the early 1960's as a cause of some cases of dwarfism and sexual immaturity. A great deal of research is being done on zinc status and health. Marginal zinc deficiency may be quite widespread and zinc treatment has been shown to improve some cases of acne.

Zinc occurs widely in plant and animal tissues and oysters are a particularly rich source. Good sources of zinc include red meat, liver, kidneys, whole grain cereals, shell fish, nuts and cheese. Zinc content of fruits, vegetables and refined foods is low. Zinc absorption is better from animal sources than plant sources due to phytic acid (see Sect. 6.2.1).

6.3.4   OTHER TRACE ELEMENTS

Other trace elements are required by the body and are shown in Table 6.3. Although required in very small amounts these trace elements are of considerable interest to nutritionists, as some appear to be essential nutrients for farm animals and may play an as yet unknown role in human nutrition.

TABLE 6.3 Trace elements in human body

Functional role in humans	Present but of no special significance in humans	Neither toxic nor with functional role in animals	Toxic
Iodine	Molybdenum	Barium	Lead
Copper	Nickel	Bromine	Mercury
Zinc	Silicon	Gold	
Cobalt	Tin	Silver	
Selenium	Vanadium	Rubidium	
Chromium	Arsenic		
Manganese			
Fluorine			

QUESTIONS

1. (a) Explain the term 'mineral'.
   (b) List the three main functions for which minerals are used in the body.
   (c) Classify minerals into two broad groups based on requirements and give two examples of each.
2. (a) Why is calcium required in the human body?
   (b) Name the major sources of calcium in the diet.
   (c) Why are both calcium and vitamin D required to prevent rickets in children?
3. (a) Which three compounds contain over 90 per cent of the body's iron?
   (b) What is the deficiency disease and the physical symptoms associated with not obtaining enough iron in the body?
   (c) Name three good dietary sources of iron.

    (d) How much of the iron we ingest is absorbed into the blood-stream?

    (e) Why does the eating of vitamin C-rich foods help iron absorption?

4. (a) Why does an adequate supply of fluorine in the diet benefit growing children?

    (b) What are the signs of an excessively high intake of fluorine?

    (c) Why do we need iodine in the diet and what happens to people who have an insufficient intake?

    (d) List three sources of iodine in the diet.

7

NUTRITION AND MENU PLANNING

7.1 INTRODUCTION

Increasing public awareness of the importance of nutrition, due to media coverage and product advertising, means that a caterer should be better informed than the public and so be able to respond to the ever-changing requirements. The shelves of the supermarkets provide evidence of the demand for healthier, more wholesome products such as wholemeal bread, low-fat spreads, margarines high in polyunsaturated fatty acids, fresh foods, etc. Similarly, the increasing number of wholefood and vegetarian restaurants. The significance of the dietary provision in a catering establishment to the overall nutrient intake of an individual will depend upon the percentage of the total diet being supplied by the establishment. As the proportion increases, so greater stress must be laid upon the connection between diet and disease and reflected in terms of the dietary provision.

In most restaurants the clientele is transient and the food provided will probably not constitute a significant proportion of the diet. Many restaurants have a 'theme' which is reflected not only by the menu but also by the overall atmosphere. If clients want to eat 'Chinese', 'Indian' or 'Mexican' then they will go to a specific restaurant to satisfy that requirement. The meals provided must then be authentic and it may be difficult to recreate particular dishes to correspond to specific dietary patterns. Indeed, if the meal constitutes a treat they may actually desire to eat something 'naughty but nice', i.e. something they know is nutritionally not very good but has an appealing taste. However, fashions in catering change and one of the current fashions, *cuisine naturelle*, is based on healthy eating practices and use of ingredients such as cream, butter, etc., is minimised. In addition, caterers are being urged to take the lead in healthy eating (see Fig. 7.1).

In contrast, in institutional catering, where the audience is 'captive' e.g. in schools, hospitals, homes for the elderly and prisons or restaurants where people eat regularly, the food provided

FIG. 7.1 Caterers are urged to take the lead in the move towards healthier eating patterns

may constitute a much greater proportion of, if not the total diet, and therefore it is critical that it corresponds to healthy varied eating patterns. One recent report has condemned canteen meals as being a hazard to health specifically on nutritional grounds (see

Sect. 5.3.10). Variations in the foods served and the days on which an item will appear become important considerations and predictability should be avoided, i.e. 'it is Monday so we'll be having...'. Caterers will need to randomise their menus, e.g. on a 14-day or 21-day cycle, to ensure that they are interesting and varied and so stimulate appetite. Nutritious, appetising menus are particularly important in schools, which cater for growing children, and hospitals, where the patients are repairing tissues after illness and surgery.

7.2   BALANCED DIET

The daily food we eat is termed our 'diet'. A balanced diet is one which provides a sufficient, but not excessive, quantity, of each of the nutrients required for health (see Table 7.1), to ensure that an individual is not prone to the development of specific deficiency diseases. Alternatively, it can be described as one which provides:

(a) An adequate amount of energy.
(b) Optimum proportions of protein, starch and fat.
(c) Sufficient dietary fibre.
(d) Adequate quantities of essential fatty acids, vitamins and minerals.

TABLE 7.1   Nutrients required in a balanced human diet

Nutrient	Use
Water	Adult humans contain about 70 % water which is used as a medium for the transport of nutrients through the body, to disperse substances within cells and to allow biochemical reactions to take place
Carbohydrate	Energy production
Protein	Dietary protein is broken down into its constituent amino acids which are used for the production of the body's own proteins; if insufficient energy is provided by the diet protein can be used for energy production
Fat	Fat is used as an energy substrate; essential fatty acids are required for cell structure and function
Vitamins	To maintain health and prevent the onset of specific deficiency diseases
Minerals	Some minerals are required in large amounts for body structure, e.g. calcium and phosphorus in bone; some, e.g. sodium and potassium, are required in the soft tissues; trace elements, e.g. zinc, are required as a component of enzymes, etc.

The recommended daily allowances of food energy and nutrients for healthy, moderately active, adults is shown on page 130. A balanced diet which provides adequate amounts of each of the

TABLE 7.2 Three main sources of nutrients in the British diet

Nutrient	Three Main Sources
Energy	Cereals and cereal products (29.6 %) meat and fish (16.9 %) butter, margarine and other fats (15.2 %)
Carbohydrate	Cereals and cereal products (48.7 %) sugars and preserves (18.1 %) vegetables (15.1 %)
Protein	Meat and fish (35.5 %) cereals and cereal products (25.2 %) milk, cream and cheese (22.3 %)
Fat	Butter, margarine and other fats (35.7 %) meat and fish (26.3 %) milk cream and cheese (22.3 %)
P.U.F.A.	Margarine (26.4 %) meat and fish (19.3 %) other fats (18.4 %)
Vitamin A	Vegetables (45.6 %) meat and fish (22.5 %) milk, cream and cheese (12.5 %)
Vitamin B e.g. thiamin	Cereals and cereal products (49.6 %) vegetables (16.7 %) meat and fish (14.6 %)
riboflavin	Milk, cream and cheese (37.4 %) cereals and cereal products (20.2 %) meat and fish (19.2 %)
Vitamin C	Vegetables (49.5 %) fruit (40.2 %) milk, cream and cheese (5.2 %)
Vitamin D	Butter, margarine and other fats (52.2 %) meat and fish (15.0 %) egg (12.1 %)
Calcium	Milk, cream and cheese (56.4 %) cereals and cereal products (25.3 %) vegetables (6.7 %)
Iron	Cereal and cereal products (41.8 %) meat and fish (22.7 %) vegetables (17.5 %)

nutrients listed should be unlikely to result in a deficiency disease of any of those which are essential to life but are not listed here. For example, recommendations are listed for calcium and iron, a diet that provides sufficient of these minerals should also provide sufficient of the others that are required for health (see Ch. 6). Recommended daily intakes tend to stress minimum values and assume that the body can adapt to any excess. For protein, minerals and the water-soluble vitamins this may well be true, but for excessive energy intakes (see Sect. 4.6) and for the fat-soluble vitamins, A and D (see Sect. 5.2), this is patently not so.

Foods are not single nutrients but are mixtures of different ones in varying proportions. There is, however, no one natural food which alone can provide the blend of nutrients which would constitute a balanced diet. Milk probably most closely approaches the overall optimum provision of each nutrient as it has to nourish the rapidly growing baby during the first months of life. It is, however, deficient in its provision of iron, ascorbic acid (vitamin C), and without supplementation of milk by other foods during weaning, deficiency problems would occur. A normal diet should be as varied as possible, in terms of the food commodities selected, to ensure that a balance of different nutrients is obtained.

In order to calculate the nutrient provision of a portion of a particular food item it is necessary to know:

1. The content (amount/100 g) of the nutrient in the particular food. For example, the vitamin C content of potatoes is about 20 mg/100 g, the protein content of bread is about 8.8 g/100 g. The nutrient content of an enormous range of foods is given in *McCance and Widdowson's The Composition of Foods* by A. A. Paul and D. A. T. Southgate, 4th revised edition, 1978, HMSO, London. Caution should be exercised in interpretation of results as different brands may vary and quality of products due to storage will affect nutrient content. Nutritional labelling on individual packs does give a good idea of nutrient content. Alternatively nutrients can be determined for particular foods of interest to the caterer by chemical analysis. This is less convenient but much more accurate. Analysis of most nutrients is a time-consuming operation.

2. The portion size. Portion sizes can be easily determined by weighing a clean dry plate and reweighing the plate after addition of the food. Portion sizes are usually carefully controlled in catering establishments to ensure that meals can be costed realistically. In order to assess intake a measurement of plate wastage is required.

The nutrient provision of the food can be calculated as follows:

$$\frac{(\text{amount nutrient}/100 \text{ g food item}) \times \text{portion size (g)}}{100}$$

For example, there are 10.9 g of fat per 100 g of chips. A 180 g portion of chips will therefore provide:

$$\frac{10.9 \times 180 \text{ g of fat}}{100}$$

i.e. 19.62 g of fat

The nutrient provision of a meal can be determined by adding together the amount of the nutrient provided by each component of the meal. For example, consider a meal of:

	Protein/100 g (g)	Portion size (g)
Roast chicken	24.8	130
Roast potato	2.8	90
Cauliflower	1.6	70
Peas	5.0	75

The protein provided by the meal is the sum of the protein provided by the roast chicken, the roast potato, the cauliflower and the peas, i.e.:

$$\frac{(24.8 \times 130)}{100} + \frac{(2.8 \times 90)}{100} + \frac{(1.6 \times 70)}{100} + \frac{(5.0 \times 75)}{100}$$
$$= \quad 32.2 + 2.5 + 1.1 + 3.7$$
$$= \quad 39.5 \text{ g protein from meal}$$

In most circumstances it would be impractical to calculate the nutrient or energy content of every food, and one way of developing a balanced diet is to use the 'food group system' in which foods are usually divided into six groups (see Fig. 7.2). Similar systems using smaller numbers of groups are possible, e.g. a three-group system – body-building foods (protein-rich foods), protective foods (foods rich in vitamins) and fuel foods (foods contributing energy). In the six-food group system shown in Fig. 7.2, by eating foods from each of the first four food groups (i.e. cereals and starchy vegetables, fruit and vegetables, meat and alternatives, milk and milk products) and limiting foods as far as possible from the last two groups (i.e. sugars, sugary foods and drinks and fats and oils), we achieve a dietary pattern which should ensure that we receive our requirement for each of the individual nutrients. The food group system has the

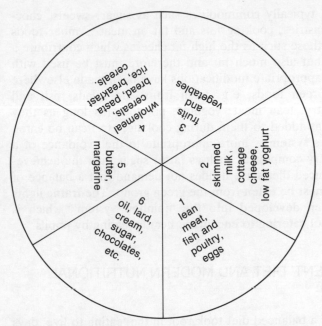

FIG. 7.2 A six food group system which can be used in the selection of a balanced diet

advantage of being simple and is applicable in a multicultural society where religious and cultural background may forbid the eating of a particular food within a certain group and an alternative can be selected from that group.

Problems are caused, however, by dividing foods simplistically into various categories. Cheese, for example, is often classified as a protein food and therefore would be contained in food group 4. Certain types of cheese, e.g. cream cheese, Cheddar, Cheshire, Gorgonzola, Gruyère and Stilton, are, however, very rich in fat, containing from 30 per cent to over 50 per cent fat. Uncritical use of cheese as a source of protein without reference to its fat content may be quite misleading.

Another system of achieving a balanced diet is the traffic lights system which can be adapted to cater for a number of different eating patterns, e.g. weight control, diabetes, low-fat diets, etc. In this system foods are divided into three groups based on their nutrient composition according to the needs of the consumer:

RED – stop and think.

AMBER – go carefully.

GREEN – go right ahead.

Red foods are typically commodities such as sugar, sweets, chocolate, cakes, pastries, cooking fats and fat on meat. Amber foods would include those such as the high-fat cheeses which contribute a lot of protein but also much fat and therefore must be used with caution unless appropriate modifications have been made elsewhere in the diet. Green foods, e.g. fresh fruits and salads, fish and seafoods, poultry, lean meat, yoghurt, potatoes (as long as they have not had fat added to them during cooking, etc.) can be eaten as desired. This system is more appropriate to the avoidance of a particular dietary component such as fat or sugar than the achievement of a balanced diet since it does not demand that a balance of various foods must be eaten from the green group. The traffic lights system has been developed into the "rainbow system" which is utilised in school catering to encourage healthy eating by pupils.

7.3   'PRUDENT' DIET AND MODERN NUTRITIONAL ADVICE

The concept of a balanced diet took root in the 'eating to live' days of nutrition when the major nutritional problems were deficiency diseases and their avoidance. Since those days, increasing knowledge of the interactions of certain foods and nutrients with the human body has resulted in a change of attitudes towards nutritional advice. Epidemiological studies of diet and corresponding disease patterns have shown that illnesses which we had come to accept as being quite a normal part of the human existence, are in fact related to specific dietary factors. By controlling or modifying our diets it may be possible to reduce the risk of suffering from particular conditions. The relationship between fibre-depleted diets and a range of diseases has already been discussed (see Sect. 1.5.1). Coronary heart disease and cancer are multifactorial diseases, i.e. there are a number of different factors which may predispose a person to them and they are major killers in modern society. Various forms of evidence are available which link coronary heart disease and several forms of cancer to specific dietary patterns. The aim of modern nutritionists and medical experts is to identify risk factors in the human diet and to attempt to draw up a set of guidelines which will help in reducing susceptibility to these diseases.

Various reports have appeared over the last few years each of which attempts to put into perspective the role of diet in the prevention of disease, e.g. the report of the Committee on Medical Aspects of Food Policy, the so-called COMA report. The reports of the National Advisory Committee on Nutrition Education and the Joint Advisory Council on Nutrition Education (the NACNE and JACNE reports) present proposals for nutritional guidelines for health education in Britain. A summary of the recommendations in these reports will effectively convey the 'state of the art' in nutritional thinking (see Table 7.3).

TABLE 7.3 'State of the Art' in nutritional thinking for adults

Dietary component	Modification
Sugar intake	Reduce
Fibre intake	Increase intake: 30 g per day is recommended which means increasing the average British person's fibre intake by 10 g per day
Fat intake	Decrease fat intake; it is now recommended that foods should be labelled with their fat content to facilitate this; the polyunsaturated fatty acid content of the diet should be increased so that the ratio of polyunsaturated fatty acids to saturated fatty acids is greater than 1.0
Dietary cholesterol	Dietary cholesterol intake should not exceed 300 mg/day
Salt intake	Should be reduced
Alcohol	Should not provide more than 4 % of total energy intake.

7.4   ACHIEVING THE NUTRITIONAL GOALS

The guidelines listed in Table 7.3 are essentially theoretical and give little information to 'the man in the street' on how to go about modifying their diet. A few simple suggestions for adults are listed below **but are not suitable for children under five**.

1. Avoid fried foods. Grill rather than fry and let as much of the fat as possible drain away from the food.
2. Avoid chips. Each chip absorbs fat increasing energy intake. Thick straight cut chips have relatively less surface area and absorb less fat than thin crinkle cut chips. Oven chips contain about 40 % less fat than conventionally fried chips. Potatoes are a valuable food commodity so try eating them baked in their jackets or just mashed (but do not add butter!). By eating baked potatoes you also increase your intake of dietary fibre.
3. Eat more bread, especially wholemeal and other high-fibre

breads. Use thick slices of high-fibre bread and spread as thinly as possible with a low-calorie spread or a spread high in polyunsaturated fatty acids. This will increase the intake of starchy foods, increase fibre intake, increase the intake of polyunsaturated fat and decrease the intake of saturated fat. Avoid slicing bread thinly and spreading thickly with butter or a butter substitute.

4. Choose leaner meats and leaner cuts of meat, e.g. chicken is lower in fat than beef. Remove as much of the visible fat as possible from the meat (see Table 7.4). Eat fish, ideally white fish, rather than meat; fish is a valuable protein source and supplies polyunsaturated rather than saturated fats. Either cut down on processed meat products, e.g. sausages, as they are often high in fat, or use low-fat alternatives.

TABLE 7.4 Percentage of fat in meat and meat products

Food	Fat in product (%)	Fat, when visible fat is removed where possible (%)
Beef		
silverside	14.2	4.9
topside	12.0	12.0
forerib	28.8	12.6
Pork	19.8	6.9
Bacon rasher (back rashers)	33.8	18.9
Gammon	12.2	5.2
Lamb cutlets	30.9	12.3
Chicken, roast	5.4	—
Goose, roast	22.4	—
Turkey, roast	2.7	—
Rabbit, stewed	7.7	—
Liver, fried	13.2	—
Kidney, fried	6.3	—
Tongue	24.0	—
Beef sausages	18.0	—
Low-fat beef sausages	9.0	—

5. Avoid cream. Single cream contains 21 per cent fat, double cream 48 per cent fat. Use skimmed (0.1 % fat) or semi-skimmed (1.5–1.8 % fat) milks in place of full cream milk (3.8 % fat). Try eating yoghurt as a topping for fresh fruit and use it in cooking instead of cream.

6. Choose low-fat cheeses, e.g. cottage cheese, Edam, Camembert and low fat Cheddars, rather than the high-fat varieties.
7. Eat more vegetables and fresh fruit. Vegetables are filling and add colour and variety to a meal but they are low in fat and high in fibre.
8. Cut down on cakes, pastries, biscuits and avoid chocolates which are often high in fat as well as sugar. If you feel peckish then try eating a piece of fresh fruit which will increase your vitamin and fibre intake and is better for your teeth.
9. Train yourself to take your drinks (tea, coffee, etc.) without sugar by gradually reducing the amount of sugar you add. Try to avoid low-calorie sweeteners. Sweetness can be addictive but if you gradually reduce your intake of sweeteners you may find that you actually prefer the flavour!
10. Reduce the amount of salt you take by not using it in cooking as well as at the table. Again, you may prefer the flavour of foods which are not laced with vast amounts of sodium chloride. Try low-sodium substitutes.
11. Try low- and no-alcohol alternatives to traditional alcoholic drinks.

7.5   MALNUTRITION (see Table 7.5)

Malnutrition, literally 'bad nutrition', describes an imbalance between the diet's supply of nutrients and the body's demand for them. This imbalance may be caused by:
1. The overall supply of nutrients, particularly the energy supply, exceeding the body's demand, resulting in overweight due to over-nutrition (see Sect. 4.6). If you find that your bodyweight is greater than it should be it is important that you decrease your energy intake or increase your energy expenditure to counteract this problem.
2. The overall supply of nutrients is less than that required and can lead to undernutrition and possible loss of weight. One cause of underweight in Britain is anorexia nervosa. This is a psychological problem which manifests itself nutritionally. Fear of weight gain and a self-imposed rigorous regime of starvation results in the attainment of dangerously low body-weights and can lead to death. The problem is increasing and the group at greatest risk are young women aged from 16 to 26 of above average intelligence.
   In other parts of the world geographical, geological, meteoro-

TABLE 7.5 Causes of malnutrition

Nutrient group	Overconsumption	Underconsumption
All nutrients	Overweight, obesity	Underweight, anorexia
Available carbohydrate	Overweight, obesity, dental caries (high sugar intakes)	Weight loss
Protein		Weight loss, kwashiorkor (**gross** protein deficiency)
Fat	Overweight, circulatory problems, e.g. coronary heart disease, cancer	Essential fatty acid deficiency results in skin problems and eczema; may also be associated with multiple sclerosis
Vitamins	Excess intake of fat-soluble vitamins results in toxicity problems, death; excess intake of vitamin C may lead to kidney stones	Specific deficiency diseases associated with each vitamin
Minerals	Excessive salt intakes associated with high blood pressure and stomach cancer	Deficiency of calcium leads to rickets, of iron to anaemia and of iodine to goitre
Dietary fibre	High intakes of fibre may reduce the bioavailability of minerals	Low intakes of dietary fibre associated with 'Western', 'diseases of affluence', e.g. hiatus hernia, diabetes, diverticular disease, etc.

logical and political problems can lead to terrible famines affecting millions of people.

Defective food intakes due to religion and culture can also lead to malnutrition. The use of fad diets, e.g. macrobiotic diets, for children can lead to gross undernourishment. Following vegan diets, which are totally plant-based, can lead to vitamin B_{12} deficiency (see Sect. 5.3.8).

3. Absorption problems may be due to a number of causes, e.g. infections, gastrointestinal disorders, gut surgery, dental troubles or the inability to produce a specific absorption factor. In pernicious anaemia (see Sect. 5.3.8) there is an inherited inability to absorb vitamin B_{12} from the gut.

Excessive alcoholism can lead to aberrant nutrient intakes

which manifest themselves as deficiencies of the water-soluble vitamins B complex and C, resulting in permanent damage particularly to the liver and brain. Alcoholic drinks contain virtually no vitamins, cause acute gastritis which impairs food absorption while metabolism of alcohol increases metabolic demand for vitamins (especially thiamin, see Sect. 5.3.2), and due to the damage done to the liver, impairs their utilisation in the body. Certain diseases, alcoholism, drug addiction, etc., may reduce the appetite or 'will to eat' and may lead to deficiency diseases.

Elderly persons, particularly those living alone, often suffer vitamin deficiencies and are one of the few groups of persons at risk of suffering scurvy (see Sect. 5.3.10). About one third of elderly patients admitted to hospital for surgery have some degree of Protein Energy Malnutrition (PEM). Obesity, another indicator of malnutrition, is also prevalent among the elderly. As people get older they tend to lose interest in food and often rely on a very limited range of food items. Difficulties in purchase, preparation and chewing, as well as high costs are all factors which determine food choice. Catering for elderly persons is a growth area due to the increase in the elderly population (10 million by 1991).

Increased demand for nutrients by the body at certain times can lead to specific problems, e.g. an increased demand for calcium during pregnancy can lead to resorption of bones and teeth and cause difficulties in later life. During growth, convalescence and illness there is increased demand for protein for the growth and repair of tissues. Table 7.6 shows a list of groups likely to be at risk

TABLE 7.6 Groups with special nutritional needs

Babies and young children
Pregnant and lactating women
Elderly persons
Athletes
Overweight and obese persons
Underweight and anorexic persons
Persons suffering from inborn errors of metabolism: e.g. lactose intolerance, phenyloketonuria
Diabetics
Persons who have had sections of their gut removed surgically: (i.e. less surface area available for absorption of nutrients)
Persons suffering from other gut and associated problems: e.g. low-fat diet for gall-bladder patients, low-residue diets
Persons with kidney problems: e.g. low-salt and low-protein regimes
Surgical patients

from nutritional deficiencies due to non-provision, malabsorption or increased demand for nutrients. The hospital caterer is most likely to come across these persons and with the aid of the dietitian must be able to provide a suitable diet for all patients.

7.6   CATERING FOR SPECIAL GROUPS

7.6.1   DIETS REQUIRING LOW INTAKES OF SPECIFIC NUTRIENTS

Diabetic diets

Diabetics have problems in controlling their blood sugar level owing to inadequate secretion of the hormone insulin. There are two groups of individuals who are classed as diabetics:

(a) Those who secrete some insulin and control the problem by modification of their diet and/or the use of tablets. These persons are called Maturity-onset diabetics.

(b) Those who have to inject themselves with insulin and must control their dietary intake of carbohydrate to balance the level of insulin. These are generally young persons.

In both types of diabetes a careful control must be made of the carbohydrate intake to ensure that there is a balance of carbohydrate and insulin in the bloodstream.

Dietary control of carbohydrate intake works on an 'exchange system'. Food portions are assessed in terms of their available carbohydrate content and given an exchange value. The doctor prescribes a certain level of carbohydrate intake and by using the exchange system, the diabetic can substitute foods according to taste in order to fulfil his requirements. Diabetic patients are introduced to this system via special clinics where a dietitian is available to explain the finer points.

Low-sodium diets

These diets are used for patients with oedema and sometimes for those with high blood pressure. High sodium intakes (see Sect. 6.2.4) are associated with retention of water in the body due to osmotic pressure. The use of a low-sodium diet should only be adopted on the advice of a doctor who will recommend a particular degree of restriction:

(a) No salt at table.

(b) No salt added during cooking or at table.

(c) The selection of foods with a low-sodium content together with no salt at table or in cooking.

Course (c) presents the most difficulties as it requires the identification of foods with a high-sodium content and their avoidance in the diet. Such foods include: cocoa, biscuits, commercial baked products (scones, buns, pastries, bread, cakes and puddings), breakfast cereals and salted porridge, cheeses, salted butter, fish, fruits, processed meats, milk, salted nuts, commercial stocks – unless otherwise stated on label.

For certain persons, salt-substitutes may be allowed but these should only be used on a doctor's recommendation.

Low-fat diets

These diets are used for persons with liver damage (e.g. hepatitis and jaundice) who cannot tolerate fats, and occasionally in the treatment of cardiovascular disease. Fats aid the palatability of foods and a low-fat diet may be unpleasant. The most common fat-modified diet is where polyunsaturated fats are used in place of saturated fats for cardiovascular problems and for gallstones. Skimmed milks, lean meats, poultry, white fish, and egg whites are all low in fat and can be used as a starting point for meals. Bread, vegetables and fruits (except avocados, olives and nuts) arc also low-fat items. Commodities with high fat contents, e.g. butter, margarine, lard, suet, vegetable oils, cream, high fat cheeses, mayonnaise, bacon and ham, chocolate, pastry, cakes and fat-based sauces should be avoided. Obviously frying is not allowed and foods should be boiled, steamed, grilled, baked or stewed without the addition of fat during preparation. Fat aids satiety and a low fat diet may increase appetite.

Low-protein diets

Individuals suffering from kidney and liver disease often require modification of their protein and salt intakes to reduce the amount of work done to maintain the internal environment of the body. The major protein providers in the diet are meat, fish, poultry, eggs, milk, cheese, bread and cereals, and pulses.

Depending on the degree of restriction permitted, daily allowances of protein foods will be prescribed by the doctor, e.g. a certain amount of milk, meat, fish, etc., may be allowed and these will be supplemented with low-protein foods such as fruits and vegetables according to the taste of the individual. It is important in low protein regimes to ensure that an adequate energy intake is maintained.

Low-residue or low-fibre diets

Fruits, whole grain cereals, nuts, pulses, stringy vegetables and stringy meat should be avoided. Fruits and vegetables must be eaten to provide vitamin C but should be taken as juices or purées which can be sieved to remove fibre. Warm milk drinks are very soothing.

Dietary intolerances

A number of conditions require the removal of a specific item from the diet owing to the patient's inability to deal with that substance in the body. Examples include lactose intolerance (more common in ethnic groups of Asian or African origin) in which lactase, the enzyme which hydrolyses lactose to glucose and galactose (see Sect. 1.2), is low or lacking and thus lactose cannot be digested and absorbed from the gut. It remains in the gut and acts as a substrate for fermentation by the gut bacteria, and the production of gases can lead to severe abdominal pain. Lactose only occurs naturally in milk and the complete avoidance of milk and milk products resolves the problem. Compensation must be made via the other dietary components to ensure adequate calcium intakes.

Phenylketonuria is a disease in which the patient is unable to metabolise the amino acid phenylalanine (see Fig. 2.2) correctly and leads to severe mental retardation if left untreated. The disease is one of the most common inborn errors of metabolism and occurs in eighty out of every million live births. Routine testing of babies at birth is utilised to diagnose the problem which is then treated by strict control of phenylalanine intake. Specific preparations based on hydrolysed casein from which phenylalanine has been removed by charcoal treatment, are available for the feeding of patients suffering from phenylketonuria. Aspartame, an artificial sweetener containing phenylalanine, should not be consumed by persons with phenylketonuria.

Coeliac disease is one of the commonest adverse reactions to food which results in damage to the intestinal surface and loss of absorptive capacity leading to massive losses of weight. The food component causing the reaction is gluten – wheat protein important in the production of doughs and bread (see Sect. 2.5.1). Food manufacturers often use wheat flour as a thickener or filler in their products, e.g. in soups and sauces. Some patients are also sensitive to barley, oats and rye. Treatment requires avoidance of gluten-containing foods, and gluten-free flours should be used for baking. A number of gluten-free products are widely available and these can be used by the coeliac patient.

7.6.2   DIETS REQUIRING HIGH INTAKES OF SPECIFIC NUTRIENTS

High-fibre diet

This type of diet can be used for the treatment of atonic constipation (a 'lazy colon', due to poor condition of the muscular walls
and low peristaltic contractions) as well as in the treatment of
certain cases of obesity and diabetes.

All the foods listed above for avoidance in the low-fibre diet form
a major part of the high-fibre diet. Raw and cooked fruits, nuts,
vegetables, wholemeal and other high-fibre breads, cereal products
such as high-bran breakfast cereals. The diet leaves a large residue
in the gut which keeps faeces soft and makes them more easily
voided. The food is satisfying and therefore the intakes of available
energy are reduced without the patient feeling hungry. Hunger
associated with low-energy diets are a major cause of the patient not
sticking to his prescribed diet. The fibre content reduces the availability and rate of absorption of carbohydrates from the gut and so
aids in the body's handling of carbohydrate and may be used as part
of the treatment for diabetic patients.

7.6.3   POPULATION GROUPS WITH SPECIAL NEEDS

Pregnant women require:
1. Slightly more energy.
2. Approximately 10 per cent more protein.
3. Approximately 100 per cent more vitamin.
4. Extra vitamin D.
5. Approximately 100 per cent more calcium.
6. More iron, especially in later pregnancy.
7. More folic acid.
   Generally more milk, cheese or eggs, more fruit and vegetables.

Convalescents require:
1. Simple appetising meals.
2. Adequate calcium and iron.
3. More protein and vitamin C.

Older people require:
1. Slightly less energy provision.
2. Adequate calcium and iron.
3. Adequate vitamin C and folic acid.
   Hot meals are useful in winter to help to maintain body temperature.

Young people require:

1. For their weight relatively more protein and energy provision (very active and growing).
2. Formation of good eating habits, avoidance of too many high-energy snack foods, sweets, soft drinks, etc.
3. Adequate calcium, especially for Asian girls bound by traditional customs.
4. Ideally school meals should provide about 30 per cent of protein and energy intake.
5. Adequate iron, especially for girls.
6. Adequate vitamin D.

Vegetarians

The number of these has increased quite dramatically in recent years, thus it is important that caterers should be able to provide at least one vegetarian meal on a menu. There are two types of vegetarian, lactovegetarians and vegans. The former will not eat meat but will take milk, cheese and eggs. The main nutritional problem is likely to be due to lack of iron. This can be supplied by eggs (if eaten), cereals, pulses and green vegetables. Generally such diets are lower in calories and high in fibre.

Vegans, however, will eat no foods of animal origin. The main problems are likely to be due to lack of iron, calcium, riboflavin and vitamin B_{12}. Supply of amino acids should be covered by complementation.

Slimmers

Typical energy requirements are for between 9240–12 600 kJ/day (2200–3000 kcal/day). In order to reduce weight, energy intake should be reduced. An appropriate level depends upon how quickly the weight needs to be lost. Often a daily intake of 4200 kJ/day (1000 kcal/day) is selected. This should be achieved by:

(a) Reducing fat intake.
(b) Reducing refined carbohydrate intake.
(c) Reducing alcohol intake.
(d) Increasing fibre intake in the form of fruit and vegetables.

Any such diet is likely to be more effective if used in conjunction with exercise.

7.7   FOOD ADDITIVES

Additives are not new, they are an extension of traditional techniques, e.g. the use of salt for preserving and the use of sodium nitrite for preserving and curing of hams. Why additives are causing concern is that their use has multiplied ten-fold over the last thirty years and it is estimated that in the United Kingdom today we each consume about 4–5 kilogrammes (8–10 lbs) of additives per year.

Without additives it would be extremely difficult to provide food in the enormous quantities required today – it is estimated that 75 per cent of the food we eat has been processed to some degree. Shelf life would not be as good, products would not be as attractive and they would be dearer. The modern housewife does not shop for food every day and expects her food to be reasonably priced, nutritious, attractive, palatable and safe. It is the relationship between food additives and safety that is the centre of the current debate.

Food manufacturers should only use additives that have been tested and found to be safe. Typically the cost of testing an additive is put at £1 million. Legally manufacturers are forbidden to add substances to food that may injure a person's health. However testing of food additives takes place in animals and on an individual basis. The exact consequences of eating mixed cocktails, or combinations of additives by humans is not known. Further, in the United Kingdom, many of the results of the additive tests are not available for outside inspection. In the final analysis it would be untrue to say that food additives are not harmful and more correct to say that some additives may present a health problem but only to a small percentage of the population. At this point it should also be remembered that some of the natural components of foods may also be harmful to a small percentage of the population. The real debate though centres on exactly what percentage of the population may be adversely affected by additives. Current thinking places this between 0.03 and 0.15 per cent of the population.

Reports of the harmful effects of foods, particularly those concerning additives, have attracted much public attention, e.g. the implications of the role of tartrazine (E102) in hyperactivity in children. Food additives are nowadays an emotive and political topic of great public concern, with a high media profile. Manufacturers are finding that they have a justify the presence of additives and demonstrate a useful role and many are redesigning their products to reduce or even omit additives. The fact that additives are not present in a food is being used as a positive advertising feature, although this can be misleading. A statement on a label that a product is free of artificial colourings means just that, and it will probably contain natural colourings, preservatives, flavourings, etc., depending upon the actual product. A wise consumer reads his labels carefully as some food manufacturers may 'play' with words to give a false impression.

It is perhaps worth considering whether under present day testing procedures and legislation a substance could be added to food if when consumed in sufficient quantities it could make you giddy, with slurred speech. If consumed in very large amounts it could lead to death or in smaller doses for a very long period of time, liver damage. Such a frightening description does, of course, apply to alcohol!

Balanced against the possible harm that additives may cause is the benefits they bring. Their use may be summarised as providing:

appeal – processed foods lose flavour, colour and texture during processing;

safety – helping to slow down the undesirable growth of micro-organisms;

convenience – in terms of an increased shelf life and a convenient format;

nutrition – some food additives help to minimise nutrient losses during processing and storage.

It is up to the consumer to balance the harmful effects against the benefits and to choose whether to eat foods containing additives or to eat natural foods or additive-free alternatives.

Public interest in food has lead to legislation requiring more informative product labelling and a listing of components in decreasing order. Many food additives have such long and complex names that label size can be a problem and so an international shorthand has been developed which numbers permitted additives for easy recognition. Entry into the European Economic Community has meant that those additives accepted for use in Europe also carry an E prefix to their number.

Some substances which are used as additives in food manufacturing do not have to appear on labels since they do not modify the properties of the final product, although they may pass through with the product. Such substances include release agents, e.g. paraffin oil, which prevent the product sticking to the machinery; bleaching agents, anti-caking agents and flow agents, e.g. in flour; and enzymes, e.g. pectinolytic enzymes used to clarify fruit juices. Solvents are used to carry colours and flavours in powdered or liquid form throughout the manufactured product and avoid 'patchiness'. Nine solvents are permitted in the United Kingdom but only one, glycerol (E422), carries an E number.

Food additives can be classified in two ways:

(a) on their role in the food

Colouring Agents (E100 – 180)

These substances are added for cosmetic reasons to make the food look more attractive. Our expectation of food quality is to a certain extent colour-dependent. Many colouring agents are natural in origin, such as chlorophyll (E140) a green pigment extracted from plants, e.g. nettles and grass and caramel (E150) which is produced by the action of heat or chemicals on carbohydrates (see Sect. 1.5). Synthetic dyes, e.g. the azo dye tartrazine and the coal tar dyes, e.g. Yellow 2G (E107) and Ponceau 4R (E124), have been recognised as causing problems in asthmatics and persons sensitive to aspirin. It is the use of synthetic dyes that has probably attracted most criticism from the anti-additive lobby.

Preservatives (E200 – 290)

These are a particularly important and beneficial group of food additives which prevent or reduce the growth of microorganisms in or on food. Bacterial growth in foods can lead to food spoilage, food poisoning or toxin production in the food (see Ch. 12). Mould growth on foods can lead to the production of dangerous mycotoxins. To remove preservatives from foods would decrease their keeping qualities and might make them potentially dangerous. Specifically the use of nitrites in food helps to minimise the risk of botulism.

Antioxidants (E300 – 321)

Atmospheric oxygen causes chemical changes to take place in the food which can make them unfit to eat, e.g. rancidity in fats and oils or colour changes in the product due to browning reactions. Antioxidants include: L-ascorbic acid – vitamin C (E300) which is used to prevent browning reactions in fruits and fruit products; vitamin E (E306) which is added to prevent rancidity in vegetable oils and polyunsaturated margarines; butylated hydroxyanisole (BHA – E320) and butylated hydroxytoluene (BHT – E321) which are also used as antioxidants in a wide range of products. These last two antioxidants have been shown to cause adverse reactions in some individuals, and are not allowed to be added to foods intended for babies and young children. The use of anti-oxidants helps to retard the degradation of oils and fats which can result in the formation of carcinogenic breakdown products.

Emulsifiers and stabilisers (E322 – 500)
These additives modify the consistency of food or stabilise it and include emulsifiers, stabilisers, thickening agents, gelling agents and delayers, dispersing agents, leavening agents, foaming and antifoaming agents. Examples include the phosphates and polyphosphates (442 – E450(c)) which are added to chickens and various meat products as stabilisers, retain water during cooking and retain succulence particularly in frozen chickens. Alginates (E400 – 407), e.g. carageenan (E407) are used as thickening, gelling, emulsifying and suspending agents in ice creams, pastries, cheeses, salad dressings and alcoholic beverages.

Sweeteners (E420 – 421)
Only two artificial sweeteners have E numbers, sorbitol and mannitol. In the United Kingdom the list of permitted sweeteners is longer and includes aspartame and thaumatin. Hydrogenated glucose syrup and certain forms of saccharin are also permitted.

Flavours and flavour enhancers
There are about 3000 flavouring substances in use in the United Kingdom and these are not currently included as additives. Flavours can be divided into five categories:
aromatics – these are obtained from plants and dried or roasted for their distinctive flavour, e.g. ginger, nutmeg, etc.
natural flavours – are extracted from aromatics to intensify the natural flavour, e.g. orange oil. These substances are not very stable.
synthetic flavours – chemists can now synthesise aromatic compounds which are identical to natural flavouring agents, e.g. vanillin which is identical to vanilla extracted from vanilla beans. Esters are produced by reaction between an alcohol and a carboxylic acid and can be used to give a product a fruity flavour, e.g. propyl ethanoate gives a pear flavour. These chemicals have the advantage of being cheap and consistent.
natural and synthetic flavours together – an artificial flavour

or 'extender' can be used in conjunction with natural flavours to give improved flavour characteristics.

treated flavours – e.g. heat treatment of hydrolysates of offal (provides amino acids) and corn syrup (provides sugars) causing the Maillard reaction to take place and production of an artificial 'roast meat' flavour.

Flavour enhancers (E620 – 635) are used to modify the taste of food, particularly when processing has reduced the natural flavour of the product. Examples include monosodium glutamate (E621) which is used widely in packet soups, sausages, meat flavour crisps and other snack foods.

(b) on their source, into natural, synthetic and artificial substances.

Natural additives are substances which are extracted from natural products and added to other foods to improve its characteristics. Examples of natural food additives include: lecithin (E322) which is produced from soya beans and is used as an emulsifier in the production of mayonnaise and sauces; and pectin which is extracted from apple residues in cider making and used for jam making.

Synthetic additives, 'nature-identical' compounds, are substances which are synthesised by biological or chemical methods to be identical to natural compounds. L-ascorbic acid (E300), vitamin C is synthesised and used as an antioxidant, a browning inhibitor in fruit drinks, a flour improver and a meat colour preservative. Riboflavin (E101) vitamin B2 is produced synthetically and used as a yellow or orange-yellow colour.

Artificial additives are substances which are synthesised by chemical methods but have no natural counterpart. This is the most contentious group of additives and the group for which manufacturers are trying hardest to find natural alternatives. One of the disadvantages of natural colouring agents is that they have to be used in much higher concentrations to achieve the same effect and they tend to be much less stable, again leading to shorter product shelf life. Whereas one can show that without preservatives foods would be potentially dangerous and have much poorer keeping qualities, the same can not be said of colouring agents which have an exclusively cosmetic role in foods.

QUESTIONS

1. (a) What is meant by the term 'balanced diet'?
   (b) List the components of a balanced diet.
   (c) What is meant by the term 'malnutrition'?
2. (a) What is a 'risk factor'?
   (b) List five risk factors which have been identified by nutritional experts.
3. Describe six ways in which you can improve your diet and bring it into line with modern healthy eating policies.
4. (a) List four conditions which may require the control of a particular dietary component and the dietary component which is involved in each case?
   (b) What is meant by the term 'dietary intolerance'?
   (c) Name two dietary components which commonly cause intolerances and name the associated condition.

Recommended daily allowances of food energy and nutrients for healthy, moderately active adults

	Men (18–34 years)	Men (35–64 years)	Women (18–54 years)
Energy MJ	12.0	11.5	9.0
Protein (g)	72	69	54
Thiamin (mg)	1.2	1.1	0.9
Riboflavin (mg)	1.6	1.6	1.3
Nicotinic acid (mg)	18	18	15
Total Folate (μg)	300	300	300
Ascorbic acid (mg)	30	30	30
Vitamin A (μg)	750	750	750
Vitamin D (μg)	—*	—*	—*
Calcium (mg)	500	500	500
Iron (mg)	10	10	12

* Assuming sufficient exposure to sunlight.

8

CLEANING AND CLEANING MATERIALS

8.1   INTRODUCTION

Cleaning is important in all areas of a hotel or restaurant and is in fact the largest routine maintenance task of a caterer. 'Cleaning is next to profit in catering'. Mechanical methods, such as vacuum cleaning, and a range of cleaning materials can be used by caterers to remove dirt from the surfaces of floors, walls, fixtures, fittings, furnishings, catering equipment, etc. Cleaning is important in all areas of a hotel or restaurant but is perhaps most critical and is a legal requirement in:

(a) Areas where food is prepared, handled or stored.

(b) Toilets and wash areas.

Consequently, in these two key areas, additional measures involving the use of disinfectants and sanitisers (see Sect. 8.7), may need to be taken to ensure that visibly clean surfaces are microbiologically clean. The cleaning operation depends upon the type of soiling, the surface involved, the cleaning materials, standards of cleanliness required and the hardness of the water. The usual stages involved in cleaning are physical removal of excess visible soil deposits, followed by the use of cleaning agents to remove residual soil, and finally, if necessary, a disinfection stage using heat or chemicals.

Cleaning agents include water, surfactant detergent powders and solutions, alkaline and acid cleaners, solvents, abrasive cleaners and bleaching agents.

8.2   DEFINITIONS

A number of terms and words, applied to cleaning, are widely used in the food industry although the precise meaning of these terms is not universally agreed. The definitions used here are the most widely accepted.

Cleaning: removal of soil from surfaces; does not include sterilisation.

Clean Surface: soil free but may still contain microorganisms.

Detergent: assists cleaning by emulsification of soil (grease) and reduction of surface tension.

Sterilisation: the complete removal of all microorganisms and spores from an object or surface. This is rarely, if ever, achieved or even necessary in catering establishments.

Sterilising agents/sterilants: chemicals leading to sterilisation. They are unlikely to live up to their name and are better described as disinfectants.

Disinfection: this is the destruction or removal of microorganisms. While not all organisms are destroyed, if it is carried out correctly any remaining microorganisms should not pose a health risk or affect the quality of perishable foods, i.e. the number of microorganisms has been reduced to an acceptable level for that particular area. Disinfection is an essential part of good hygiene and may be achieved by cleaning, heat or chemicals.

Disinfectant: a chemical capable of disinfecting, i.e. killing or retarding the growth of microorganisms.

Germicide: literally, a chemical capable of killing germs (harmful microorganisms) and is really the same as a disinfectant.

Antiseptic: literally meaning 'against infection', antiseptics (skin disinfectants) are chemicals that kill or retard the growth of microorganisms and are tolerated by the skin.

Sanitising: cleaning process, of equipment or premises, with an element of disinfection incorporated, i.e. after sanitising, microbial contamination will be at a low residual level.

Sanitizer: chemical used in sanitation. Really a combined detergent/disinfectant.

Soil: matter out of place, e.g. grease and particulate material, commonly referred to as dirt.

8.3   WATER

Water is the commonest compound on Earth making up two-thirds of its surface and about three-quarters of the human body. Water is an oxide of hydrogen, H_2O, and between the temperatures of 0 °C and 100 °C is a colourless liquid without taste or smell. There are very few substances that do not dissolve in water, at least slightly, and it is often called the 'universal solvent'. In cleaning, detergents are used in conjunction with water to improve its cleansing properties. There are various forms of natural water as shown in the water cycle in Fig. 8.1 and these differ in the level of dissolved substances,

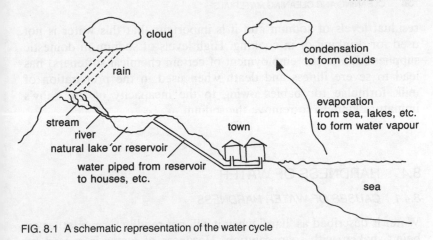

FIG. 8.1 A schematic representation of the water cycle

or impurities, that they contain. The dissolved solids which contribute to hardness of water (see Sect. 8.4) are probably of greatest
significance, particularly in cleaning.

Tap water is produced for us by the local water authorities in the
various parts of the country and is mainly derived from rivers and
streams which are dammed to form resevoirs. At some stage during
its passage from the resevoir to the consumer the water authority
treats the water, e.g. by adding chlorine, to ensure that it is
microbiologically safe. Levels of water contamination are closely
monitored by the Public Health Laboratory Service in Great Britain.
Water is supplied to various premises via a 'mains' pipe which runs
beneath streets and roads. A service pipe leads the water into the
building, a stopvalve or stopcock is provided outside so that water
can be turned off at this point, and a second stopvalve is fitted
inside, near the point of entry of the service pipe.

Inside the premises at least one tap is fed directly from the mains
and this should be used as drinking water. Other taps are supplied
from a cold water storage tank in the roof of the building to give a
head of water above the taps. Tap water is not chemically pure but
is an extremely dilute solution of a number of different salts.
Some of the dissolved substances are of nutritional significance and
deficiency can result in illness (see Sect. 6.3.1). Dissolved substances
may be removed by distillation, i.e. boiling to produce steam which
is then condensed, or by deionisation, treatment with various chemicals called 'deionisers'. In hard water areas where excessive dissolved
solids are found the whole water supply, inside a building, apart
from the mains-supplied tap, may be treated to avoid problems
associated with the use of hard water (see Sect. 8.4.2). Some
methods of chemical softening (see Sect. 8.4.3) may leave high

residual levels of sodium and it is important that this water is not used for drinking or in cooking. High levels of sodium in domestic supplies (due to the employment of certain chemical softeners) has lead to severe illness and death when used in the preparation of milk formulae for babies owing to the incapacity of the baby's immature kidneys to remove the sodium.

8.4 HARDNESS OF WATER

8.4.1 CAUSES OF WATER HARDNESS

Water is described as 'hard' when it will not readily form a lather on being shaken with soap solution. Hardness of water is caused by dissolved metallic ions, principally calcium and magnesium, which react with soap producing a scum. The principal salts causing hardness are calcium hydrogen carbonate (calcium bicarbonate), magnesium hydrogen carbonate (magnesium bicarbonate), calcium sulphate and magnesium sulphate. Salts are leached out of the soil as rain water percolates through. Carbon dioxide dissolves in rain water as it falls producing a weakly acidic solution of carbonic acid (H_2CO_3). Carbonic acid dissolves chalk deposits (calcium carbonate) to produce calcium hydrogen carbonate:

$$CaCO_3 \quad + \quad H_2CO_3 \quad \rightarrow \quad Ca(HCO_3)_2$$
calcium   carbonic   calcium hydrogen
 carbonate   acid   carbonate

Variations in soil composition in different parts of the country lead to differences in the degree of water hardness. Waters are classified according to their content of dissolved calcium and magnesium ions, and these are expressed as parts per million (ppm) of calcium carbonate. Water in Devon is soft (less than 50 ppm), in London very hard (more than 200 ppm), in Wales soft to moderately soft (50–100 ppm), and in Berkshire moderate to very hard (100–200 ppm).

Hardness caused by calcium and magnesium hydrogen carbonates is described as 'temporary hardness' since it can be removed by boiling.

$$Ca(HCO_3)_2 \quad \rightarrow \quad CaCO_3 \quad + \quad H_2O + CO_2$$
soluble   insoluble
 calcium hydrogen   calcium carbonte
 carbonate   forms precipitate
                             a component of scale

The calcium or magnesium hydrogen carbonate is converted to an insoluble precipitate of calcium or magnesium carbonate, respectively, by boiling. In contrast, calcium and magnesium sulphates are not decomposed by boiling and their presence in water is termed 'permanent hardness'.

8.4.2   PROBLEMS ASSOCIATED WITH HARDNESS OF WATER

Scum formation
The reaction of dissolved calcium and magnesium ions with soap, e.g. sodium stearate produces calcium or magnesium stearate, an insoluble grey scum, which deposits on sinks, skin and objects being washed.

calcium	+	sodium	→	calcium	+	sodium
sulphate		stearate		stearate		sulphate
soluble		soluble		insoluble		soluble

Soapless detergents can be used in hard water areas to avoid problems of scum formation.

Excessive consumption of detergent
Scum formation uses up a large excess of soap before a reasonable lather is achieved. This results in wastage of soap and increased costs. Modern cleaning materials contain builders which remove calcium and magnesium ions. There are two groups of builders:
 (i) precipitant builders e.g. sodium carbonate and tetrasodium pyrophosphate,
(ii) true complexing builders, which include inorganic sequestrants, e.g. sodium tripolyphosphate and organic chelating agents e.g. ethylene diamine tetra acetic acid (EDTA) and sodium gluconate.
A combination of builders is added to washing powders but this is an expensive method of water softening as a high concentration has to be added.

Redeposition
Calcium and magnesium salts tend to cause flocculation, i.e. the dirt suspended in the water is apt to be redeposited on the cleaned surface. Antiredeposition (suspending) agents, e.g. sodium carboxymethycellulose, are used particularly in low lather washing powders to disperse insoluble materials and maintain them in suspension.

Scaling
Temporary hardness of water is removed by boiling, as soluble

hydrogen carbonates are converted to insoluble carbonates which are precipitated on to heating elements as a scale or 'fur'. Build up of the deposit on the element acts as an insulating layer and decreases the efficiency of heat transfer from the element to the water. This can cause overheating and consequent failure as well as increasing fuel bills. Excessive fur build up decreases the internal dimensions of boilers and can lead to blocking of pipes. A thin layer of scale can be beneficial in reducing corrosion in iron and steel pipes which corrode quicker in soft water areas. Scale build up in central heating systems and boilers can result in noisy systems. A typical descaling agent involves an acidic formulation of 31 % phosphoric acid, 68.7 % water and 0.3 % non-ionic surfactant.

8.4.3   WATER SOFTENING

'Water softening' processes result in the removal of hardness from water. Water softening methods lower the calcium and magnesium content of the water but usually result in an increase in sodium content, and so softened water should not be used for drinking or in cooking. Water softeners may result in precipitation of 'hardness' ions, e.g. calcium and magnesium ions are precipitated as their insoluble carbonates by addition of sodium carbonate (washing soda). Soap powders and bath salts contain sodium carbonate.

$$CaSO_4 \quad + \quad Na_2CO_3 \quad \rightarrow \quad Na_2SO_4 \quad + \quad CaCO_3$$

calcium	sodium	sodium	calcium
sulphate	carbonate	sulphate	carbonate

Alternatively, and most widely used in hotels, water softening utilises the ion exchange system which involves the exchange of 'hardness' ions for sodium ions by passing the hard water through a column containing an ion-exchange resin, e.g. Permutit (a complex sodium aluminium silicate):

$$Ca^{2+} \quad + \quad 2Na^+ \quad \rightarrow \quad 2Na^+ \quad + \quad Ca^{2+}$$

soluble	on resin	soluble	on resin

The use of sodium hexametaphosphate (Calgon) results in the formation of a soluble complex of the 'hardness' ion so preventing the interference of the ion with soap and the formation of scum.

8.5   WATER IN CLEANING

Water is a very poor wetting agent since it tends to remain as a drop even when placed on a surface. This is because water has a high

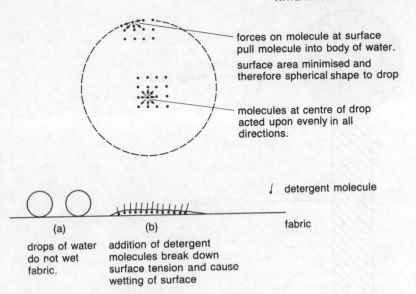

forces on molecule at surface pull molecule into body of water.

surface area minimised and therefore spherical shape to drop

molecules at centre of drop acted upon evenly in all directions.

detergent molecule

fabric

(a)   (b)

drops of water do not wet fabric.

addition of detergent molecules break down surface tension and cause wetting of surface

FIG. 8.2 Intermolecular forces acting in a drop of water

surface tension. A drop of water (see Fig. 8.2) is composed of innumerable molecules which are attracted to one another. In the body of the drop, these forces operate evenly in all directions. At the surface of the water drop, however, all the forces on the molecules are exerted inwards and between the molecules of the surface, pulling these molecules into the body of the liquid. The surface area of the drop is reduced to a minimum and so it takes on a spherical shape. Objects, such as a needle, can be made to float on the surface of water due to surface tension (see Fig. 8.3).

Certain substances, called 'surface active agents' (or surfactants), can be used to reduce surface tension. Surfactant molecules have two parts, a water-loving (hydrophilic) 'head' and a water-hating (hydrophobic) 'tail' (see Fig. 8.4).

intermolecular forces sufficiently strong to form 'skin' on which small objects can 'float'.

needle

surface of water

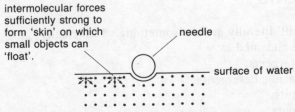

FIG. 8.3 Intermolecular forces at the surface of water are sufficient to allow small objects, e.g. a needle, to be suspended

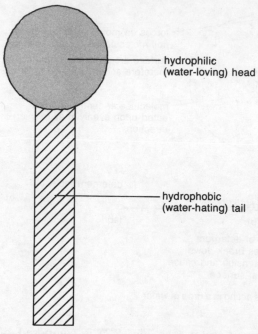

FIG. 8.4 A schematic representation of a surfactant molecule

In water, the hydrophilic heads arrange themselves at the surface of the liquid so that the hydrophobic tails can stick out of the water into the air. The surfactant molecules force the water molecules of the surface further apart, reducing the attraction between them and so decreasing surface tension. Detergents are surface-active agents. Addition of detergent to a drop of water causes the spherical shape to collapse and allows the drop to 'wet' the surface. When detergent is added to water on which a needle is supported the surface tension is reduced and the needle, being no longer supported, drops through the liquid to the bottom.

8.6   DETERGENTS

The term 'detergent' literally means 'something which cleans'. Detergents can be classified as:
  (i) surfactant detergents,
 (ii) alkaline and acidic detergents,
(iii) bleaching agents,
(iv) abrasive cleaners,
 (v) solvents.

8.6.1   SURFACTANT DETERGENTS

Action of surfactant detergents

Detergents are substances which act with water to cleanse by:
1. *Reducing surface tension*. This allows water to wet the surface being cleaned (see Fig. 8.3).
2. *Emulsifying greasy dirt*. The hydrophobic tails of the detergent molecules bury themselves in the grease leaving the hydrophilic heads at the water–grease interface. The like charges of the hydrophilic heads repel each other and cause rolling up of the grease to form suspended droplets. Detergent molecules act as emulsifying agents (see Sect. 3.5.1) since adding a detergent solution to grease produces two immiscible liquid phases, one dispersed in the other (see Fig. 8.5).

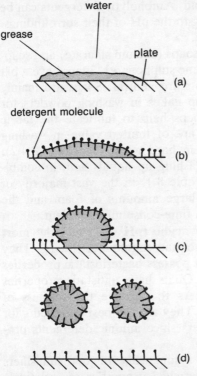

FIG. 8.5 Emulsification of grease by detergent action (a) grease does not dissolve even in hot water (b) addition of detergent molecules causes hydrophilic heads to remain at grease – water interface and hydrophobic tails to bury themselves in the grease (c) repulsion of hydrophilic heads rolls up the grease (d) grease droplets become suspended and cannot coalesce or redeposit themselves on the surface due to repulsion between hydrophilic heads. Articles should be rinsed well after washing and before drying to remove detergent molecules

3. *Suspending greasy dirt particles.* Detergent molecules become associated with the cleaned surface as well as with the greasy dirt particles. Forces of repulsion between the heads of the detergent molecules prevent the dirt particles flocculating and redepositing themselves on the cleaned surface and so they remain suspended and can be rinsed away. Residual detergent molecules on crockery may be passed onto food and have been implicated in certain types of gut irritation.

TYPES OF DETERGENTS

Detergents are classified according to the charge carried on the hydrophilic head of the molecule. Anionic detergents have a negatively charged hydrophilic head and cationic detergents have a positively charged hydrophobic head. Ampholytic detergents can be either anionic or cationic according to the pH of their surroundings. Non-ionic detergents do not ionise.

Anionic detergents include the soaps (sodium stearate) and soapless detergents (sodium alkyl benzene sulphonate). Soaps have a pH of 8–9 whereas soapless detergents are neutral. Soaps are mainly used in hand washing and as soap flakes in washing powders for fabrics such as wool and silk. Soaps help to lubricate the fabric fibres and maintain softness but are of limited value in washing powders since they form a scum in hard water (see Sect. 8.4.2). Soapless detergents are used in washing up liquids and, in combination with other ingredients in Table 8.1, in the vast majority of washing powders. They produce large amounts of foam and the removal of this by rinsing can be a time-consuming problem.

Cationic detergents are slightly acidic (pH 6–7) and the most important are the quaternary ammonium compounds (quats). They have limited detergency power but possess bacteriostatic properties and can be used for disinfection. Quats have antistatic properties and are used as fabric conditioners to improve the softness of laundered articles and aid ironing. They are the best detergents for washing plastic glasses and tumblers since anionic detergents produce clouding.

Ampholytic detergents based on amino acids are good emulsifiers and although possesing some bactericidal properties are relatively expensive. They are frequently used in medicated liquid soaps and oven cleaners.

Non-ionic detergents have good scum dispersing properties and can be used in conjunction with anionic detergents to produce low – lather products which are particularly suitable for automatic washing

TABLE 8.1 Composition of a soapless washing powder

Function	Property	Examples
Surfactant detergent	Cleaning	Sodium alkyl benzene sulphonate
Builder	Soften water, suspend soil and improve cleaning.	Sodium tripolyphosphate
Conditioner	Improves flow of powder, maintains alkalinity, and protects metal machine parts	Anhydrous sodium silicate
Filler	Bulking agent, keeps granules crisp	Anhydrous sodium sulphate
Bleaching agent	Stain removal	Sodium perborate
Bleach precursor	Enables bleach action to start at lower temperatures	Tetra acetyl ethylene diamine (TAED)
Anti-redeposition agent	Helps suspend dirt particles	Sodium carboxy methyl cellulose
Foam stabiliser	Improves lather	Ethanolamide
Fluorescing agent	Improves whiteness	
Perfumes and dyes	Increase consumer acceptability but can cause skin allergies	
Enzymes	Digest protein based stains	

machines and floor cleaning machines. Large amounts of foam affect machine operation and the foam can overflow from front loading and some top loading machines.

The choice of a particular detergent will depend on the application, one proviso being that products designed for hand cleaning should avoid components likely to cause allergic reactions. Some anionic detergents, e.g. sodium lauryl sulphate, cause skin allergies as do some perfumes and dyes incorporated into soapless washing powders. Proteolytic enzymes, extracted from bacteria, are added to some biological washing powders and may cause allergic reactions. They are used to remove protein soil, e.g. blood, egg and gravy at low temperatures to prevent inactivation of the enzymes. Protein-based fabrics, e.g. wool and silk, should not be soaked in biological powders. Properties of the various types of surfactant detergent are summarised in Table 8.2.

TABLE 8.2

Anionic		Non-ionic	Cationic
Soaps	*Soapless*		
hydrophobic tail	hydrophobic tail	hydrophobic tail	hydrophobic tail
(COO⁻) hydrophilic head	(SO₃⁻) or (SO₄⁻) hydrophilic head	(OH) [ether] hydrophilic head	CH_3—(N⁺)—CH_3 CH_3 hydrophilic head
Negatively charged ion	Negative charged ion	Does not ionise	Positively charged ion
e.g. sodium stearate, potassium laurate	e.g. alkylbenzene sulphate	e.g. alkylphenol ethoxylate	e.g. cetyl trimethyl ammonium bromide (cetrimide)

Notes:-

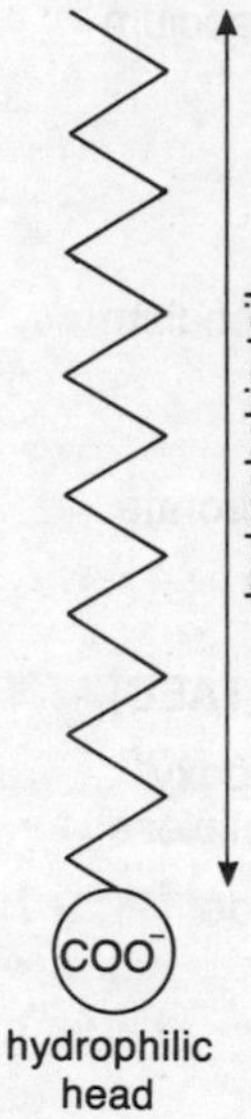	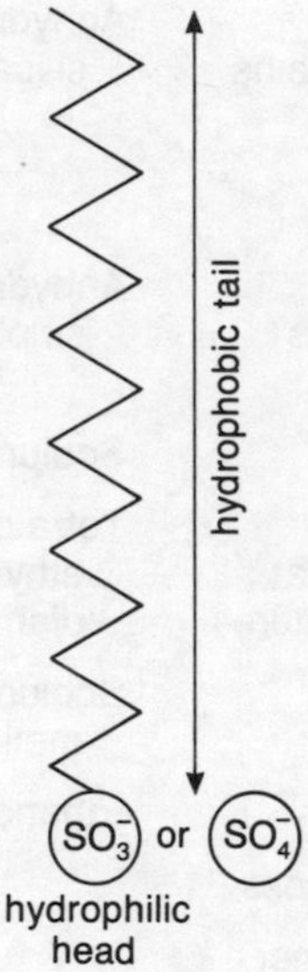	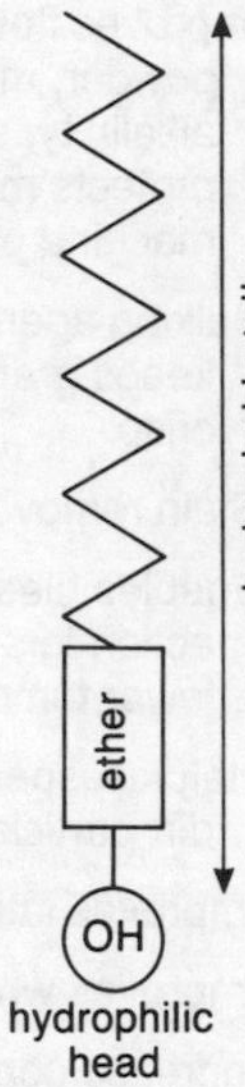	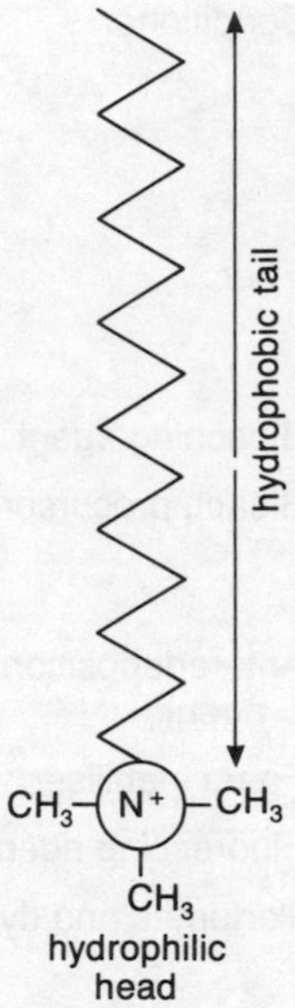
Forms scum in hard water	May cause skin problems e.g. contact dermatitis	Expensive	Inactivated by hard water
Expensive			Expensive
	Cheap		Good antistatic agent
			Good bactericidal properties

INCOMPATIBILITY OF ANIONIC AND CATIONIC CLEANERS

The mixing of an anionic and a cationic detergent and the attraction of the oppositely charged heads, results in the formation of complex insoluble products which are precipitated from solution and their detergent effect lost. The production of a lather and roll up of grease depends upon repulsion of like charges. The mixing of anionic and cationic detergents causes lather to collapse. Where an anionic and a cationic product need to be used in the same situation, the first product should be carefully rinsed to ensure activity of the second, e.g. hypochlorites must not be mixed with cationic detergents.

8.6.2   ALKALINE AND ACID CLEANERS

Alkaline Detergents (Degreasing Agents)
These have a pH of 9–12 and clean by converting fatty soil (grease) to soap, a process known as saponification. Alkaline detergents are used to remove grease from ovens and stoves, for clearing blocked drains and at lower concentrations, in dish washing powders. The alkalis most commonly used are sodium hydroxide (in crystalline, solution or aerosol form), sodium metasilicate (crystals) and sodium carbonate (crystals and solution). All alkaline detergents must be handled with great care, particularly sodium hydroxide, and protective clothing should be worn. Manufacturers usually give advice on appropriate safety precautions on the product's container. Alkaline detergents cannot be used on aluminium and galvanised surfaces and strong alkalis damage wool, silk, cotton and skin.

Sodium hydroxide is extremely caustic and corrosive and should only be used in situations where a very strong alkali is needed, e.g. for oven cleaning.

Sodium metasilicate is non-caustic but still corrosive and is the detergent most commonly used in dish washing formulations to emulsify grease. Dishwashing detergents are corrosive and poisonous and are so powerful that they may remove the pattern from crockery not specifically designed for use in dishwashers.

Sodium carbonate is the least corrosive, and is recommended for use in crystal form for unblocking drains.

Acid cleaners
Strong inorganic acids, pH 1–3, are widely used for the removal of limescale from toilet bowls (see Sect. 8.4.2). Acids react with limescale and mineral deposits to give water-soluble salts. Acid cleaners should be handled with care and should not be allowed to

come in contact with skin. They must never be used in conjunction with toilet cleaners and disinfectants based on hypochlorite as they react to form the highly toxic gas chlorine. Acid toilet cleaners are usually in powdered form and are based on acid salts such as sodium bisulphite and sodium persulphate which release sulphuric acid on contact with water. Moderately strong acids, such as phosphoric and sulphamic, can be used to remove all but the most excessive limescale build up. Acid cleaners usually require a contact time of 2–3 hours to be effective.

Weaker organic acids, such as citric, acetic and tartaric acids, pH 3–5, are much safer to handle. A dilute solution of acetic acid can be used to clean plastic laminates, e.g. on table tops and work surfaces. A mixture of citric acid and salt can be used to remove rust and for cleaning copper. Badly stained copper can be cleaned with a very dilute solution of hydrochloric acid.

8.6.3   BLEACHING AGENTS

Bleaches are oxidising agents which react chemically with stains to remove colour and make subsequent removal of the stain with a detergent easier. Bleaches are based on the production of either chlorine or an active form of oxygen in solution.

The most common liquid bleach is a solution of sodium hypochlorite (see Sect. 8.7.4) which breaks down to release free chlorine in solution. This can be used at appropriate concentrations for removal of stains from textiles, sinks, and lavatory bowls. Alternative sources of chlorine are chloramines and dichlorodimethyl hydantoin which can be used in dishwashing powders and scouring powders.

Sodium perborate is a solid form of hydrogen peroxide which breaks down to release active oxygen in solution and is used at approximately 10 % in washing powders to bleach stains. Sodium perborate is only really efficient at high temperatures (80 °C) which are unsuitable for coloured and synthetic fabrics. Most washing powders now incorporate a 'bleach precursor', e.g. tetra acetyl ethylene diamine (TAED), which enables sodium perborate to operate efficiently at 50–60 °C giving 'boil wash' results at lower temperatures together with energy savings of about 8 %.

8.6.4   ABRASIVE CLEANERS

These involve the use of an abrasive powder as part of a mixture which is rubbed onto a soiled surface for cleaning. The particle size of the powder determines the degree of abrasiveness.

Fine particulate powders, such as iron oxide (Jeweller's Rouge) or china clay are used together with a suitable solvent and ammonia in metal polishes.

Coarser powders, such as powdered pumice are used in scouring powders and cream cleaners, for the cleaning of hard surfaces. Scouring powders contain abrasive powder, surfactant and a chlorine compound and being abrasive are limited in use to certain hard surfaces, e.g. ceramic tiles. Cream cleansers contain very fine abrasive powders, e.g. calcite, mixed with detergent and ammonia or sodium carbonate to maintain alkalinity. Even those cream cleansers described as being 'non-scratch' must be used with caution on polished surfaces.

8.6.5   SOLVENTS AS CLEANING AGENTS

The term solvent includes any liquid capable of dissolving a solute, and many aqueous solvents are used in cleaning. However, an extremely important group of compounds used for the removal of grease and other stains are the organic solvents (see Table 8.3), which are used where water would be undesirable or ineffective. All organic solvents are volatile and some are flammable. Care needs to be taken to ensure adequate ventilation during use to prevent staff being overcome by fumes. Always test a small, inconspicuous part of the material being cleaned before treating the whole object.

8.6.6   PRIMERS, SEALERS AND POLISHES

Although these are technically not cleaning agents many manufacturers list primers and sealers under the heading of cleaning agents. They are applied to porous surfaces such as wood and cork to make the surface impervious to grease and dirt. The surfaces are initially primed to give a strong bond to the material being used as a sealant. Sealers can be resins, plastics (polyurethane) synthetic rubbers or silicates. Breakdown of the sealed surface during subsequent cleaning leads to hygiene risks.

Polishes for floors, furniture and metals are either solvent-based (e.g. natural or synthetic wax plus turpentine) or water-based (emulsions) where the main active ingredients are wax and a polymer resin.

TABLE 8.3 Solvents as cleaning agents

Aqueous solvents

Water	Universal solvent. Removes fresh fruit, beer and wine stains
Warm detergent solution	Removes fresh paint stains, and fresh mildew stains
Salt solution	Removes meat juices, gravy and egg-white stains
Laundry Borax solution (3 %)	Removes cocoa, coffee and beer stains and scorch marks
Ammonia solution (25 %)	General household cleaner.
Glycerol solution (30 %)	Removes obstinate (dried) cocoa and coffee stains

Organic Solvents
All these solvents are volatile and some are flammable

Trichloroethylene	Main solvent for drycleaning. Removes oils, fats, grease, tar, wax resins and some paints
Tetrachloroethylene	As for trichloroethylene
Industrial methylated spirit	Solvent for some dyes, resins, ball point pen marks FLAMMABLE
Propanol	Window/mirror cleaner FLAMMABLE
White spirit	Solvent for oils, fats, grease, tar, wax, paints. FLAMMABLE
Turpentine	As for white spirit. FLAMMABLE
Petrol	Removes tar, pitch and contact adhesives. FLAMMABLE
Acetone or Amyl Acetate	Solvent for some dyes, paints, lipstick and nail varnish. FLAMMABLE

8.6.7 STORAGE OF CLEANING MATERIALS

The following set of simple rules can be followed:
1. Store cleaning materials in a separate locked room which should be:
   (a) dry and cool;

(b) adequately sized;

(c) provided with a sink, water supply and adequate drainage.

2. Acid and alkaline products should never be mixed.

3. Store acid materials separately from chlorine-based products.

4. Store chlorine-based products in dark conditions.

5. Clearly label ALL containers.

6. Do not transfer cleaning products to alternative containers for storage. The product may react with the material of the new container.

7. Take care in cleaning out containers, e.g. vessels containing sugar cleaned with sodium hydroxide, produce carbon monoxide gas.

8.7 DISINFECTION

8.7.1 DISINFECTION BY CLEANING

If correctly carried out, thorough cleaning may remove a high proportion of the microbial contamination from surfaces. However, much depends on the design, construction and condition of the surface being cleaned. Soft, porous, chipped and worn surfaces are far more difficult to clean. Cleaning materials, e.g. cloths, mops, etc., must themselves be clean and cleaning solutions correctly made up. In the two key areas, i.e. food-preparation areas and washing/ toilet facilities, disinfection by cleaning may not be adequate to reduce microorganisms to a sufficiently low level necessary to prevent cross-contamination. In such cases heat or chemical disinfection is required as well.

8.7.2 DISINFECTION BY HEAT

Bacteria taken above their maximum temperature for growth for any period of time will be destroyed, and disinfection by heat is a reliable method for disposing of most pathogenic organisms. Pathogens, apart from spore formers, are usually heat sensitive. For this reason disinfection by heat is incorporated in a number of sanitising procedures, e.g. washing of dishes by hand or machine incorporates a hot water rinse, knives and cloths can be disinfected by boiling in water for about 10 min. Disinfection of parts of catering premises can be achieved by the use of steam or hot water hoses for about 5–10 min.

8.7.3   DISINFECTION BY CHEMICALS

In some cases it is impractical to disinfect by heat, and for sanitisation cleaning may need to be combined with the use of a chemical disinfectant. Care must be taken in catering in the choice and use of disinfectants. No one disinfectant is ideal despite manufacturers claims to the contrary! Some are not suitable for food-preparation areas, others are expensive, all may have their efficiency greatly reduced if not used correctly.

Disinfectants vary both in the way in which they affect microorganisms and in the type of microorganisms destroyed. Good disinfectants have a wide range (broad spectrum) of activity, killing many types of organisms. Others have a much more limited range and few have any significant effect on bacterial spores. Some disinfectants are bacteriocidal – actually killing bacteria, others are bacteriostatic – merely preventing the growth of bacteria (similarly mycocidal' and 'mycostatic' refer to fungi, 'viricidal' to viruses and 'sporicidal' to spores). Disinfectants do not work instantly. A minimum of 2 min contact time is necessary and that is for a good disinfectant. Other disinfectants may require much longer contact times.

Disinfectant solutions should be made up correctly, following the manufacturers instructions. Solutions that are too dilute will be ineffective, those that are too concentrated may be dangerous to use. Some disinfectant solutions deteriorate rapidly if left and it is better to make them up daily. Dirty diluted disinfectant solutions can actually contain large numbers of growing bacteria! Chemical disinfectants perform less well when diluted with hard rather than soft water are more effective at high temperatures and are affected by changes in pH.

It is important that surfaces should be cleaned thoroughly before application of disinfectants (just as somebody who fell and cut his knee would clean the cut before applying antiseptic). Organic debris, e.g. food particles, gravy, grease, etc., both reduce the efficiency of disinfectants as well as surrounding and protecting the microorganisms by preventing the chemical access to function. For this reason sanitisers, i.e. chemicals with a combined detergent/disinfectant action, are best used only for surfaces subject to light soiling. Care should be taken in the formulation of sanitisers as some disinfectants should not be mixed with certain types of detergents due to incompatibility (see Sect. 8.6.1).

8.7.4   TYPES OF DISINFECTANTS

A range of disinfectants are available, the most common ones being based on the following chemicals:

Hypochlorites

These owe their antimicrobial action to the release of free chlorine in solution. As a group they have many advantages recommending their use in catering. They are relatively inexpensive and have a wide range of antimicrobial activity (including viricidal and limited sporicidal activity). In working concentrations, used on food-preparation surfaces, they have relatively little taste or smell. Hypochlorite solutions may deteriorate on storage and can have a corrosive effect on some surfaces. Their biggest disadvantage is that they are more readily inactivated by organic debris than most other disinfectants. Hypochlorite solutions are often purchased at concentrations of about 100 000 ppm (parts per million – 10 %) of available chlorine, although some cheaper brands may only be half as strong. For disinfecting clean work surfaces, this will need dilution to between 100 and 200 ppm. More heavily soiled surfaces require solutions of about 1000 ppm. (or in some hospital situations even stronger ones). Hypochlorites are anionic and must not be mixed with cationic detergents (see Sect. 8.6.1). Hypochlorites should not be mixed with acid cleansers since chlorine is produced, inhalation of which can lead to irritation and damage of the lining of the respiratory tract. Hypochlorites should not be used on fabrics as they remove colour. Examples of disinfectants based on hypochlorite solutions include Brobat and Domestos. Thickening agents are added to some products to make them cling to surfaces e.g. toilet bowls.

Quaternary ammonium detergents (QAC or Quats)

These are cationic detergents but do possess some antibacterial properties and are used for disinfection in some catering situations being more effective in alkaline conditions. Generally, they have a more limited range of activity than hypochlorites and some tend to be bacteriostatic rather than bacteriocidal. QAC are more expensive than hypochlorites and some are relatively easily inactivated by organic soil and anionic detergents. They can be used on most work surfaces or for rinsing equipment as they are virtually odourless and tasteless. Examples of QAC disinfectants include Deogen, Hytox and Dettox.

Iodophors

These are soluble iodine complexes incorporating a non-ionic detergent and phosphoric acid buffer to maintain a pH of 3–5 where they are most active. They have bactericidal action with a wide range of activity, are non-corrosive, non-irritating, non-toxic but are expensive. They are used widely in some food premises, e.g. breweries and dairies. Examples include Betadine.

Phenolic disinfectants

A number of different types of phenolic disinfectants are available, all of which are anionic, including:

    (a) White fluid phenolics, e.g. Izal.
    (b) Clear soluble phenolics, e.g. Hycolin.
    (c) Chlorinated phenols, e.g. Dettol.
    (d) Complex phenols, e.g. Hexachlorophene.

As a rule (a) and (b) are good disinfectants, possessing a broad spectrum of activity but can be toxic to unprotected skin. Unlike hypochlorites, phenolics are not so readily inactivated by organic debris **but their strong smell and residual after-taste on work surfaces limits their use in catering premises to drains, floors and toilets.** Chlorination of phenols reduces their range of antimicrobial activity and makes them more susceptible to organic debris but does allow them to be used on the skin.

Pine fluids

Disinfectants based on pine fluids often have poor antimicrobial activity but their clean pine smell makes them a popular household disinfectant, e.g. stores' own brands. Pine fluids may be blended with phenolic disinfectants to give better antimicrobial activity. Their use is not generally recommended in catering premises.

8.7.5   SUMMARY OF RULES OF DISINFECTION

1. Is cleaning alone sufficient or is there a need for extra disinfection?
2. Choose heat for disinfection where possible.
3. If a chemical disinfectant is to be used clean surfaces first. Choose a reputable brand (for food surfaces a type without taste or smell).
4. Make up disinfectant solutions daily in clean containers, following the manufacturer's instructions and using soft water. Equipment for applying disinfectants should itself be clean.

5. Apply disinfectant solutions liberally.
6. Allow sufficient time for the disinfectant to work.
7. Discard any left-over disinfectant.

8.8   APPLICATIONS OF CLEANING AND DISINFECTION TO CATERING PRACTICES

8.8.1   WASHING UP PROCEDURES FOR CROCKERY AND SMALL ITEMS OF EQUIPMENT

Washing up is regarded as a menial task but is vital to the smooth running of a hotel. A hotel is often judged on its standards of hygiene by the cleanliness of its glassware and crockery. Washing up should not be carried out in areas of food preparation because of possible cross contamination (see Sect. 14.3.3). After washing up, crockery and cutlery must be stored in a dust-free environment.

Manual washing up
This normally utilises the Two-Sink system. Crockery/utensils are prepared by scraping to rcmovc food dcbris (into a suitable waste container) then rinsing with cold water. In the three sink system an extra sink is utilised for rinsing in this preparation stage.

Sink 1 This is a cleaning stage and the sink contains hot water (plus appropriate detergent) at 50–60 °C. Gloves should be worn. The scraped crockery and utensils are washed in this sink, then removed and loaded into baskets/racks which are placed in sink 2.

Sink 2 This is a rinsing/disinfecting stage and the sink contains water at 77–82 °C. Baskets containing crockery are immersed for 1–2 minutes. This phase has three functions:
  (a) to disinfect by heat any remaining bacteria;
  (b) to rinse off any remaining detergent;
  (c) after removal from this sink items will air dry so avoiding use of a tea towel which could cause recontamination.

Washing up and rinsing water should be changed frequently and gloves, sinks, drainers and all other surfaces should also be cleaned. The approximate throughput for a manual system is 600 pieces per hour. The order of washing up must be carefully planned, e.g. lightly soiled articles such as glasses should be cleaned first. The process is slow, costly (labour intensive) and mechanical dish-washing may be preferable and often more economic. Cloth drying of washed items should be avoided and handling of items should be minimal to avoid recontamination. Care should be taken not to recontaminate the surfaces of washed items during storage or laying up of tables.

Dish washing machines

There are various types available depending on the size of the cleaning operation. These include:

(a) single tank;
(b) multi-tank with racks on conveyor;
(c) multi-tank with conveyor belt (direct feed).

Excess food should be removed from all items before loading into machines.

Single-tank machines involve hand loading/unloading of racks of tableware. The cleaning cycle is similar to manual washing up, i.e. detergent is sprayed onto items at 50–60 °C followed by a hot water (82 °C) rinse. Usual throughput for this machine is approximately 45 meals/hour.

Multi-tank machines have racks on conveyors, the tableware is loaded into the racks which are placed on the conveyor belt. This gives a much higher throughput of approximately 250–300 meals/hour. This type of dishwasher has a pre-wash section, followed by a detergent spray, a power rinse at 70 °C to remove detergent and a final hot disinfecting rinse at 82 °C.

In very large restaurants and many hospitals dishes are loaded directly onto a specially constructed conveyor belt directly feeding the multi-tank.

All machines should be serviced regularly and periodic checks made to ensure that temperatures on the dials are an accurate record of actual water temperatures.

Washed items should be checked for correct cleaning and faults in dish washing such as greasy/spotted crockery and starch deposits can be overcome by using the appropriate detergent (e.g. incorporating an oxidising agent to remove starch) and varying the temperature and amount of wash and rinse water.

Glass washing is often carried out separately because of the fragile nature of glass, the possibility of smearing and for beer glasses the 'head' of beer affects the foaming agents used in detergents. Some glass washing machines utilise a cleaning action whereby revolving brushes clean the glass while it is held in place by hand. A sanitiser should be added and brushes must be kept clean and well maintained. On a larger scale fully automatic glass washers have high pressure water jets at appropriate temperatures to wash, rinse and disinfect.

Cooking vessels, pans, etc., must be washed separately from tableware. Detergents/scouring pads may be used although care must be taken in the cleaning of certain metal surfaces. Sodium hydrogen carbonate (bicarbonate) – a degreasing agent – can be used to remove grease from heavily soiled items.

8.8.2 CLEANING SCHEDULES

Cleaning must be planned to be economical and effective. Cleaning schedules should clearly identify the method and frequency of cleaning, the chemicals to be used and the personnel involved. The latter should have suitable training and be aware of the standard required, have good communication with and back up from management. Planning of any cleaning schedule should take into consideration the following points (see also Table 8.4):

(a) clear definition of areas to be cleaned, kitchen, toilets, etc;

(b) a cleaning routine for equipment and surfaces designed to remove all contamination. This should identify the type of soil. Sugar, fat, protein and salts are the main types of food soil. It should provide the necessary information on the equipment to be used for cleaning, the correct concentration, application time and optimum temperature of chemical cleaners (detergents and disinfectants, as required). The order of cleaning equipment and surfaces must ensure that no recontamination of the cleaned surface occurs;

(c) for equipment there should be information on constructional materials and how the equipment should be dismantled for cleaning. Many manufacturers provide cleaning schedules for their equipment. Maintenance of equipment will need to be considered with cleaning schedules as damaged equipment harbours dirt;

(d) the time required for each cleaning operation and the manpower involved should be stated. There should be a clear identification of personnel involved in cleaning;

(e) problem areas must be identified and extra care taken.

(f) cleaning operatives should record the frequency of cleaning together with materials used and these should be retained by the management;

TABLE 8.4 Example of a cleaning schedule for a final food preparation area. Precise instructions should take note of constructional materials and cleaning materials to be used.

Area/Equipment to be cleaned	Method	Materials	Frequency	Personnel Responsible Signature/ Date/Time
Work surfaces e.g. formica – mixed food soil.	Remove food debris or soil. Wash with clean hot water plus detergent Rinse with hot clean water and clean cloth Apply suitable disinfectant and allow sufficient contact time Rinse off with fresh water and disposable paper towel Allow to air dry	Brush or cloth Suitable detergent* Suitable disinfectant**	Clean as you go, i.e. after completion of each food preparation task.	Kitchen Staff – take care on joints
Larder Refrigerator – mixed food soil	Switch off at mains Remove all loose food debris Wash with clean hot water plus detergent Rinse with hot water and clean cloth Apply suitable disinfectant allowing sufficient contact time	as above	Once a week	Kitchen Staff – check door seals.

Item	Method	Cleaning agent	Frequency	Personnel
	Rinse off with fresh water and disposable paper towel Leave door open to allow air drying			
Oven – mainly fat, grease and charred food	Remove shelves Turn on oven and heat to 65 °C Switch off Spray with oven cleaner, allow time for action, e.g. 20 minutes Remove loose grease and soil Rinse with fresh water Air dry	Wear rubber gloves Use suitable proprietary cleaner, following manufacturers instructions	Twice weekly, depending upon use	Kitchen Staff – take care with shelf brackets and door hinges
Wash hand basins – mainly soap and scum	Remove loose debris, e.g. soap, from drain outlet Wash with clean hot water plus detergent, inside and out Rinse with clean hot water Fill sink with hypochlorite** solution and allow sufficient contact time Rinse and air dry	as above	Minimum of three times weekly	Kitchen Staff – overflow and drain outlets need special attention
	Wipe hand operated tap handles	Suitable sanitiser***	Daily	Kitchen Staff

TABLE 8.4 Contd

Area/Equipment to be cleaned	Method	Materials	Frequency	Personnel Responsible Signature/ Date/Time
Walls – ceramic tiled – mixed food soil and grease.	Clean with hot water plus detergent Rinse with fresh hot water Apply suitable disinfectant allowing sufficient contact time Rinse off with fresh water and disposable paper towel Air dry	as above	Up to a height of two feet above work surface twice weekly Upper parts at monthly intervals	Kitchen Staff – examine for cracks. Take care with grouting Check behind equipment
Floors – quarry tiles – mixed food soil/dirt and grit	Spillages to be removed Brush to remove loose debris Mop with clean hot water plus detergent Mop off excess water Air dry Mop with hypochlorite	Brush or cloth Brush Mop	As they occur Daily, at end of day Weekly intervals	Kitchen Staff – pay attention to areas around and under equipment.

*suitable detergent – a wide range suitable for food premises are available from different manufacturers, e.g. Diversey Ltd.

**suitable disinfectant – many available, e.g. hypochlorite solution at 1000 ppm (approximately 1 in 100 dilution of neat Domestos – 0.1 % available chorine).

***a sanitiser may be used to combine detergent and disinfectant action.

(g) the cost involved including labour, chemicals, heat, equipment should be noted;

(h) efficiency of cleaning should be monitored by a random visual inspection by management personnel which will reveal whether cleaning procedures are adequate. Microbiological assessment of cleaning can be carried out where necessary, e.g. in cook-chill units, using swabs, dip slides or contact plates.

Contact plates are small plastic dishes containing nutrient media – agars (for cultivating pathogens, spoilage or indicator organisms). The lid is removed thus exposing the agar which is pressed firmly against the surface being examined. The dish is incubated in an inverted position. Bacteria from the surface having been transferred onto the medium, will grow and become visible as colonies.

Dip slides are thin rectangular plastic trays containing agar which can be pressed against the surface or food under test. Alternatively, they can be used for sampling liquids (foods, washing up water, etc.) by dipping the slide into the liquid. After incubation the developing colonies are counted and examined.

Swabbing involves the use of a sterile cotton wool swab moistened with sterile liquid being rubbed over an area of 100 cm^2 (4 in^2). The swab is returned to the laboratory and the surface of an agar plate inoculated, incubated and the growing colonies counted and examined.

TABLE 8.5 Specifications for maximum acceptable levels of contamination of a range of catering situations

Situation	Maximum acceptable numbers of bacteria
Surface of worktops:	
used for raw food	$100/\text{cm}^2$
used for cooked foods	$10/\text{cm}^2$
used for other purposes	$50/\text{cm}^2$
Surfaces of equipment in direct contact with food	$10/\text{cm}^2$
Contact surfaces of taps, fridges, etc.	$50/\text{cm}^2$
Sinks, washbasins and overflows	$50/\text{cm}^2$

There are no legal standards but suggested specifications for the maximum acceptable counts on a range of surfaces of importance in catering are shown in Table 8.5.

QUESTIONS

1. State which type of cleaning agent is used for the following and give one example of each:
   (a) Toilet cleaners.
   (b) Removal of grease from ovens and blocked drains.
   (c) Removal of grease from fabrics.
2. (a) Name the substances that cause: (i) temporary hardness of water; (ii) permanent hardness of water.
   (b) Why is one type of hardness called 'temporary' and the other 'permanent'?
   (c) What happens when soap is used with hard water?
   (d) Why does temporary hardness of water cause problems in catering establishments?
   (e) List two methods of softening water.
3. (a) Explain the meaning of the terms: (i) 'cleaning'; (ii) 'disinfection'.
   (b) List four factors to be taken into account when selecting a disinfectant to be used in a food-preparation area.
   (c) Name and briefly discuss the use of two chemical disinfectants.
   (d) Comment on the value of the word 'sterilant' used to describe some chemicals.
4. (a) Describe the structure of a detergent.
   (b) Why are detergents said to emulsify greasy dirt?

9

MICROBIAL GROWTH, SURVIVAL AND DEATH

9.1 INTRODUCTION

Microorganisms are widely distributed in nature and are universally present, unless precautions have been taken to remove them. It should not be surprising, therefore, to learn that most foods are contaminated with microorganisms, often in large numbers (see Table 9.1).

TABLE 9.1 Bacteria in foods

Food	Typical acceptable numbers of bacteria per gram of food
Dried soup	10^4
Fresh fish	10^6
Fresh vegetables (consumed raw)	$10^1–10^2$
Frozen vegetables (for cooking)	10^4
Frozen desserts	10^4
Ice-cream (vanilla)	10^3
Ice-cream (with added ingredients e.g. rum and raisin)	10^4
UHT milk	10
Ordinary milk	3×10^4
Raw carcass meat	10^6
Soft drinks	10^2

If foods are stored in conditions suitable for bacterial growth then numbers will increase. Counts in excess of 10^7 usually make food unacceptable.

The association between food and microorganisms can be a desirable one, in that the latter may actually have been used in the production of the food (see Ch. 10). Alternatively, and often more publicised, the relationship can be an undesirable one (see Chs. 11 and 12) resulting in illness.

Whether the association is judged to be desirable or undesirable, the important point in both cases is the ability of the microorganisms to grow and multiply (population growth, an increase in numbers) and survive in the food.

When making yoghurt optimum conditions for the starter culture to grow in the milk need to be known so that a high quality product can be obtained, about 2×10^8 bacteria/cm^3.

On other occasions caterers need to know about conditions for bacterial growth so that they can prevent it from taking place and a possible case of food poisoning from occurring.

It is impossible to study and understand the principles of food production, food preservation or food hygiene. without first having some elementary knowledge of microbial growth, survival and death.

9.2   CONDITIONS REQUIRED FOR MICROBIAL GROWTH

Environmental factors including nutritional (chemical factors), moisture level, pH, availability of oxygen and temperature play an important part in determining the rate and type of microbial growth that can occur in foods.

9.2.1   NUTRITIONAL REQUIREMENTS

Microorganisms may be autotrophic or heterotrophic, but in the food industry it is the heterotrophic ones which are of concern. Heterotrophic organisms require preformed organic nutrients in order to obtain energy and to act as a source of chemicals from which new cellular material can be produced. Some micro-organisms, e.g. some moulds, require only one organic chemical for growth to take place, others, e.g. some parasitic bacteria, require a complex assortment of organic molecules (see Fig. 9.1).

The most important chemical elements needed for growth are carbon, hydrogen, oxygen, nitrogen, sulphur and phosphorus, as well as a variety of others required in much smaller quantities. These elements are combined together to supply a heterotrophic organism with an energy source (often a carbon source), a source of nitrogen, and minerals as well as any vitamins and growth factors. Large organic molecules must first be broken down, by extracellular enzymes, into smaller, simpler molecules which can be transported into the cell, across the cell membrane.

Some microorganisms grow as saprophytes and can spoil foods intended for human consumption, the effect of their extracellular enzymes and growth ultimately lead to the visible signs of food spoilage (see Ch. 11). As they grow on the food, microorganisms produce waste products some of which are considered desirable,

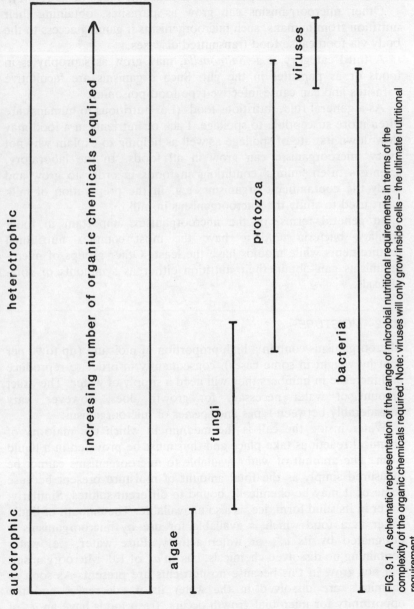

FIG. 9.1 A schematic representation of the range of microbial nutritional requirements in terms of the complexity of the organic chemicals required. Note: viruses will only grow inside cells – the ultimate nutritional requirement

e.g. lactic acid in cheese making, alcohol production in wine making. Not all waste products are desirable and some, known as 'toxins', are harmful, or poisonous, if consumed (see Sect. 12.5.2).

Other microorganisms can grow as parasites, obtaining their nutrition from humans, such microorganisms if gaining access to the body via food cause food-transmitted diseases.

A third category, e.g. *Salmonella*, may grow as saprophytes in foods or as parasites in the gut. Such organisms are facultative parasites and can cause infective-type food poisoning.

As a general rule, nutritious foods (i.e. nutritious to humans) are often more susceptible to spoilage. Lack of nutrients in a food may slow down its rate of spoilage as well as helping to explain why not every microorganism can grow in all foods. In the laboratory, scientists often 'mimic' conditions in foods in order to grow and study the contaminant organisms, e.g. in the preparation of milk agar, used to study the microorganisms in milk.

In general terms, of the microorganisms important in food-spoilage bacteria tend to have the most complex nutritional requirements while moulds have the least. Other groups of microorganisms can obtain their nutrition either as symbionts or commensals.

9.2.2 MOISTURE

Microorganisms contain a high proportion of moisture (up to 90 per cent by weight in some cases), consequently in order to reproduce and increase in numbers they will need a supply of water. The exact amount of water necessary for growth does, however, vary considerably between types and species of microorganism.

Water inside the cell is the medium in which the majority of chemical reactions take place and thus must be provided in a liquid form. The amount of water available to microorganisms cannot be measured simply as the total amount of moisture present because some of it may be chemically bound to different solutes. Similarly, water in its solid form, ice, is also unavailable. The amount of liquid water in a food which is available for use by microorganisms is designated by its a_w, or water activity. Pure water, i.e. water containing no dissolved chemicals, has an a_w of 1.0. Microorganisms will not grow in this because no nutrients are present. As soon as chemicals are dissolved in the water its a_w decreases and the opportunity for microbial growth occurs, fresh foods have an a_w of 0.99 or above. If so many chemicals are present that the a_w falls below 0.6 then no living things are capable of growth. Table 9.2

TABLE 9.2 Important levels of a_w

	a_w	
Pure water	1.0	
Fresh foods	0.99+	Increasing
Minimum a_w for most bacteria	0.91	levels of
Minimum a_w for most yeasts	0.85	solute;
Minimum a_w for most moulds	0.80	decreasing
Minimum a_w for most halophilic bacteria	0.75	concentration
Minimum a_w for most xerophilic bacteria	0.65	of water
Minimum a_w for most osmophilic yeasts	0.60	

shows the effect of decreasing a_w on the growth potential of a range of microorganisms.

As a general rule, bacteria need more moisture for growth than yeasts, which in turn usually require more than moulds. Hence spoilage of drier foods is usually caused by yeasts or moulds. The values quoted in Table 9.2 are approximate normal minimum values. Exceptions to the normal values exist in the form of micro-organisms especially adapted to growing at low available moisture levels. These include organisms that are halophilic (literally, salt loving), xerophilic (literally, dry loving) and osmophilic (literally, liking a high osmotic pressure).

Altering the level of available moisture can be a useful method of food preservation. Dehydration, or drying of foods, e.g. spray-dried milk, provides an environment unsuitable for the growth of micro-organisms (provided that the food is stored correctly). Similary, the addition of sugar or salt to foods preserves them by decreasing the a_w and increasing the osmotic pressure of the food – contaminant microorganisms are thus unable to obtain sufficient moisture for growth. **Note the values quoted in Table 9.2 are for growth, not survival.** Many microorganisms can survive perfectly well in dry conditions (see Table 9.1), i.e. dry foods may contain thousands of viable but non-growing bacteria.

Apart from methods of dehydration, such as spray drying or freeze drying, smoking of foods also lowers their a_w.

Thus it can be seen that the a_w of a food is important in determining its type of spoilage and the ease with which it might occur.

9.2.3   pH

Another property of food which determines its ease of spoilage is its pH. Although wide variations can exist between different microorganisms, the majority are classified as neutrophiles, i.e. they like relatively neutral conditions, somewhere between pH 5–8, in which to grow. Most foods are neutral-to-slightly acid and are thus likely to be spoilt by neutrophilic microorganisms. Such foods can be preserved by acidifying them, i.e. lowering their pH, pickling involves preserving the food by the addition of vinegar (acetic acid). An alternative is to allow the controlled development of microbial acids, e.g. the production of lactic acid in yoghurt or sauerkraut. However, even acidified foods can be spoilt, specially adapted microorganisms, known as 'acidophilic' (literally, acid loving), will only grow in acid conditions, pH 2–5. Aciduric organisms are those that **survive** low pH values without actually **growing** well at a low pH.

As a general rule, moulds and yeasts tolerate acid conditions better than bacteria which normally stop growing below a pH of about 5.3. Thus 'acidic foods', e.g. oranges, strawberries, etc., are more likely to suffer from mould spoilage. Apart from certain exceptions, e.g. the bacterium causing cholera, most microorganisms do not grow well above pH 8.0. As few foods are alkaline (see Table 9.4) this latter group are not important to the food industry.

9.2.4   AVAILABILITY OF OXYGEN

All microorganisms, apart from viruses, respire, i.e. they carry out energy-yielding reactions. Many microorganisms require molecular oxygen for respiration and are described as 'aerobic'. Other microorganisms carry out respiration only in the absence of oxygen and are termed 'anaerobic'. A third group can respire with or without oxygen and are termed 'facultative anaerobes'. As far as the food industry is concerned nearly all moulds are aerobic, yeasts are facultatively anaerobic, and bacteria can be aerobic, anaerobic or facultatively anaerobic.

Specific attempts can be made to reduce aerobic spoilage by vacuum packaging susceptible foods. Hard cheeses, such as Cheddar which are susceptible to mould growth, are vacuum packaged to increase their shelf-life. Similarly, storage of a variety of foods such as fruit, meat and fish, in an atmosphere of carbon dioxide has been shown to retard microbial spoilage (see Sect. 11.6.2).

The most important group of anaerobic bacteria in the food industry are those belonging to the genus *Clostridium* which are also able to produce heat resistant spores. Some, e.g. *Clostridium butyricum*, are important in food spoilage while *Clostridium perfringens* and *Clostridium botulinum* are important in causing food poisoning. *Clostridium perfringens* is associated with food poisoning by foods such as stews and casseroles which have been heated for quite long periods of time. A slow process of heating drives off all the oxygen from a food, producing anaerobic conditions for the germination of *Clostridium* spores during cooling. Similarly, *Clostridium botulinum* is often associated with canned foods which also tend to be low in oxygen, having been heated during canning. A fourth category of microorganisms are described as microaerophilic. These like to grow at slightly reduced oxygen levels, some with extra carbon dioxide, e.g. the mould *Penicillium roquefortii* used in making veined cheeses, as well as lactobacillus bacteria used in starter cultures (see Sect. 10.5.2).

9.2.5 TEMPERATURE

Even if a food provides a microorganism with the correct nutrient, pH, water and oxygen levels, it will not grow unless the food is stored at a temperature suitable for its growth.

Every microorganism (see Fig. 9.2) has:

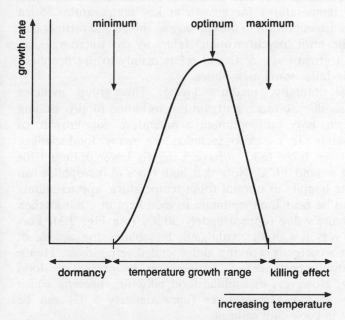

FIG. 9.2 The effect of temperature on microbial growth

(a) A minimum temperature for growth – a temperature below which it is dormant and will not grow.
(b) An optimum temperature for growth – a temperature at which it grows best (most rapidly).
(c) A maximum temperature for growth above which it will not grow and is likely to be destroyed.

The difference between the minimum and the maximum is known as the 'temperature range' for growth.

Depending upon their temperature requirements for growth, microorganisms can be allocated to one of three broad categories (see Table 9.3):

TABLE 9.3

Type of organism	Optimum for growth between	Growth range somewhere between
Psychrophilic	10 to 20 °C	−6 to +30 °C
Mesophilic	30 to 42 °C	6 to 44 °C
Thermophilic	55 to 65 °C	45 to 80 °C

Figures quoted are approximate values only.

1. *Psychrophilic (cryophilic)*, literally, cold loving. These are microorganisms which like colder conditions and have their optimum temperatures for growth at low temperatures. Such organisms are important in the spoilage of chilled and refrigerated foods. The term 'psychrotrophic' refers to any microorganism capable of growth at +5 °C and refers mainly to psychrophiles but also includes some mesophiles.
2. *Mesophilic*, literally, medium loving. This group includes pathogenic, disease-causing organisms, including food-poisoning ones which have an optimum temperature for growth of approximately 37 °C. Also included are many food-spoilage organisms but these tend to have a slightly lower optimum for growth at around 30 °C. Note that both types of mesophiles can grow quite happily at normal room temperature, approximately 18 °C, and be near their optimum in food kept in a hot kitchen on a summer's day (approximately 30 °C) (see Fig. 9.3). For-tunately, very few of the pathogenic mesophiles are capable of growth in a correctly working and operated refrigerator. Hence the utmost importance of refrigeration in preventing food poisoning. However, mesophilic food poisoning bacteria which can grow at low temperatures (approximately 5 °C) can be important in cook chill catering.
3. *Thermophilic bacteria*, literally, heat loving. These bacteria will

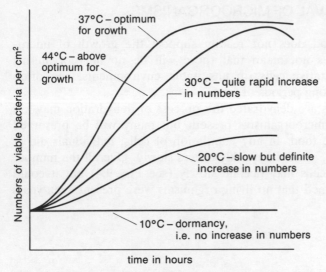

FIG. 9.3 The effect of 10 °C temperature increases on the growth of a mesophilic bacterium with a growth range of 10-44 °C

only grow at high temperatures, usually in excess of 45 °C and some can actually grow at temperatures as high as 75 °C. Such thermophilic bacteria are important in the spoilage of some canned foods.

9.2.6 TIME

Given a suitable environment, microorganisms do not instantaneously increase in number but first need time to adapt to the conditions and then actually to reproduce. Bacteria are the quickest growing of the microorganisms some being able to double in number every 12 min under optimum conditions, longer in non-optimum ones (see Fig. 9.3). Bacteria growing in food at this rate would number millions within a few hours, thus in suitable foods they are the first spoilage organisms to accumulate. One hundred bacteria doubling in number every 20 minutes become more than two million bacteria in five hours. However, bacteria are often the most demanding in their conditions for growth (moisture, pH, nutrients) and in commodities that do not meet their specific requirements (e.g. acid foods, dried foods), the slower growing yeasts and moulds will be the primary spoilage organisms.

Wise caterers know about microbial growth and do their best to limit its occurrence, using temperature in particular as a weapon.

9.3   SURVIVAL OF MICROORGANISMS

Because a food does not readily support the growth of micro-organisms does not mean that there will be no microorganisms present. Vegetative cells, in unsuitable environments, can often survive quite long periods of time.

When foods are dehydrated the process of dehydration may kill some of the microorganisms present but many will be preserved along with the food. In any population of cells, individuals die at different rates, some die quickly others slowly. Overall the number of vegetative cells may decline slowly (see Fig. 9.4) but it could never be assumed that no living organisms were present even years later.

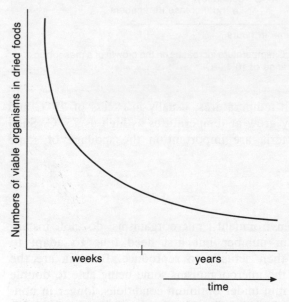

FIG. 9.4 A graphical representation of the effect of dehydration on the survival of microorganisms. Graph shows initial rapid drop in numbers of viable cells on storage but continuing low levels years later

Similarly, when food is frozen some microorganisms in the food may die as a result of 'cold shock', others may lose viability during cold storage. More hardy members of the community might remain potentially viable for years, and if transferred back to a suitable environment would revive and start to reproduce. The exact number of microorganisms dying from cold shock would depend on the food, the type of microorganisms involved and the manner of freezing. For this reason it is possible (see Sect. 12.6.1) to isolate food-poisoning bacteria from stored frozen poultry.

The discussion so far has been concentrated on vegetative microorganisms (normal growing forms). Certain types of bacteria, along with moulds and yeasts, are capable of producing spores. Spores are dormant (not actively growing) and to varying degrees resistant. Bacterial spores, produced by *Bacillus* and *Clostridium* bacteria, are potentially the most resistant, with mould spores usually being less resistant. However, all spores are likely to be more resistant than the organism that produced them.

While subjecting microorganisms to drying or to low temperatures induces dormancy, most microorganisms if taken above their maximum temperature for growth and kept there for any length of time will be destroyed.

9.4   DEATH OF MICROORGANISMS

The term 'disinfection' means the removal or destruction of microorganisms and can be achieved as a result of heat, chemicals (known as disinfectants, see Ch. 8) and irradiation. The term 'sterilisation' means the complete destruction of all viable organisms (including microorganisms and their spores) from an object and is best achieved by heat.

Pasteurisation, cooking and canning are all methods of food processing that rely on the destructive effect of heat. The killing effect of heat on microorganisms varies in efficiency, depending on the presence or absence of moisture. Moist heat is far more effective for killing microorganisms than dry heat. Using dry heat, a time-temperature programme of 121 °C for up to 8 hr is required for sterilisation. Using moist heat at 121 °C (i.e. under pressure) a time of only 15 min is needed. On excessive exposure to dry heat, microorganisms become dehydrated and oxidised, moist heat causes coagulation and denaturation of cell proteins.

9.4.1   HEAT RESISTANCE OF MICROORGANISMS

The relative heat resistance of microorganisms can be compared in terms of their thermal death times (TDT). The thermal death time of an organism is defined as the time required to kill all of a given number of microorganisms at a specified temperature. For example, the thermal death time of a non-sporing bacterium at 60 °C might be as short as several minutes for a bacterium very susceptible to heat, or as long as several hours for more resistant bacteria. As the temperature increases so the thermal death time decreases, i.e. the higher the temperature the quicker the killing.

In general terms, the ability of an organism to withstand heat is related to its optimum temperature for growth, i.e. the higher the organism's optimum temperature for growth the more likely it is to be resistant to heat. Microorganisms can be placed into three broad categories based on their ability to survive heat: (a) heat sensitive, (b) thermoduric, and (c) heat resistant.

Heat-sensitive microorganisms

The term 'heat-sensitive' can be applied to many types of bacteria and most types of moulds and yeasts. Such organisms, depending on circumstances, would normally be destroyed after exposure to a temperature of 63 °C for about 30 min (or even less). Fortunately, most non-sporing pathogens are heat-sensitive. Pasteurisation is a process widely used in the food industry and it employs relatively low temperatures for short periods of time. Its function is either to kill heat-sensitive spoilage organisms (as in beer) or to kill food-borne pathogens (e.g. pasteurisation of milk to kill the tuberculosis organisms).

Thermoduric microorganisms (literally, heat enduring)

This term is applied to those microorganisms which although preferring to grow at medium temperatures (approximately 30–37 °C) have the ability to tolerate or endure a short period of exposure to higher temperatures which would destroy heat-sensitive bacteria. A typical thermal death time for a thermoduric organism kept at between 80 and 100 °C would be 10 min or less. Thus, such organisms will be important in the spoilage of mildly heat-processed foods. The times and temperatures used to pasteurise milk are sufficient to destroy only a relatively small number of thermoduric organisms which are mainly responsible for the spoilage of pasteurised milk stored at ambient (room) temperatures.

Heat-resistant organisms

This term is usually reserved for the description of types of endospores produced by certain species of bacteria (see Sect. 9.3) which are capable of surviving 100 °C for at least 10 minutes. Although three major food poisoning bacteria can produce endospores (i.e. *Clostridium botulinum*, *Clostridium perfringens* and *Bacillus cereus*, see Sect. 12.6) particular care has to be taken with the spores of *Clostridium botulinum* in canned foods. Spores of

Clostridium botulinum are able to survive boiling at 100 °C for 3 hr or more. To achieve safety, susceptible canned foods need to be heated at temperatures in excess of 100 °C for varying lengths of time depending on the nature of the food, e.g. tinned meat is processed at approximately 115–121 °C.

It must be made clear that the sensitivity of a microorganism to heat is greatly dependent on the environment, e.g. in terms of the nutrients present, proteins, fats and sugars all have a protective effect on any microorganisms present. Probably the most important factor to the food industry is the cooperative destroying effect of temperature and pH. Acid foods need less heat processing than neutral foods because a low pH enhances the killing effect of the heat (see Table 9.4). However, all canned foods of pH 4.5 and above must receive a certain minimal heat treatment – known as the '*botulinum* cook'. This ensures the product will be free of the spores of *Clostridium botulinum* and is equivalent to the coldest point in the can being subjected to 121 °C for a minimum of 2.5 min (often for additional safety 3 min). In practice because of the possibility of more heat resistant spoilage organisms being present most canned foods receive heat processing well in excess of this minimum heat treatment.

TABLE 9.4 pH, time and temperature in the destruction of microorganisms

Food	pH	Classification	Heat processing
Milk and meat products	5.3+	Low acid	115 °C for approx. 15 min
Soups and sauces	4.5–5.3	Medium acid	decreasing to
Tomatoes/pineapples	3.7–4.5	Acid	
Citrus fruits and rhubarb	Below 3.7	High acid	100 °C for 2–3 min

9.4.2 OTHER METHODS OF DISINFECTION

Other methods of destroying microorganisms are based on the use of chemicals toxic to microbial cells (see Ch. 8) or of certain types of radiation. The possible use of irradiation as a means of preserving foods has been discussed for about 30 years but is not currently permitted for general use in the U.K. largely due to worries about the safety of irradiated food. Use is made of irradiation in other

E.E.C. countries. However, since 1981 there has been renewed interest in irradiation for food preservation and many countries, including the United Kingdom, are actively re-examining its possible use.

QUESTIONS

1. (a) Explain the symbol a_w.
   (b) Why might a reduction in a_w be useful in minimising the risk of food spoilage?
   (c) State two different ways of reducing the a_w of some peeled apple pieces for use in convenience foods.
2. Explain the principle behind the preservation of food by pickling.
3. Distinguish between the following terms applied to micro-organisms: thermophilic and thermoduric; aerobic and anaerobic; mesophilic and psychrophilic.
4. (a) Explain the meaning of the initials 'TDT'.
   (b) A bacterium has a TDT of 20 min at 70 °C. Will the TDT of the bacterium be shorter or longer at 85 °C?
   (c) Explain the function of pasteurisation in the processing of: (i) beer; (ii) milk.

10
DESIRABLE GROWTH OF MICROORGANISMS

10.1 INTRODUCTION

In many instances the growth of microorganisms in food is un-desirable (see Chs. 11 and 12) but there are a number of food-related occasions where growth or survival is actively encouraged. These can be grouped into three main areas:
(a) Manufacture of foods, e.g. cheese, yoghurts.
(b) Source of foods, nutrients or food additives.
(c) Agriculture or soil fertility.

The first group is the most important in relation to catering, microbial growth resulting in desirable changes in food raw materials. The new or microbially altered food has acceptable qualities to the consumer, possibly combined with an extended shelf-life.

10.2 RESPIRATION AND FERMENTATION

In order to appreciate the way in which microbial growth may be desirable in food, it is necessary briefly to examine the way in which they metabolise.

Microorganisms, like all other living organisms, require energy and those important in the manufacture of foods achieve this by breaking down organic chemicals. Any process involving the release of energy from the breakdown of chemicals is known as 'respiration'. The main chemical broken down is glucose and if this takes place in the presence of oxygen it is termed 'aerobic respiration'.

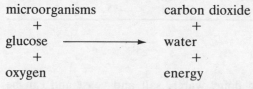

microorganisms   carbon dioxide
+   +
glucose   ⟶   water
+   +
oxygen   energy

Most instances of desirable microbial growth do not follow this type of reaction but involve the microorganisms breaking down the sugar without the use of oxygen, i.e. a type of anaerobic respiration known as 'fermentation'. For example, fermentation by yeasts:

yeast   alcohol
                        +

+   ⟶   carbon dioxide
                        +

glucose   small amount of energy

Fermentation reactions yield less energy than aerobic respiration but result in the formation of a diverse variety of chemicals e.g. alcohol, lactic acid, propionic acid which can contribute to, or determine, the characteristics of a wide range of food products (see Table 10.1).

TABLE 10.1 Some microbial food fermentations

Organisms	Substrate	Product
Lactic acid bacteria	Cabbage	Sauerkraut
	Cucumber	Pickles
	Red meat	Sausages – salami, Thuringer, Pepperoni
	Milk products	
	(a) cream	Sour cream
	(b) milk	Yoghurt
	(c) milk	Cheese – unripened, e.g. cottage cheese
	(d) milk	Cheese – ripened, e.g. Cheddar
Acetic acid bacteria	Alcoholic liquors	Vinegar
Lactic acid bacteria and yeasts	Flour (dough)	Sour dough bread
	Beans	Vermicelli
Yeasts and moulds	Soya beans	Soy sauce
Yeasts	Malt	Beer, stout, lager
	Fruit	Wines, vermouth, cider
	Wines	Brandy ⎱
	Molasses	Rum ⎰ require distillation
	Grain mash	Whisky
	Flour dough	Bread

10.3 BREAD MAKING

Bread is made by mixing flour, water, salt and yeast and can be regarded as a solid foam (bubbles of carbon dioxide trapped in a

TABLE 10.2 Enzymes in bread making

Starch in flour	diastase*	Maltose	maltase†	Glucose	zymase‡	Carbon dioxide, alcohol, flavouring
	→		→		→	

* Diastase: a mixture of amylase enzymes which break down starch – found in flour
† Maltase: enzymes produced by yeasts – found outside the yeast cells.
‡ Zymase: a sequence of enzymes found inside the yeast cells.

solid). The overall reactions taking place can be summarised as shown in Table 10.2.

Strains of the yeast *Saccharomyces cerevisiae* are used in bread making. The yeast reproduces by budding and apart from producing carbon dioxide to raise the dough, the yeast has two other functions: as an ingredient it contributes flavour and it helps to modify (condition, mature or ripen) the gluten (dough protein). Modification involves making the gluten more elastic and capable of retaining the evolved carbon dioxide. In bread making the yeast breaks down the glucose by a combination of fermentation and respiration (see equations below):

$$C_6H_{12}O_6 + 6O_2 \longrightarrow 6CO_2 + 6H_2O \qquad \text{aerobic respiration}$$
$$C_6H_{12}O_6 \longrightarrow 2CO_2 + 2C_2H_5OH \qquad \text{fermentation}$$

Aerobic respiration depends upon oxygen and is more likely to occur at an early stage in the process, especially near the outside surface of the dough. Fermentation is more likely to take place in the interior of the dough and when the oxygen has been used up. Bread is not noted for its high alcohol content and this is because as the temperature of the loaf in the oven increases most of the alcohol is driven off (boiling point of alcohol is 80 °C). It has been estimated that considerable quantities of alcohol enter the atmosphere daily from bakeries. Alcohol and other fermentation products contribute to the characteristic aroma of freshly baked bread.

The traditional method of baking (bulk fermentation process) is relatively slow and involves a number of critical stages and in many cases has now been replaced by shorter bread making processes, including Activated Dough Development (ADD), modern no-time doughs and the Chorleywood process (see Table 10.3). This latter method employs high-speed mechanical mixing of the dough. Larger quantities of yeast and water are added together with fat and chemical improvers, e.g. ascorbic acid. Production times are decreased by up to 60 per cent, the loaf produced has a slower staling rate, a larger variety of flours can be used (including those cheaper flours with a lower protein content, i.e. weak flours), and temperature control throughout the whole process is less critical. ADD requires the addition of a reducing agent, L-cysteine. ADD and modern no-time doughs can be mixed on slower, open pan machines, e.g. the spiral.

It is interesting to examine the changes taking place during baking as they illustrate some of the reactions discussed earlier (see Chs. 1 and 2).

Bread is baked in an oven set at about 230 °C for a period of

TABLE 10.3 Comparison of traditional (bulk fermentation) bread making with the Chorleywood bread making process

Bulk fermentation (straight dough technique)	Chorleywood bread making process
Mixing of ingredients	Mixing of ingredients (plus fat and vitamin C), additional water and yeast*
↓	↓
Fermentation (approx. 2 hr)	High-speed mechanical mixing (approx. 5 min)
↓	↓
Knocking back	Division into pieces and shaping
↓	↓
Fermentation (approx. 1 hr)	First proof (6–10 min)
↓	↓
Division into pieces and shaping	Moulding and placing into tins
↓	↓
First proof (fermentation) (approx. 10 min)	Final proof (50–60 min)
↓	↓
Moulding into final shape, placing into baking tins	Baking
↓	
Final proof (approx. 45 min) (fermentation here replaces carbon dioxide lost in moulding and shaping)	
↓	
Baking	

* It is important to use strains of yeast capable of rapid carbohydrate fermentation.

between 22 and 40 min. The temperature in the dough rises as heat is conducted towards the centre. Higher temperatures cause:

1. The yeast to be killed off (cell destruction starts at about 44 °C).
2. Starch granules swell (due to water absorption) followed by bursting and gelatinisation (see Sect. 1.3.3). The gelatinising starch helps to support the still soft gluten structure.
3. The gluten molecules start to coagulate at about 70 °C (see Sect. 2.5.4).
4. Dextrinisation (see Sect. 1.3.3) occurs on the outside of the loaf as a result of the combined action of heat and steam on the starch.

5. Caramelisation (see Sect. 1.4.2) gives an attractive brown colour to the crust.

10.4 ALCOHOLIC BEVERAGES

Ethanol is the essential component of alcoholic beverages and is produced in drinks as a result of a yeast fermentation (in some more exotic beverages, e.g. some South African beers, bacteria may also contribute to the fermentation). A variety of starting materials can be used although all possess a source of fermentable carbohydrate (e.g. grapes for wine making contains glucose, cereals for beer contain starch).

10.4.1 BEERS AND LAGERS

Beers and lagers are made by fermenting a hop-flavoured extract of barley malt using yeast. The production of the two beverages is similar although not identical, and whereas the brewing of beer utilises strains of *Saccharomyces cerevisiae*, strains of *Saccharomyces carlsbergensis* are used in lager making.

The starting commodity for both beers and lagers is barley which is converted into malt by soaking, or by steeping the barley seeds in water. This initiates the germination process and leads to the activation of amylase enzymes which break down starch to maltose. Malting is terminated by raising the temperature and allowing the 'green malt' to dry out. The actual temperature used is important. Darker beers and stouts originate from malt 'kilned' or dried out at a higher temperature. After drying, the malt is ground or crushed and is known as 'grist'.

The brewing process 'proper' starts with the mashing stage. Here grist is mixed with water at approximately 70 °C (the type of mixing and temperature of the water varies between different types of beers and beer and lager). Enzymes formed during germination now start to break down the starch to maltose. This liquid extract of malt is known as 'wort', hops are added for flavouring and the mixture is boiled. After cooling and filtration the wort is run into vats ready for fermentation. Traditionally, different types of vat and different strains of yeast have been used for the production of beers and lagers. For brewing a British type of beer *Saccharomyces cerevisiae* is used (the process of addition to the wort is known as 'pitching') This yeast tends to grow on the surface of the wort. Initially carbon dioxide is produced by aerobic respiration but as conditions change and become anaerobic the result is a fermentation reaction and the production of ethanol. For the manufacture of lager, *Saccharomyces carlsbergensis* is used and this yeast tends to settle out at the bottom of the fermentation vessel. Lager fermentation is carried out at a lower temperature and for a slightly longer time than beer fermentation. Carbon dioxide produced during the whole process can be collected and used for other purposes, e.g. soft drinks, dry ice, carbonation of beers, etc. After fermentation is complete, the yeast is separated from the immature or green beer which is run into storage tanks and left to 'condition'. After conditioning or 'maturing', the beer is ready for filtration, pasteurisation and packaging into cans, bottles, barrels or kegs.

The alcohol content of beer (2–5 per cent) is low compared to other alcoholic beverages.

10.4.2 WINES

Production of wine also depends upon the action of alcoholic fermentation. This time the yeast ferments glucose and fructose naturally found in grapes (or other fruits) (see Sect. 1.2).

Grapes are crushed and the grape juice or 'must' (really a concentrated solution of sugars with fruit acids) is treated with sulphur dioxide to inhibit the growth of undesirable spoilage organisms. If white wine is to be produced the grape skins and pulp are removed at this stage.

Fermentation now starts, traditionally carried out by yeasts derived from the surface of the grape (collectively known as the 'bloom') but this can sometimes give unreliable results. Usually in modern wine making a specially selected starter culture of yeast – often *Saccharomyces cerevisiae* var. *ellipsoideus* – is added. The yeast soon respires anaerobically and ferments, leading to the production of alcohol. In the making of red wine, pigments called 'anthocyanins' found in the grape skins are extracted giving the wine a characteristic colour. The conversion of sugar to alcohol slows down as the alcohol content exceeds 10 per cent (typically most table wines have alcohol contents between 9–12 per cent). The length of time required for fermentation varies, depending on the variety of yeast used, the type of grape, temperature, etc., but generally takes several weeks. Sweet wines, which still contain some unfermented sugar, may be fermented for shorter periods.

After fermentation the new wine is drawn off into vats. The most important post-fermentation treatment of wine is clarification and involves:

(a) Fining: addition of substances to precipitate out yeast cells and pectic substances.
(b) Racking: separation of the wine from the deposit.
(c) Filtration: to remove fine particulate material.

After filtration wines may be pasteurised to improve keeping quality and finally bottled and corked.

Different types of grape can be used for fermentation giving a wine its distinctive characteristics. Blending of grape varieties takes place. Chianti is a blend of three different varieties and Chateauneuf du Pape involves ten different grape varieties.

Contrary to popular belief many wines are best consumed when they are still fairly young and only the more expensive wines (e.g. Chateauneuf du Pape and St Emilion) improve in quality on long storage. Volatile substances produced during fermentation contribute to the alcoholic content and bouquet of a wine, the type of grape used adding more to underlying taste and character.

Wines are used in food preparation both for the purposes of marination – important in improving the texture of cheaper cuts of meat and in cooking. During cooking, the alcohol in the wine evaporates and contributes to the aroma. The remainder of the wine – tannins, acids, etc., enhance the flavour (combination of taste and aroma) of the dish.

10.4.3 OTHER ALCOHOLIC BEVERAGES

Fortified wines, e.g. sherry
These are made by adding alcohol (often in the form of brandy) to certain natural wines. This increases the alcohol content to about 16–20 per cent.

Spirits
These are alcoholic beverages (see Table 10.1) which have undergone distillation and contain 40 % alcohol w/v. Brandy and whisky, particularly, improve with aging which can take up to 20 years or even more.

Liqueurs
These are produced by combining a spirit with flavouring and adding syrup for sweetening, e.g. cherry liqueur, crème de menthe (mint and peppermint).

10.4.4 VINEGAR

The production of vinegar first involves a fermentation process, wine vinegar being made from grapes, cider vinegar from apples, malt vinegar from malt. Subsequently, bacteria belonging to the genus *Acetobacter* convert the ethanol to ethanoic (acetic) acid. This latter stage takes place in the presence of oxygen and is an oxidation reaction.

10.5 ACID FERMENTATIONS

A number of different types of bacteria ferment carbohydrates and while some produce alcohol or other neutral products, often the major end products of the fermentation are acidic e.g. lactic acid. Some bacteria produce almost exclusively lactic acid – 'homolactic fermentation', while others produce a mixture of acids plus neutral products and are termed 'heterolactic fermentations' (see Table 10.4).

TABLE 10.4 Acid fermentations

Homolactic fermentation		
Glucose ——————▶ Lactic acid		
Heterolactic fermentation		
Glucose ——————▶ Lactic acid		
	Acetic acid	
	Formic acid	Some possible
	Propionic acid	end-products from
	Ethanol	heterolactic
	Diacetyl	fermentation
	Acetaldehyde	

10.5.1 CHEESE

Cheese manufacture is a convenient way of converting milk into a nutritious product with improved keeping qualities. Lactic acid producing bacteria play an important role in this process. Milk is first pasteurised, this has only taken place since about 1965. Prior to this time manufacturers believed that the heat processing involved affected the flavour of the cheese. Pasteurised milk for cheese making is not sterile but should be free from harmful organisms. A starter culture of bacteria (selected strains and species of homolactic or heterolactic bacteria) is added to the milk at a temperature of about 30 °C. The starter culture may consist of a single strain of bacterium, e.g. *Streptococcus lactis* or *Streptococcus cremoris*, or a mixture of these possibly even combined with other bacteria. These soon break down the lactose in the milk and produce lactic acid.

This initial fermentation is important because it:
(a) Decreases the pH of the milk.
(b) Contributes to the curdling of the milk.
(c) Enhances drainage of whey from the curd.
(d) Contributes to a change in texture and flavour.

Rennet (contains the milk-clotting enzyme rennin), an extract from calf stomach, is added. This causes casein (the main protein in the milk) to clot or coagulate (see Sect. 2.6.1). The coagulum or curd is cut into small pieces to release the liquid whey. The pieces of curd are gathered together and pressed, after which they are broken up into small pieces and salted. The salted immature cheese is then packed into moulds (shapes), date stamped and stored. During the storage period the cheese ripens or matures and flavour develops. This is brought about by the action of microorganisms and enzymes and the cheese gains its final characteristic texture and flavour. The length of the ripening period varies between cheeses. Caerphilly cheese may be ready in from 2 to 3 weeks, a mild Cheddar in about 3 months, and a mature 'farmhouse' Cheddar with a strong flavour may be left for 10 months or more. Most of the typical English cheeses, Cheddar, Cheshire, Double Gloucester, etc., are bacterially ripened, bacteria already present in the immature cheese contributing to the ripening process. Other cheeses, however, are mould ripened. Moulds, especially species of *Penicillium*, are allowed either to develop on the outside of the cheese, e.g. Brie and Camembert, or within the cheese, a process that is encouraged by piercing the cheese with metal skewers. The mould develops and often gives rise to blue – green coloration typical of Danish Blue or Blue Stilton.

Cream cheese is made from cream, and cottage cheese is a low-fat, acid curd made from skimmed milk.

10.5.2 OTHER DAIRY PRODUCTS

Other dairy products can be produced using lactic fermentations. Yoghurt is a fermented milk beverage originating centuries ago in Eastern Europe and Western Asia, although present-day United Kingdom yoghurt differs somewhat from the original product. Most yoghurt in the UK is made from a blend of milk and skimmed milk and has a low fat content. Yoghurt made from full-fat milk is also available but on a much more limited scale. The production of yoghurt is outlined in Table 10.5.

One of the starter culture bacteria is *Streptococcus thermophilus* which produces diacetyl as part of the fermentation end products.

TABLE 10.5 Manufacture of yoghurt

Stage	Events taking place
Milk mix	Blending of milk and skimmed milk
Heat treatment	Equivalent to pasteurisation carried out for hygiene reasons and also to remove air and coagulate some proteins
Homogenisation	Breaking up of fat into small globules to prevent separation
Cooling	37–44 °C
Inoculation with starter bacteria	Equal proportions of *Streptococcus thermophilus* and *Lactobacillus bulgaricus*
Incubation	37–44 °C for approximately 6 hours – fermentation takes place. Most yoghurts are pasteurised at this stage
Cooling	4.5 °C
Addition of fruit and/or flavour	The end product varies in pH from 3.7–4.3 and contains approx. equal quantities
Packaging	(10^8/g) of each starter culture bacteria
Dispatch	

Diacetyl gives a creamy – buttery aroma and flavour to the finished product. *Lactobacillus bulgaricus*, the other starter culture bacterium, gives, in addition to considerable quantities of lactic acid, acetaldehyde which helps to give yoghurt its characteristic flavour. Diacetyl and acetaldehyde are examples of non-acid flavouring substances produced during fermentation. A variety of other fermented products similar to yoghurt can be made using cow's milk, goat's milk, etc. Examples of other fermented milk products include kefir (from the Balkans) and koumiss (from Russia).

Butter is produced from separated cream which may or may not be soured by bacteria prior to churning. The bulk of butter produced in the UK (and New Zealand and Ireland) comes from unripened cream and is known as sweet cream butter. On the continent, especially in Scandinavian countries, many of the butters are made from ripened cream, a starter culture of bacteria being added to the cream. During the fermentation, some acid is produced but so is diacetyl which gives the product a more pronounced buttery flavour than that of sweet cream butter.

10.5.3 OTHER LACTIC FERMENTED PRODUCTS

Lactic fermentations are important in a range of non-dairy foods (see Table 10.1).

1. *Fermented Eastern foods and beverages*: involve fermentation by moulds, yeasts or bacteria of a wide range of substances, e.g. tempeh from soya beans, bongkrek from coconut press cake.

2. *Pickled vegetable products*. In the UK the term 'pickle' covers all savoury vegetable foods with any sourness (acidity) in their taste. Some are simply packed in vinegar (unfermented pickles) while other pickled vegetables undergo a lactic fermentation, e.g. sauerkraut, olives, cucumber. In the making of sauerkraut, cabbages are washed, shredded and mixed with brine. The liquid is then fermented by a mixture of homo- and heterofermentative bacteria.

3. *Fermentation of beans*. Complex fermentations take place in the processing of coffee and cocoa beans.

10.6 MICROBIAL PROTEINS AND VITAMINS

Apart from their role in producing other foods, microorganisms can themselves be used as a source of protein or vitamins. Microbial protein, sometimes referred to as 'single cell' protein, offers a long-term hope of producing large quantities relatively cheaply (its yield and speed of production far exceeding that of conventional protein sources, such as meat or soya bean production). Countries world-wide are investigating the possibility of producing protein from bacteria, moulds, yeasts and algae. A variety of substances, including wastes from paper mills, sugar refining, the oil industry as well as natural gas (methane), have been used to cultivate the microorganisms. The present role of microbial protein is mainly restricted to animal feed where Pruteen, made by ICI from bacteria grown on natural gas, has achieved limited commercial success and is now accepted as suitable for human consumption. More recently Rank Hovis McDougall have incorporated specially produced mycoprotein (protein extracted from the hyphae of *Fusarium graminarium*) in foods for human consumption. Large-scale production of the mycoprotein now takes place and analysis shows it to be generally similar in its amino acid content to plant and animal protein although in some instances its digestibility may be lower (see Sect. 2.7.1). Savoury pies containing mycoprotein with beef or chicken flavouring are now widely available in the U.K. Other food uses of microorganisms include their role as vitamin sources, e.g. Marmite is a yeast extract rich in B vitamins, the manufacture of vitamins, e.g. B complex, and the production of food additives, e.g. citric acid and glutamic acid.

Thus although much attention in catering is devoted to the undesirable aspects of microbial growth it must be remembered that the majority are harmless and some are beneficial.

QUESTIONS

1. Distinguish between fermentation and respiration.
2. Outline the role of yeast in the baking of bread. Briefly describe how modern bread making techniques differ from the traditional bulk fermentation methods.
3. (a) Compare and contrast the brewing of traditional British beer with that of lager.
   (b) What is the typical alcohol content of: (i) pale ale; (ii) dry white wine; (iii) sherry; (iv) whisky. How is the alcohol content of (iii) and (iv) achieved and what effect does this have on shelf-life?
4. In the making of what food might *Streptococcus cremoris* be important? Explain the importance of this organism in its food-production 'role'.

11

FOOD SPOILAGE AND FOOD PRESERVATION

11.1 INTRODUCTION

Food spoilage can be defined as having occurred when a food is no longer safe or desirable to eat. This simple definition is a useful working guide in catering but it must be realised that when food is considered desirable or attractive can be subjective, depending upon the person doing the judging. Similarly, in some cases food safe for one person to eat can be unsafe for another.

Food laden with food-poisoning organisms is likely to be unsafe, no matter who eats it but in other cases the concept of safety is not so clear cut. A diabetic who eats a restaurant meal could be ill as a result of taking in too much sugar – another customer eating the same meal would suffer no ill effects. Similarly some people are allergic to certain types of food or components of foods and develop unpleasant symptoms if they consume them. Other examples could be given but the caterer should realise that all foods are not universally safe for all people.

The term 'organoleptically acceptable' refers to the total sensations involved in eating or drinking. The total sensations involved are a combination of sight, smell, taste, touch and hearing. It must be realised that what is pleasing or acceptable to one customer may not necessarily suit another. In Scandinavian countries, sour herring is regarded as a delicacy yet people have been known to be ill just by seeing and smelling it! Yoghurt is liked by many people yet intensely disliked by others who regard it as spoiled milk. Pheasant is deliberately left to hang to develop a 'high' flavour before it is considered to be at its best for cooking. Most people consider mouldy bread as undesirable yet moulds are deliberately added to cheeses to allow them to develop flavour (see Sect. 10.5.1) and become highly prized. Thus 'when food is spoilt' is a value judgement which may vary depending on an individual's personal opinion, or more generally within communities.

However, with possible exceptions, there is a broad agreement in the United Kingdom as to when food is spoilt or not. This consensus is important, as a caterer serving spoilt food risks customer complaints, loss of trade and income, bad publicity as well as legal problems. The Food Act 1984 states that it is an offence to sell food which is unfit or not of a nature, substance or quality demanded by the purchaser. Food that has deteriorated due to chemical, microbiological or other spoilage may be investigated by the Environmental Health Officer (see Sect. 15.1) and it is his duty to form a judgement on its condition. If a magistrate agrees with the Environmental Health Officer, the food can be destroyed. Thus it is an offence to sell, or be in possession of, for the purposes of sale, unfit food.

11.2   FOOD SPOILAGE IN MODERN SOCIETY

Food spoilage is more significant today than at any other time in the past. The World Health Organisation estimates that world-wide 25 per cent of food (up to 50 per cent in some tropical countries) is spoilt before consumption. Spoilage occurs in the interval between food being harvested or slaughtered, and being consumed. Anything that lengthens this delay period increases the opportunity for food to deteriorate in quality and possibly become unsafe or undesirable to eat. While food travelling from distant parts of the world can be regarded as an inevitable delay before consumption, e.g. butter and lamb from New Zealand, fruit from Australia, other aspects of modern society, e.g. storage of European Economic Community food surpluses for years, are more controversial.

Causes of food spoilage can be grouped into three separate but related groups:

   (a) Physical spoilage.
   (b) Chemical spoilage.
   (c) Microbiological spoilage.

11.3   PHYSICAL SPOILAGE

11.3.1   PHYSICAL DAMAGE AND FOOD SPOILAGE

All potential foods have on their surface some form of protective barrier or layer, and damage to this layer can both in itself cause food spoilage, or increase the chances of chemical or microbiological spoilage. A wise caterer checks carefully the quality of tomatoes, peaches, eggs, etc., on delivery to his establishment to identify damage or breakage. Similarly, cans of food should be examined for rusting or denting.

Such physical damage can occur in harvesting, processing or distribution and illustrates the importance of good packaging and careful handling. Another contributer to physical damage is the presence of pests, e.g. rodents, cockroaches, etc. Pests can spoil foods by breaking their outer protective layers, e.g. a rat gnawing at food or more simply by coming into contact with it. Apart from spoilage in its own right, physical spoilage increases the opportunity for chemical and microbiological damage (see Fig. 11.1).

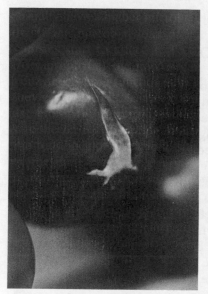 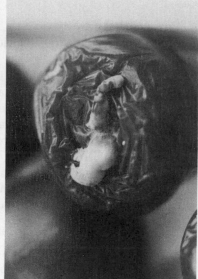

FIG. 11.1 Physical damage promotes food spoilage allowing micro-organisms entry past the protective outer coating as seen on these tomatoes

11.3.2 WATER CONTENT

Water is the predominant component in most foods and if not stored in conditions of correct relative humidity (RH) then there will be a tendency for foods either to gain or to lose water to the atmosphere. Gaining of water from the atmosphere can result in various forms of spoilage. Biscuits or dried foods can become soggy, or worse in cases where the level of surface water increases to a point where mould growth is initiated. Fresh foods with a high moisture content can lose moisture to the atmosphere, becoming shrivelled or dried in appearance with possible surface caking or hardening. Prevention of this type of physical spoilage requires care in storing and packaging. Apart from checking stock on arrival and removing any spoilt products, a good caterer should operate a system of stock control ('first in first out') as well as making sure that food is stored in clean, well ventilated conditions (see Sect. 14.3.2).

11.4 CHEMICAL SPOILAGE

This can be considered under four headings:
  (a) Chemical contamination.
  (b) Enzymic spoilage.
  (c) Rancidity.
  (d) Non-enzymic browning.

11.4.1 CHEMICAL CONTAMINATION

This can occur as a result of poor storage or cleaning practices. The storage of open food (see Sect. 15.2.3) near disinfectants, solvents or cleaning materials, will result in them picking up unpleasant odours and smells (see also Sect. 11.4.3). Utensils or equipment not properly rinsed may pass on traces of detergent to other foods and may cause toxicity problems. Chemical contamination can occur accidentally, e.g. insecticides and herbicides, and this can be potentially harmful (see Sect. 12.4.2).

11.4.2 ENZYMIC SPOILAGE

Many foods, e.g. meat, fruit, vegetables, etc., are made up of intact cells which, like all cells, contain enzymes. After slaughter or harvesting, the cell enzymes continue to function and in many cases bring about desirable changes. e.g. conditioning of meat during hanging, ripening of fruit. If stored for too long, then enzymic activity can become undesirable and result in spoilage. Autolytic (literally, self-breakdown) enzymes destroy the desirability of foods as well as increasing the opportunity for other types of spoilage. As the cellular nature of the food disintegrates water and other nutrients are released on to the surface and the risk of microbial spoilage occurs. Bananas are green with little flavour when picked but as they ripen they turn yellow with more taste, if left for too long they overripen and become black and mushy.

Enzymic spoilage can be slowed down by reducing the temperature, and in some cases by altering the gaseous environment (ratio of oxygen to carbon dioxide). However, the reactions do not cease at low temperatures and therefore vegetables, if stored frozen for a long period of time, need to be blanched. It is not feasible to blanch meat and this is the main reason why vegetables have a longer deep freeze life than most meat or fish products.

Enzymes are also responsible for some browning reactions, e.g. in cut potatoes and apples, as well as the loss of nutrients, such as ascorbic acid (vitamic C). Vitamin C is destroyed on storage by the enzyme ascorbic acid oxidase (see Sect. 5.3.10).

An enzyme in fruits and vegetables, e.g. apples and potatoes, called polyphenol oxidase can oxidise phenolic substances, such as the amino acid tyrosine (see Fig. 2.2), to produce polymerised brown pigments. This type of reaction is very important in the browning of fruits and vegetables, especially after cell damage has taken place, e.g. by mechanical damage to potatoes during harvesting and storage and at the cut surface of an apple or banana. In undamaged cells the phenolic substances and enzymes are kept separate and so there is no browning. After damage the enzyme and substrate are brought together and so browning takes place.

Enzymic browning in fruits and vegetables during preparation can be reduced by several methods.

1. Heat treatment of the product to denature the enzymes, e.g. in the manufacture of fruit juices and purées, and the blanching of fruits and vegetables prior to freezing. Heat treatment can alter flavour and so may be unsuitable for fresh fruit products.

2. Sulphur dioxide gas or sodium metabisulphite solutions inhibit the enzyme action and can be used for the preparation of pre-peeled potatoes for catering purposes. At high concentrations, sulphite treatment can alter the taste of foods, but it is effective at inhibiting enzymic browning at much lower concentrations. Sulphites do breakdown vitamin B_1 (thiamin – see Sect. 5.3.2) but cereal products rather than fresh fruit and vegetables are the major providers of thiamin. Sulphur dioxide may bring about adverse reactions in some consumers.

3. Excluding oxygen from cut surfaces, e.g. by immersing potatoes in water, can reduce browning but also reduces the water-soluble vitamin content (see Sect. 5.4). Antioxidants, such as ascorbic acid (vitamin C), can be used to treat products. The ascorbic acid is preferentially oxidised and so browning is avoided. It has the advantage of being undetectable by taste at effective concentrations and has a nutritional value in its own right.

4. Alteration of pH, e.g. by the use of citric and ascorbic acids, decreases the rate of browning. Polyphenol oxidase has its

optimum pH in the region of 6–7, and below pH 3 there is virtually no activity. Lemon juice contains both citric and ascorbic acids as well as a refreshing flavour and can be used for the treatment of cut fruits, e.g. in the preparation of fresh fruit salad.

Enzymic browning is actively encouraged in the fermentation of tea and cocoa by keeping the dried, rolled leaves or beans at 25 °C.

11.4.3 RANCIDITY

This refers specifically to the spoilage of oils and fats and products containing them. There are three main types of rancidity: absorption, hydrolytic and oxidative (see Sect. 3.4.2).

1. *Absorption rancidity* occurs when fats or oils are stored next to strongly smelling chemicals or foods. For this reason lipid products should be stored in sealed containers away from cleaning chemicals or strongly smelling foods such as mackerel or onions.
2. *Hydrolytic rancidity* is caused by the breakdown of triacylglycerols (triglycerides – found in fats and oils) into glycerol and free fatty acids. Frcc fatty acids with a chain length of less than fourteen carbon atoms give food an unpleasant rancid flavour. This type of rancidity can be found in cream, nuts and some biscuits.
3. *Oxidative rancidity* is the most common type of rancidity and occurs due to the oxidation of double bonds present in unsaturated fatty acids (see Sect. 3.2.2) found in triacylglycerols. Characteristically, lipids exposed to air react only slowly initially but once rancidity has started thc rate increases quite rapidly. This results in the formation of aldehydes and ketones which not only give the fat a rancid, tallowy flavour but may also make it harmful. For this reason antioxidants are often added to susceptible food items such as margarine and crisps. To prevent oxidation, lipids are best stored in non-metal containers in cool dark conditions.

11.4.4 NON-ENZYMIC BROWNING – THE MAILLARD REACTION

This reaction (see Sect. 1.4.1) takes place between reducing sugars and amino groups (in proteins and amino acids) and can be desirable in baking, toasting and malting. Unwanted Maillard reactions can spoil or discolour dry foods, e.g. dehydrated milk, fruit, fruit juices and vegetables.

11.5 MICROBIAL SPOILAGE

Microbial spoilage is the most significant single cause of food spoilage. The organisms responsible are bacteria, moulds and yeasts. Growth of these organisms in or on food (see Table 11.1) can result in visible growth, surface slime, off colours, decomposition, as well as possible production of toxins or poisons.

11.5.1 CAUSES OF MICROBIAL SPOILAGE

The number and types of microorganisms in or on food is known as the 'microbial load'. Raw foods usually have a higher microbial load than processed or cooked foods. If the microbial load of a food becomes excessive the microorganisms start to affect it. To obtain nutrients (spoilage organisms are saprophytic) the microorganisms produce a range of extracellular enzymes whose function is to break down the food into a form that they can utilise, i.e. carbohydrates to sugars, proteins to amino acids, etc. At this stage food quality deteriorates and spoilage starts to become detectable. Sources of microorganisms contaminating the food include the air, soil, water, equipment, work surfaces, personnel and even other ingredients, e.g. spices. The microbial load can become excessive as a result of poor hygiene standards, i.e. too many contaminating microorganisms in the food environment. Alternatively, failure to store foods correctly so that a small number of contaminant organisms grow and multiply has the same effect, i.e. the number of microorganisms becomes excessive.

11.5.2 MICROORGANISMS AND THE FOODS THEY SPOIL (see Table 11.1)

Bacteria

Bacteria are, as a rule, the fussiest of the spoilage organisms and their growth may often be prevented by low pH, a_w, etc. (see Ch. 9). However, bacteria are the fastest growing of the microorganisms and if their growth is supported they will usually spoil foods rapidly, this occurs with meat, fish, poultry, milk and many vegetables.

Moulds

Moulds tend to be the least fastidious but the slowest growing of the microorganisms. Moulds often spoil foods which are unsuitable for the growth of bacteria, those foods which have a low pH or drier foods. Because they are aerobic, mould growth occurs on the surface of foods such as bread, fruits and some vegetables.

Yeasts

Yeasts are not as demanding as bacteria and as many like quite high levels of sugar, they can spoil high-sugar products such as jams or syrups as well as other foods, e.g. alcoholic beverages and fruit juices.

11.5.3 FOODS AND THEIR EASE OF SPOILAGE

Not all foods are as susceptible to microbial food spoilage. Commodities such as milk, meat, etc., spoil quickly and are termed 'perishable' whereas those that do not, sugar, flour, etc., are termed 'non-perishable'. In between are foods such as root vegetables and some fruits that are 'semi-perishable', and which if stored correctly will keep for a number of months. Properties of a food influencing its ease of spoilage include:

(a) pH. Neutral foods are usually more likely to spoil easily, acid foods less easily.
(b) a_w. Foods with a low a_w (either as a result of dehydration or the addition of sugar or salt) spoil less readily.
(c) Nutrient content. Foods with a wide range of nutrients tend to spoil more easily.
(d) Temperature. Foods kept at lower temperatures usually spoil less rapidly.

These properties of the food relate to how suitable a growth environment they provide for any contaminant microorganisms and manipulation or alteration of these properties can enhance food preservation.

11.6   PRINCIPLES OF FOOD PRESERVATION

11.6.1 AIMS

The aim of food preservation is to extend the safe storage life (period of consumer acceptability). Prevention of microbial spoilage is based on three broad principles.

11.6.2 MINIMISING CONTAMINATION OF FOOD (ASEPSIS)

For microorganisms to spoil food they must contaminate the food. A food manufacturer who wishes to produce a food with a long shelf-life should keep the microbial load to a low level and handle food as aseptically (literally, without infection) as possible.

Hygiene

Good hygiene standards minimise the number of microorganisms in

TABLE 11.1 Examples of microorganisms and the foods they spoil

Type of food spoilage	Name of microorganism	Type of organism	Typical food involved	Effect on the food
Fermentation	*Streptococcus cremoris*	Bacterium	Raw milk	Carbohydrate in food attacked, results in souring due to lactic acid production
	Lactobacillus sp.	Bacterium	Sausages	Off flavour due to chemical called diacetyl
	Pediococcus	Bacterium	Beer	'Flat souring' of canned foods; lactic acid produced
	Bacillus sp.	Bacterium	Canned foods	
	Saccharomyces sp.	Yeast	Jams and syrups	Spoilage due to production of alcohol and carbon dioxide
Oxidation	*Acetobacter* sp.	Bacterium	Wines, beers fruit juices	Acetification – production of acetic acid
	Lactobacillus sp.	Bacterium	Cured meats	Greening of cured meats
	Candida sp.	Yeast	Wines and beers	'Film yeasts' grow on surface of alcholic products
Ropiness	*Bacillus* sp.	Bacterium	Bread	Organism causing spoilage produces a capsule (sticky outer layer) causes the formation of sticky strands
	Leuconostoc sp.	Bacterium	Sugar products	
	Lactobacillus sp.	Bacterium	Beer	
	Alcaligenes sp.	Bacterium	Milk	
Putrefaction	*Clostridium* sp.	Bacterium	Poorly canned foods	Anaerobic breakdown causes breakdown of proteins and production of foul odours
Mouldiness/ whiskers	*Penicillium* sp.	Mould	Bread, fruits some vegetables	Food covered in fungal growth – mycelium; may become discoloured due to the the production of spores (see below)
	Aspergillus sp.	Mould		
	Rhizopus sp.	Mould		

Type of spoilage	Organism	Type	Food	Description
Colour changes	Serratia marcescens	Bacterium	Bread	Bloody bread – reddish spots on the bread
	Pseudomonas	Bacterium	Meat, fish, eggs	Variety of pigments produced, e.g. yellow, blue, green
	Aspergillus niger	Mould	Fruit	For example, black mould on oranges
	Neurospora sp.	Mould	Bread	Pink
	Penicillium sp.	Mould	Bread	Initially white, then becoming grey-green
Rot*	Rhizopus sp.	Mould	Carrots	Black rot of fruit and vegetables
	Aspergillus sp.	Mould	Fruit and vegetables	Soft rot
	Penicillium sp.	Mould	Citrus fruits	Soft rot of carrots, black leg of potatoes
	Erwinia sp.	Bacterium	Vegetables	Especially of chilled meats
	Pseudomonas sp.	Bacterium	Meat	Ring rot of potatoes
	Corynebacterium sp.	Bacterium	Potato	
Sliminess	Pseudomonas sp.	Bacterium	Meat	Growth of microorganisms in moist conditions; may involve the production of extracellular slime
	Alcaligenes sp.	Bacterium	Poultry	
	Lactobacillus sp.	Bacterium	Frankfurter sausages	

* Rot is a general word used to describe spoilage especially if there is some breakdown of cell structure and the food becomes soft and mushy.

the food environment. Apart from proper cleaning, etc. (see Ch. 8), the simple act of removing rotten fruit and vegetables from bags or sacks, or the disposal of mouldy bread can help to reduce the number of spoilage organisms in the vicinity of food.

Food packaging

Food packaging preserves and protects the packaged food by helping to prevent contaminant microorganisms in the environment from reaching it. The overriding criterion in the selection of a suitable packaging material for a particular product is to ensure that it is kept in a sound condition for its anticipated shelf-life. However, in a modern sophisticated society it is naïve to imagine that these are the only functions of packaging and increasingly two more functions are becoming important – convenience (especially in portion control) and selling and marketing considerations. Attractive and suitable food packaging enables caterers to optimise their use of food, minimise waste, as well as increasing its visual and sales appeal. It is not surprising therefore to learn that the food industry is the largest user of packaging at the consumer level.

A correctly selected food packaging material reduces microbial and insect attack as well as maintaining the sensory and nutritive properties of the food, e.g. by exclusion of oxygen, control of moisture loss or gain, exclusion of dust and dirt.

There are many ways of classifying packaging materials, e.g. into rigid or flexible packaging, by material – plastic, wood, metal or glass, etc. Primary food packaging comes into contact with the food whereas secondary food packaging does not (e.g. shipping crates, outer cardboard cartons, etc.) Thus, for reasons which are self-evident, greater care has to be taken in the choice of primary packaging materials. There is no single perfect packaging material and different types have advantages and disadvantages (see Table 11.2).

In deciding which packaging material to use various factors need to be considered – the product itself, method of transport, properties of the packaging material as well as marketing considerations (see Table 11.3).

Minimising contamination has in itself only a short-term effect in preventing spoilage and the shelf-life of the product will depend upon any additional measures taken at the time of packaging. One relatively recent innovation is the use of controlled atmosphere packaging (CAP). CAP has been used for improving the keeping quality of processed foods such as dried milks, instant mashed potato and dried coffee. Gas flushing with carbon dioxide or nitro-

TABLE 11.2 Advantages and disadvantages of various food packaging materials

1. *Paper and board*, e.g. paper bags, cardboard boxes, Kraft paper
   Varying degrees of stiffness
   Absorbent
   Tear easily
   Low density
   Relatively low cost
   Easy to design and print packaging
   Usually need coating to give a good barrier
   Foods can be reheated in a microwave oven

2. *Metal*, e.g. tinned steel and aluminium
   Rigid
   High density
   May react with food unless coated
   Good tensile strength
   Joints need closing carefully for a good seal
   Foods have to be removed to a second container before reheating in a
     microwave oven

3. *Plastics*, e.g. glass fibre, reinforced polyesters, polyethylene,
     polypropylene, polyvinyl chloride
   Low density
   Can be rigid or flexible
   Transparent or opaque
   Usually low stiffness
   Variable tensile and tear strengths
   Wide range of permeable/impermeable properties

4. *Glass*, e.g. glass jars, glass bottles
   Near perfect barrier (provided there is a good lid seal)
   Rigid
   Brittle
   High density
   Inert to foods
   Transparent

Note: plastics offer the most versatile form of packaging and may in the future supersede other forms, e.g. replacement of tin cans with plastic containers or plastic laminates combined with aluminium foil. Concern has been voiced that chemicals added as plasticisers, to give the packaging material improved properties, may pass into the food and prove to be toxic.

gen is used to replace air in the product and like vacuum packaging limits oxidative rancidity as well as vitamin and colour loss. More recently, CAP has been applied to the packaging of fresh meats, e.g. mince and stewing steak, the extra carbon dioxide in the atmosphere retards bacterial growth extending the shelf life of the meat, if temperature control is also maintained, by up to four days. The typical combination of the gases used for fresh meat products would be 20 % carbon dioxide and 80 % oxygen or 20 % carbon

TABLE 11.3 Factors considered in the choice of packaging

1. *The food itself*
   State (solid or liquid)
   Size
   Shape
   Density
   Ease of chemical spoilage
   Ease of physical spoilage
   Effect of moisture

2. *Distribution hazards*
   Effect of handling
   Effect of dropping
   Effect of stacking
   Method of transport
   Effect of vibration
   Method of handling (hooks, puncturing)

3. *Packaging itself* (properties in relation to product requirements)
   Effect of light
   Effect of oxygen
   Effect of chemicals
   Effect of moisture

4. *Marketing considerations*
   Shape and colour (effect on attractiveness)
   Price
   Consumer (age, income, etc.)
   Convenience in use
   Ease for inspection of faults
   Competition
   Type of outlet (e.g. hotel, supermarket)
   Ease and safety of reclosure (economy considerations)
   Disposal

dioxide, 69 % oxygen and 11 % nitrogen, the oxygen present is required to maintain the myoglobin as oxymyoglobin to give the meat a fresh, red appearance. Similarly, CAP has been used for fish, bakery products and cheeses.

In canning heat processing in a container may give a shelf-life of up to 5 years or more. Storage of packaged food in a freezer may give a shelf-life of 1 year or more.

If such additional measures are not taken then the number of microorganisms on susceptible foods will increase as a result of growth.

11.6.3 KILLING OR REMOVING MICROORGANISMS

Removal
Physical removal of microorganisms has a limited application in

food preservation. Wines and beers can be filtered to remove microorganisms, while water supplies are filtered through sand beds before chlorination. Washing of food products reduces the number of microorganisms present. After washing it is important to dry the surface properly or there can be an increased risk of microbial growth. Meat and other foods can be trimmed to remove excessively contaminated portions, this process is often carried out as part of normal catering practice. However, all these procedures only have a minimal effect on the overall shelf-life of the product.

Destruction/killing of microorganisms
At present this is most successfully achieved by the use of heat but it seems likely that the United Kingdom will follow the trend started in other countries and in the near future there will be an increased use of ionising radiation (either γ-rays or beams of electrons) for food preservation (see Table 11.4). If the trouble is taken to remove the microorganisms from a product then it is usual to package the food to prevent recontamination. Depending on the degree of heat or radiation used, the shelf-life can be extended for either a short or a long term (see Table 11.4).

Pasteurisation is only a mild heat treatment (using temperatures between 60 °C and 80 °C) given to some foods either to extend their shelf-life, e.g. beers, or to make the foods safe. Milk is normally pasteurised at 71.7 °C for 15 seconds. This is known as high temperature short time pasteurisation (H.T.S.T.) and is followed by rapid cooling to less than 10 °C. The older low temperature long time method (L.T.S.T. or 'holder') method of 62.8 °C for 30 minutes is now little used. The relatively mild heat treatment used destroys the heat-sensitive organisms but most thermoduric and heat-resistant organisms (see Ch. 9) survive quite easily. The times and temperatures used were originally devised to destroy the tuberculosis organism which occurred in raw milk.

In cooking, temperatures of between 70 and 100 °C are reached. The internal temperature achieved during roasting varies from about 60 °C, when a rare finish is desired, up to about 80 °C in well-done meat. Baking requires temperatures of about 100 °C, the internal temperature of a loaf of bread is approximately 97 °C, while stewing temperatures are considerably less. Frying needs higher temperatures, slightly above 100 °C, and this is associated with shorter cooking times and leads to greater weight loss in the cooked food. Cooking, however, in its own right is not really employed as a food preservative measure unless combined with a low storage temperature as well, e.g. cook freeze and cook chill (see Sect. 13.5).

TABLE 11.4 Destruction of microorganisms and its use in food preservation

Method of destruction	Degree of severity	Name of process	Shelf-life of food
Heat	Mild, 60–80 °C	Pasteurisation	Usually short-term for perishable food items; may be longer for other food and drinks; only heat-sensitive organisms destroyed
	Medium, 70–100 °C	Cooking/baking	Used to make food safe and to make it more appetising, used in combination with low temperatures for food preservation.
	Severe, 100–120 °C	Canning	Long-term, up to 5 years or more
	Severe, 130–150 °C	UHT	Employ high temperatures for short periods of time; long-term storage with minimal changes in food quality
Ionising radiation	Mild	Radurization (0.1–1 mrad, 1–10 kGy)	Short-term, equivalent to pasteurisation extends shelf-life of product
		Radicidation (1 mrad, 10 kGy)	Uses sufficient radiation to destroy non-sporing pathogens
	Severe	Radappertisation (3–5 mrad, 30–50 kGy)	Long-term, equivalent to canning but food quality may deteriorate
Ultra-violet radiation			Treatment of water, surface of bread, cakes, bacon

The cooking part of these processes should be sufficient to destroy the vegetative (i.e. non-sporing) stages of any food-poisoning bacteria. During regeneration of cook-chilled foods a temperature of at least 70 °C at the centre of the food is necessary.

Canning involves more severe heat treatments. Food in sealed metal containers is subject (depending on pH, size, type of food, etc.) to varying degrees of heat. Canned food is commercially sterile, i.e. safe with no vegetative organisms surviving, although small numbers of bacterial spores may be present. These should be incapable of germination (usually spores of thermophilic organisms) and thus should not spoil the can contents. Tinned tomatoes, which have a very low pH, receive relatively little heat treatment, about 100 °C for several minutes, while neutral foods may be heated to 115–120 °C for much longer. The heating process is usually carried out in a retort or steriliser, the domestic equivalent being the pressure cooker.

Ultra heat treatments (UHT) are a type of processing which can be used for liquid foods, e.g. milk. The process involves heating the product in a heat exchanger to a high temperature for a short period of time (high temperature short time, HTST) then aseptically adding the product to a previously sterilised container. UHT milk is heated to a minimum of 132.2 °C for 1 sec, and is capable of being stored at room temperature for 6 months without deterioration. UHT or long-life milk coupled with tea-making machines are responsible for the near elimination of the early morning tea maid service in hotels.

11.6.4 PREVENTION OF MICROBIAL GROWTH

In order, to spoil foods, microorganisms need the correct conditions for growth (see Ch. 9). By altering the conditions so that micro-organisms cannot grow food preservation is achieved (see Table 11.5).

Temperature reduction
The degree of temperature reduction controls the shelf-life of the product. In cellar storage usually no artificial means of reducing the temperature are employed. It is important in the United Kingdom for semi-perishable items, such as fruit, vegetables, beer, etc., but it is even more necessary in those parts of the world where refrigeration and electricity, are not readily available.

Refrigerators operate at temperatures between 1 and 4 °C and are useful in the short-term storage of perishable food items. The

TABLE 11.5 Prevention of microbial growth and its use in food preservation

Method of preventing growth	Degree of severity	Name of process	Shelf-life of food
Reduction in temperature	Very slight, 12–16 °C	Cellar storage	Used mainly for improving shelf-life of semi-perishable items only; no artificial means of reducing the temperature
	Moderate, 1–4 °C	Refrigeration	Used for short-term storage of perishable items
	Considerable, −6 °C, −12 °C, or −18 °C	Freezing	Long-term; for three-star freezer vegetables up to 1 year, meats up to 8 months (except pork up to 3 months)
Reduction in a_w	Moderate	Salting, addition of sugar	Shelf-life depends upon amount added
	Severe	Dehydration	Long-term if a_w goes below 0.6
Presence of chemicals with antimicrobial effect		Addition of preservatives	For example, propionates in bread
		Development of acidity	For example, yoghurt
		Addition of acids – pickling	For example, pickled eggs
Control of food atmosphere		Addition of CO_2 or N_2, reduction of O_2	Used in combination with other preservative measures, e.g. for fruit,
		Vacuum packaging	For example, bacon, cheese

growth of psychrophilic food-spoilage organisms is not prevented and perishable food items, e.g. raw meat, will visibly deteriorate in quality after about 48 hr (as the number of microorganisms increases.). What is important, is that most food-poisoning bacteria will not grow and thus foods will be safe to eat. 'Chilling', a widely used term in the food industry, is less precise and the temperature of storage of chilled items varies with the commodity and the person describing it. Chilled meat is at -1 °C, most other foods between 0–10 °C, cook chill 0–3 °C.

Freezing requires lower temperatures and the exact level determines the star rating of the freezer. One-star freezers operate at -6 °C, two-star freezers at -12 °C, and three-star freezers at -18 °C. Storage in a three-star freezer is long term, even psychrophilic spoilage organisms cannot grow, although some enzymic activity may continue (see Sect. 11.4.2). The best frozen food looks, tastes and is nutritionally better. Food should reach -18 °C within 1 hr. This is achieved commercially by blast freezing where very cold air (approximately -20 °C) is blown over or up through the product, or alternatively by the use of very low temperature, -33 °C in a multiple plate freezer (for beef-burgers, fish fingers, etc.). Cryogenic freezing utilises liquid nitrogen (boiling point -196 °C) and enables food to freeze very rapidly, sometimes within 30 sec. True rapid freezing is not possible with domestic equipment. Many bacteria and other microorganisms in or on food can survive freezing and when the food is defrosted the bacteria are capable of growth again. Russian scientists claim to have defrosted and cultivated frozen bacteria originally 12 000 years old! As some bacteria remain viable in frozen foods, **items once frozen and allowed to thaw must not be refrozen.** If this practice were allowed, the refrozen foods could contain millions of bacteria which on further thawing could give rise to food spoilage or food poisoning. Combining freezing with cooking in the cook freeze system enables whole meals to be centrally prepared, cooked, frozen and then stored for long periods. A recent development also likely to have a major impact is the 'freeze flo' process which allows the freezing of some foods without the development of solid ice crystals. The advantages to the caterer, particularly in confectionery items, is that portions of frozen gateaux, etc., can be cut from the products without the need to raise the temperature, i.e. to defrost. The basis of the process is the chemical binding of the liquid water to proteins and sugars in the food so that it never turns to solid ice. Thus, 'freeze flo' foods are at -18 °C but are not frozen hard and solid.

Dehydration
Microorganisms can survive but are unable grow without free liquid water. The latter can be reduced by the addition of sugar or salt which makes it unavailable for microbial growth (lowers the a_w) and creates an osmotic effect. Alternatively, the total moisture content can be reduced by dehydration. This can be achieved by a variety of means, e.g. spray drying of milk and mashed potatoes, and more recently by accelerated freeze drying (AFD) e.g. meat, vegetable and fruit products. In accelerated freeze drying the product is first frozen and then heated gently in a vacuum. The ice crystals sublime and are converted directly into water vapour. AFD is a more expensive method of dehydration than spray drying giving a superior product.

Chemical preservation
A number of chemical substances can be found in foods which slow down or halt microbial growth (see Sect. 7.7). Many of these are used in combination with other food-preservation techniques. Sulphur dioxide, in addition to inhibiting microbial growth, maintains the colour of processed vegetables and British sausages. It can be added to a wide variety of foods, e.g. dehydrated vegetables, dried fruits, fruit juices and wines (see Sect. 10.4.2). Sodium and potassium nitrates and nitrites are used as curing salts for bacon, ham and other meats. The nitrite is particularly important due to its inhibitory effect on *Clostridium botulinum*. Organic acids, such as benzoic acid and citric acid in soft drinks and propionic acid in bread, find use as preservatives. The main preservative effect is due to the undissociated acid molecule. Acetic acid has been traditionally used in pickling. An alternative method is to allow the controlled development of acid in the product (see Sect. 10.5.2).

At one time it was thought that antibiotics might find wide use as food preservatives. Problems associated with allergic reactions and the selection or development of resistant strains have halted this application for medically important antibiotics. One antibiotic, nisin, not of medical importance, is permitted in the United Kingdom and can be found in a variety of foods including cheeses and canned peas.

Control of food atmosphere
Microorganisms have different gaseous requirements and control of the food atmosphere can help to delay spoilage (see Sect. 11.6.2). This is particularly true of foods subject primarily to aerobic spoil-

age, these include hard cheeses liable to mould spoilage and fresh meat infected by superficial bacterial slime.

Storage of fruit in an atmosphere containing extra carbon dioxide slows down the rate of ripening and hence deterioration. Carbon dioxide packaging can also be used to control moisture loss without promoting mould growth in baked goods.

QUESTIONS

1. (a) Explain, using named examples, the term 'physical spoilage of food'.
   (b) Define the term 'autolytic enzymes' and explain how they cause deterioration in foods.
   (c) Describe the aim of food preservation and briefly discuss the three broad principles upon which it is based.
2. Explain why the addition of a little lemon juice can help maintain the desirable colour of fruit in a fresh fruit salad.
3. A reaction can occur in foods between reducing sugars and the amino groups of some of the amino acids in proteins.
   (a) What is this reaction known as?
   (b) What colour change is likely to take place?
   (c) State two instances when it is desirable.
   (d) State two instances when it is undesirable.
4. Explain the reasons for the following statements:
   (a) Milk is spoilt initially by bacteria.
   (b) Yeasts can cause spoilage in syrups.
   (c) When oranges spoil it is usually as a result of mould growth.
   (d) The surface of bread is likely to be spoilt by mould growth.
   (e) Raw meat might be spoilt by psychrotrophic organisms.

FOOD-TRANSMITTED AND OTHER DISEASES IMPORTANT IN CATERING

12.1 INTRODUCTION

It has been realised for centuries that the eating of food can sometimes result in illness. Illnesses carried by food are described as 'food-transmitted diseases'. In addition modern day caterers need to be informed of certain other infectious diseases.

12.2 TYPES OF FOOD-TRANSMITTED DISEASE

There are many reasons why consumption of food may result in illness and the causes can be considered in two main categories (see Table 12.1):
(a) Food-borne infections.
(b) Food poisoning.

While food poisoning probably occurs with greater frequency in the United Kingdom and is of more immediate concern to the caterer, food-borne infections are likely to be more serious and within the context of world tourism are important. The main differences between food poisoning and food-borne infections are summarised in Table 12.2.

12.3 TYPES OF FOOD-BORNE INFECTION

A number of parasitic organisms (see Table 12.3) can use food as a means of gaining access to their human host. Such parasites do not increase in numbers in the food and often only require a small infective dose, i.e. a small number consumed, to initiate illness. Some of these diseases may also be transmitted via contaminated water or by gaining direct access to the mouth without food even being involved. For example, direct contamination from animals or indirectly from infected objects such as toilets. Many food-borne infections (and some cases of food poisoning) are examples of

TABLE 12.1 Food-transmitted diseases

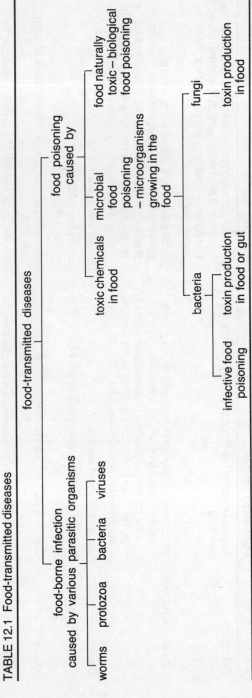

TABLE 12.2 Differences between food borne infection and food poisoning

	Food-borne infection	Food poisoning
Definition	Any illness other than food poisoning transmitted in food	An illness following immediately or shortly after the ingestion of food and having some of the following symptoms – vomiting, diarrhoea, fever, nausea, abdominal pain
Causes/role of food	Various parasitic organisms; these do not grow in the food and it only acts as a vehicle or agent in the transmission of the disease; illness classed as food-borne infection can often be transmitted in other ways not involving food	Can be caused by the food being naturally poisonous, by the presence of toxic chemicals in the food or by microorganisms; microbial food poisoning is the most important in the UK and the microorganisms actually grow in the food
Severity	Likely to be more severe	Usually less severe
Site of illness	Starts in the gut but can spread to other parts of the body	Usually limited to the gut
Incubation period	Can be quite long, up to several weeks	Relatively short usually within 24 hours of eating the food
Note on prevention	Are not prevented by refrigeration as causative organism does *not* have to grow in the food	Microbial food poisoning is usually prevented by refrigeration; low temperatures prevent growth of *most* food-poisoning bacteria

TABLE 12.3 Some examples of food borne infections

Type of organism	Illness	Name of causative organism	Points of interest
Worm	Beef tapeworm	*Taenia saginata*	Can reach up to 7 m in length
	Hydatid disease	*Echinococcus granulosus*	Dog tapeworm
	Trichinosis	*Trichinella spiralis*	Spread by infected pork and rodents; can be difficult to detect in meat
Protozoa	Amoebic dysentery	*Entamoeba histolytica*	Common in tropical countries
	Giardiasis	*Giardia lamblia*	'Traveller's diarrhoea' after return from abroad
	Toxoplasmosis	*Toxoplasma gondii*	Possibly up to one-third of the population has been infected – does not often result in illness
Bacteria	'Enteric fever', i.e. typhoid and paratyphoid	*Salmonella typhi, Salmonella paratyphi*	Tourists to certain countries abroad may need TAB immunisation – against typhoid and paratyphoid A and B
	Bacterial dysentery	*Shigella species,* mainly *Sh. sonnei*	Mainly spread in UK by direct contamination not involving food
	Brucellosis	*Brucella abortus*	Occurs in cattle mainly, but also goats, sheep and pigs
	Cholera	*Vibrio cholerae* or *V. el Tor*	Tourists abroad may need immunisation; recent outbreaks in Tunisia, Portugal, Italy and Spain
Viruses	Epidemic jaundice, 'infectious hepatitis'	Hepatitis A virus	Not the same virus found in drug addicts, etc., that is hepatitis B virus
	Poliomyelitis	Polio virus	Largely eradicated in UK due to immunisation ('sugar lump') and improved hygiene
	Viral gastroenteritis	Various types of enteroviruses including echo, coxsackie viruses	Difficult to assess how commonly food is involved in their spread; more research needed

zoonoses – diseases acquired from animals – having an animal reservoir of infection. Worm (mainly tapeworm and roundworm) infections can be transmitted to Man by a variety of foods including meat and fish. Fortunately, food-transmitted worm infections are relatively rare in the UK and most reported cases have been contracted abroad. Proper inspection of meat in abattoirs plus good standards of hygiene have done much to reduce the incidence of these infections. Proper cooking of food, or freezing at −18 °C, will usually destroy these parasites.

Protozoan infections include amoebic dysentery, which although world-wide in incidence, occur more frequently in tropical and subtropical than temperate climates, the small number of cases reported in the UK having been acquired abroad. Giardiasis is a protozoan infection and is more common in the UK but far less so than in some other European countries. Giardiasis is one of the many causes of traveller's stomach upsets suffered by people spending holidays abroad.

Most of the bacterial food-borne infections are also more common abroad than in the UK with the exception of *Campylobacter* infections (see Sect. 12.6.6). For this reason travellers to certain countries may need to be immunised against food-borne diseases such as typhoid and cholera. The last major outbreak of typhoid in the UK occurred in Aberdeen in 1964 as a result of people eating contaminated canned corned beef imported from Argentina. Europe is relatively free of cholera the exception being certain Mediterranean countries, outbreaks having occurred relatively recently in Portugal, Spain, Tunisia and Italy. Often contaminated water or shellfish have been involved. Brucellosis is a bacterial disease of cattle which is spread to humans via infected raw milk (also by direct contact and is an occupational hazard in veterinary surgeons). Cattle in the UK have been declared brucellosis-free (less than 0.01 per cent infected) although sporadic incidents still occur. Bacterial dysentery is caused by *Shigella* bacteria and is different from amoebic dysentery. Most cases occurring in the UK are contracted by direct contact rather than by consuming contaminated food.

It is difficult to assess how many cases of viral food-borne diseases occur, mainly because viruses are far more difficult to cultivate from food samples than are bacteria. It is thought, however, that viruses are responsible for a number of cases of gastro-enteritis at present recorded as having 'unknown aetiology', i.e. as having an unknown cause. In addition, many cases of viral enteritis are likely to go unreported. Infectious hepatitis is one of the more serious viral diseases transmitted in food. Surveys have shown that many sufferers of this disease consumed shellfish, and caterers may have to revise their methods of cooking to ensure that shellfish are safe to eat. Obviously more research is needed on this subject and some scientists believe that in the future viral food-borne diseases will be considered even more important in catering. Note viruses do not actually grow in food as they are obligate intracellular parasites, i.e. they need intact living cells.

12.4 FOOD POISONING

Food poisoning can occur (see Table 12.1) because:
  (a) Certain foods are naturally toxic.
  (b) They have become contaminated with toxic chemicals.
  (c) They have become contaminated with food poisoning bacteria.
In the UK the vast majority of cases of food poisoning are due to bacteria, i.e. (c) above.

12.4.1 NATURALLY TOXIC FOODS

Parts of certain foods are naturally toxic, such as rhubarb leaves which contain high levels of oxalic acid. People who eat the death cap fungus, mistaking it for mushroom, are likely to die as a result. One health-conscious individual in Birmingham came close to death after accidentally gathering poisonous foxglove leaves instead of comfrey leaves (used to make herbal tea). Table 12.4 illustrates some 'foods' which may be poisonous.

Research has recently shown that consumption, over a period of time, of mildly toxic foods of plant origin may contribute to a number of chronic illnesses including cerebrovascular disease (strokes), allergies and even cancer. Modern processing and refining of foods may contribute to these toxicological problems.

The muscle of dark-meated Scrombroid fish, e.g. mackerel, is high in histidine. Bacteria acting on the muscle produce a histamine-like substance which if consumed causes illness within about 4 h. This emphasises the need for caterers only to serve fresh mackerel. Any fish showing signs of staleness or tasting peppery should not be used.

12.4.2 CHEMICAL FOOD POISONING

Toxic chemicals can find their way into food in a number of different ways (see Table 12.5). Toxic industrial waste can

TABLE 12.4 Some causes of 'natural' or biological food poisoning

Food	Illness
Potatoes	Solanine poisoning caused by accumulation of alkaloid poisons in potato skins; do not use potatoes with green patches for baking
Rhubarb	Leaves contain high levels of oxalic acid
Red kidney beans	Raw beans contain a toxic substance (haemagglutinin) which is destroyed by proper cooking
Poisonous fungi	Picked and eaten in mistake for mushrooms; mainly fungi of the Amanita group
Poisonous weeds	Hemlock, monkshood mistaken for parsley or horseradish
Mackerel	Scrombrotoxic fish poisoning due to the presence of a histamine-like substance in the fish
Ciguatera poisoning	Occurs in West Indies, caused by eating fish containing poisonous plankton; a similar illness – paralytic shellfish poisoning – has occurred in Europe from eating similarly affected shellfish
Other seafood poisoning	From eating toxic parts of various seafoods, e.g. crab, etc.

accidentally contaminate food. Sometimes, food is picked and eaten too soon after being sprayed with pesticides or other chemicals. A recent example of this in the United States of America led to the destruction of over 10 million melons. Whatever the cause, the symptoms of food poisoning, mainly vomiting and nausea, often appear within a short space of time. The time interval between food being eaten and the appearance of symptoms is known as the 'incubation period' and may be as short as a few minutes for chemical food poisoning.

One very large-scale incident involving toxic chemicals contaminating food occurred in the United States in 1973. A poisonous chemical polybrominated biphenyl, PBB for short, was accidently used in livestock feed. The contaminated feed was eaten by a variety of farm animals resulting in the slaughter of 30 000 cattle and 1.5 million sheep. By this time, the chemical had unfortunately been consumed by humans in meat and dairy products and up to 97 per cent of the population of Michigan were believed to have been affected. Reports of various illnesses in farmers started appearing in the late 1970s but the long-term effects on the population may be even more worrying as PBB can be carcinogenic (cancer inducing).

TABLE 12.5 Examples of some causes of chemical food poisoning

Food	Poison
Various acid foods, e.g. fruits stored or cooked in incorrect metal containers	Zinc poisoning after storage in galvanised iron containers Antimony poisoning from chipped enamel containers Copper poisoning from copper-lined vessels
Fruit and vegetables, e.g. apples	Insecticides, fungicides need time to decompose and become harmless after spraying; if food is picked and eaten too soon after spraying illness can result
Fish and vegetables	Contamination by toxic industrial waste, e.g. containing lead, mercury and cadmium salts
Various foods	Accidental contamination with cleaning materials, germicides
Various foods	Accidental contamination with toxic chemicals mistaken for food ingredients, e.g. pesticide, sodium fluoride, added instead of baking powder

Also of concern are instances where toxic chemicals are added to food on purpose. Two recent examples of this have occurred in Europe. In Spain, sale of deliberately contaminated olive oil led to over 200 deaths and more than 20 000 people became ill. In 1985 bottles of German and Austrian wine were found to be intentionally contaminated with diethylene glycol (used in antifreeze) to make it sweeter. Excessive consumption of this chemical could lead to kidney damage or even death.

12.5 MICROBIAL FOOD POISONING

Microbial food poisoning can be caused by the growth of bacteria or moulds in or on food. Bacterial food poisoning is the most important type of food poisoning and the most significant food-transmitted disease in the United Kingdom.

There are two major categories of bacterial food poisoning and both are characterised by illness following the consumption of contaminated or 'unsafe' food. Such food is unsafe either due to the accumulation of a large number of certain types of living bacteria or of bacterial toxins (poisons).

12.5.1 INFECTIVE BACTERIAL FOOD POISONING

In infective bacterial food poisoning, food becomes contaminated with certain bacteria. These then grow in the food (due to improper storage) and when consumed they continue to grow in the gut of the person eating the food. Their growth and death in the human gut leads to the unpleasant symptoms associated with food poisoning. An example of infective food poisoning is that caused by the bacterium *Salmonella*. A person eating food infected with large numbers of Salmonella – in excess of 100 000 – is likely to get food poisoning. A figure of 100 000 may seem large but remember bacteria grow and multiply very rapidly (often doubling in number in less than 20 min). Food causing food poisoning may have in excess of 100 million bacteria per gram and a typical portion of chicken or meat off the bone will weigh about 110 g!

12.5.2 TOXIN-TYPE BACTERIAL FOOD POISONING

This occurs when certain types of bacteria grow in the food producing chemical poisons or toxins which are separate and distinct from the bacterium itself. If food containing these toxins is eaten then food poisoning will result. Note it is not necessary for living bacteria to be consumed, just the toxins or poisons they have produced. An example of toxin-type food poisoning is that caused by certain strains of *Staphylococcus aureus*. Normally at least 1 million of these Staphylococci are required to be growing in the food to produce sufficient toxin, approximately 1 μM toxin, to cause illness. Such a toxin is called an 'exotoxin' because it is separate from the cell producing it (literally outside toxin) and an 'enterotoxin' because it causes enteritis, i.e. inflammation of the lining of the alimentary canal.

The difference between a food-borne infection and the two types of food poisoning is illustrated in Fig. 12.1. In this diagram three imaginary bottles of raw milk are contaminated by three different bacteria. Depending on the type of bacterium, a food-borne infection, infective food poisoning or toxin food poisoning would result if the milk were to be consumed. These examples also illustrate why raw milk or cream should not be served to customers in catering establishments.

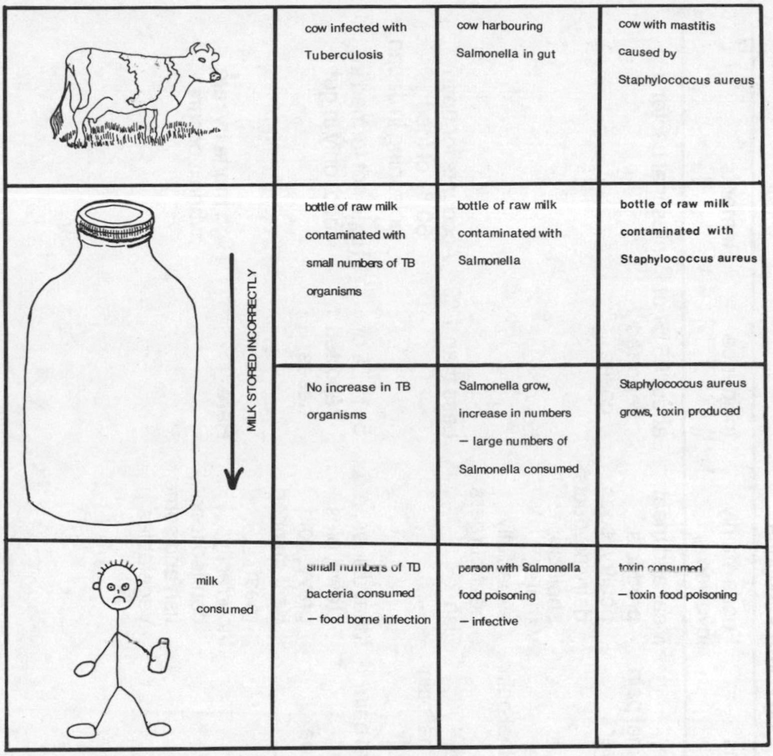

FIG. 12.1 Comparison of food-borne infections and bacterial food poisoning

12.6   BACTERIA CAUSING FOOD POISONING AND FOOD-BORNE INFECTIONS

A range of bacteria (see Table 12.6) have been found to cause food poisoning and food-borne infections but in the United Kingdom the vast majority of all incidents are usually caused by a small range of bacteria (see Table 12.7). Note, in other countries patterns of food poisoning differ considerably because eating habits can be quite dissimilar and food-poisoning bacteria are often associated with specific foods.

12.6.1 SALMONELLA FOOD POISONING

Incidence
Salmonella food poisoning is the most commonly reported type of food poisoning in the UK and is normally responsible for approxi-

TABLE 12.6 Summary of bacteria causing food poisoning and food borne infections

Type	Bacterium	Incubation period and duration	Symptoms	Foods mainly involved	Incidence	Remarks
Infective food poisoning	Salmonella species, e.g. S. typhimurium	10–72 hr, normally 12–24 hr, duration 1–7 days	Diarrhoea, abdominal pain and fever	Meat and meat products, poultry, eggs, dairy products, shellfish	about 85 % of reported cases	Intestinal bacteria
	E. coli	12–72 hr, duration 1–7 days	Diarrhoea, abdominal pain	Various, especially beef burgers	Low	
	Vibrio parahaemolyticus	2–48 hr, duration 2–5 days	Diarrhoea, abdominal pain and fever	Fish	Less than 1 %	Accounts for up to 60 % of food poisoning in Japan
Toxin food poisoning	Clostridium perfringens	8–22 hr duration 1–2 days	Abdominal pain, nausea, diarrhoea	Meat dishes, e.g. stews, pies, gravy, cold beef, minced meat	5–11 % of reported cases	Toxin not formed in food, only in gut
	Clostridium botulinum			Incorrectly canned foods, fish and some vegetables	Rare	High mortality rate when it occurs

Staphylococcus aureus	From 30 min to 6 hr; normally 2–3 hr; duration 6–24 hr	Vomiting, nausea, sometimes collapse and dehydration	Cold cooked meats, also cream/custard items	Approx. 2 %	Many cases likely to be unreported
Bacillus cereus	1–6 hr, duration up to 24 hr	Vomiting, nausea, diarrhoea	Rice	Approx. 1 %	Can cause another type of food poisoning found in USA and other countries
Campylobacter	Incubation period 1–10 days, normally 3–4 days, duration 5–7 days	Diarrhoea, malaise, abdominal pain, fever	Raw or improperly pasteurised milk; frozen poultry	Approx. 35 000 cases per year	Intestinal bacterium but limited survival ability
Yersinia enterocolitica	Incubation period 1–3 days, duration approx. 3–5 days	Abdominal pain, diarrhoea and fever	Various including raw milk	Low	Can grow on food even if refrigerated
Listeria monocytogenes	Incubation period 3 days–2 months	Flue type illness, meningitis	Undercooked poultry and soft cheeses (unpasteurised)	Approx 150–300 cases per year	Minority of people at risk (old, young or pregnant). When cases occur 30% mortality. Can cause miscarriage in pregnant women. Psychrotrophic.

Food-borne infections

mately 85 per cent of all *reported* cases (see Table 12.7). Note that these figures do not represent *all* cases of food poisoning in the UK since the majority of food-poisoning cases go unreported (see Sect. 12.7).

Salmonella bacteria

Salmonellae are short rod-shaped bacteria and there are approximately 2000 different sub-types. *Salmonella* was first isolated by an American microbiologist named Dr Salmon, and Salmonellae sub-types are often named after the place where they were first isolated, the place where they first caused food poisoning, or the person who first isolated them. For many years *Salmonella typhimurium* was the most commonly occurring food poisoning type but in recent years this has been overtaken by *Salmonella enteriditis phage type 4*. *Salmonella* are mesophilic bacteria and although they are relatively easily destroyed by heat can survive freezing and drying for considerable periods.

Distribution, origins and sources

Salmonella bacteria are widely distributed in nature but are primarily associated with the gut of animals. These include farm animals such as cattle, poultry and pigs. Thus food products derived from these animals may be affected, e.g. meat, milk, eggs, etc. In one recent survey a consumer association found 79 per cent of frozen poultry contaminated with *Salmonella*. Farm animals fed contaminated food and kept in crowded conditions are most likely to be infected. At the time of slaughter it is difficult to prevent *Salmonella* from the gut of a dead contaminated animal being transferred to the carcass. Infected food products, inadequately cooked are probably the most important cause of Salmonella food poisoning. Domestic pets, e.g. cats and dogs, and pests, e.g. rats and cockroaches, as well as birds, may also harbour *Salmonella*. Certain humans may carry *Salmonella* in their intestines, and therefore must not handle food – this is a legal requirement! (see Ch. 15). People who may carry, *Salmonella* include victims of *Salmonella* food poisoning, hence an individual who has an unexplained stomach upset should not handle food (another legal requirement). Persons, known as 'convalescent carriers', who are recovering or have recovered from *Salmonella* food poisoning may feel well but can still be egesting the organism and may thus easily contaminate food. Chronic carriers continue to harbour the organism for over a year after having been ill. Some people may have become symptomless carriers, i.e. carriers of *Salmonella* without ever having been ill.

Whatever the reason for an individual harbouring the organism, it is important to exclude carriers from catering premises as they egest the organism in their faeces and even with reasonable standards of hygiene they may harbour the bacterium on their hands. This could lead to the contamination of food or fellow workers, as well as bins, sewers, waste pipes, etc. Individuals can be checked to see if they are carriers by submitting to a stool test.

Symptoms and illness

The symptoms and severity of Salmonella food poisoning vary from person to person, depending on their level of immunity, the strain of *Salmonella* involved, as well as the actual numbers consumed. The incubation period, i.e. the time between the food being eaten and the appearance of the symptoms, is between 6–72 hr, normally 12–24 hr. The main symptoms are fever, headache, aching limbs, diarrhoea and abdominal pain. The illness may last from 1–7 days after which the person will either recover, with a slight chance of remaining a carrier (more likely in females), or the victim may die. The mortality rate for Salmonella food poisoning is slightly less than 1 per cent and people most at risk are the old, very young or ill.

In the developed countries the most important reservoir of infection remains food animals themselves. The commodities most often associated with Salmonella food poisoning are meat, poultry, eggs, milk and milk products.

12.6.2 CLOSTRIDIUM PERFRINGENS FOOD POISONING

Incidence

Clostridium perfringens is currently responsible for up to 11 per cent of reported food-poisoning cases in England, although as recently as 1975 it was responsible for over 20 per cent of the reported cases. Although Clostridium food poisoning is described as a toxin-type food poisoning, the toxin is not produced in the food, but only in the gut of the person who has eaten contaminated food.

Clostridium *bacteria*

These are spore-forming, rod-shaped, anaerobic bacteria. Probably a minimum of 100 million bacteria need to be consumed before sufficient toxin is likely to be produced in the gut to cause food poisoning. *Clostridium perfringens* is capable of very rapid cell division (every 12 min), hence large numbers can accumulate in a short space of time. The optimum temperature for growth of *Clostridium perfringens* is about 45 °C.

Distribution, origins and sources

Clostridium perfringens is found in the gut of many animals including farm animals, domestic pets, pests and humans. From the gut, spores of the *Clostridium* can pass into soil, dirt, sewage as well as on to a variety of foods including meat and vegetables.

Disease symptoms

The incubation period for *Clostridium* food poisoning is normally between 8 and 22 hr and the symptoms include abdominal pain, which can be quite severe, nausea and diarrhoea. The illness is relatively mild and rarely lasts more than 24 hr.

Most cases of *Clostridium perfringens* food poisoning are associated with meat dishes, particularly those cooked in advance of requirements. These are then served cold or reheated. Spores contaminating the original meat survive cooking. The meat dish will become anaerobic during cooking and the spores, given time, will germinate. The germinating spores produce bacteria which grow and multiply rapidly in food left unrefrigerated. A quick 'warming up' of such meat dishes fails to destroy the bacteria present and food poisoning will result. Rapid cooling of meat dishes followed by refrigeration and thorough reheating would virtually eliminate *Clostridium perfringens* food poisoning.

12.6.3 CLOSTRIDIUM BOTULINUM FOOD POISONING

Botulism is a rare but deadly form of food poisoning caused by the growth of *Clostridium botulinum* in food. An outbreak occurred in Birmingham in 1978 and attracted wide publicity. Four people became ill and two died as a result of eating a tin of infected salmon. More recently an outbreak in 1989 involved contaminated hazelnut puree used to make hazelnut yoghurt. *Clostridium botulinum* produces a classical toxin-type food poisoning and the toxin produced is one of the most deadly poisons known. Botulism is typically associated with incorrectly canned foods and some fish and vegetable products.

12.6.4 STAPHYLOCOCCUS AUREUS FOOD POISONING

Incidence

Staphylococcus aureus is responsible for about 1 per cent of the reported cases of food poisoning in the United Kingdom. However, being a mild type of food poisoning most cases are likely to go unreported making it difficult to assess how common it is.

Staphylococcus aureus *bacteria*
These are round-shaped bacteria that grow in clusters. Fortunately, not all strains of *Staphylococcus aureus* can cause food poisoning, only those strains capable of producing a heat-stable toxin. Although *Staphylococcus aureus* is relatively easily destroyed by heat, the toxin it produces is quite resistant, and once formed in food can persist (toxin survives boiling for 30 min). *Staphylococcus aureus* is relatively resistant to the effects of freezing, drying and salt. The organism is normally slow growing but owing to its tolerance of salt, it can increase in numbers more rapidly than competing bacteria when growing on cooked meats or other foods with a high salt content. Between 1 and 5 million bacteria are required to produce sufficient toxin to cause food poisoning.

Distribution, origin and sources
With the exception of outbreaks involving raw milk, staphylococcal food poisoning nearly always has a human origin. The organism is found as a commensal on the human skin. It is also likely to be found in very large numbers in the nose (up to 70 per cent of the population), on the hands (up to 40 per cent of the population), as well as the throat and infected cuts and minor infections such as boils and spots. Staphylococci are difficult to wash off and can penetrate into the deeper layers of the skin associated with sweat ducts and hair follicles. Hands so infected may harbour staphylococci even though vigorously washed. When perspiration occurs, as in a busy humid hot kitchen, the staphylococci rise to the surface of the skin. Thus many rules of personal hygiene aim specifically to prevent contamination of the food by this organism, e.g. no smoking in the food preparation areas, no coughing or sneezing over food, the use of waterproof, protective plasters to cover infected skin lesions.

Disease symptoms
Staphylococcal food poisoning has a short incubation period, normally from 1–6 hr, and the main symptom is vomiting. This may be so severe as to lead to collapse and dehydration. The vomiting actually helps to cut short the illness by getting rid of the toxin from the body. The vomiting is followed by a short period of weakness and then a rapid recovery within 8–24 hr. Some, more severe, cases may last several days. Foods most frequently associated with outbreaks include cold cooked meats, e.g. ham, as well as foods containing cream and custard. Canned foods have an extremely good safety record but most cases of food poisoning associated with them

are caused by staphylococci entering the can during handling in the cooling period after heat processing.

12.6.5 BACILLUS CEREUS FOOD POISONING

Incidence
This organism was only recognised as causing food poisoning in the early 1970s and is now responsible for approximately 1 per cent of reported cases in the United Kingdom.

Bacterium
Bacillus cereus is an aerobic spore-forming rod-shaped bacterium which can produce a toxin in food. At least 1 million bacteria per gram of food need to be present to produce sufficient toxin to cause illness.

Distribution, origin and sources
It is a common soil organism and can be found in dust, soil, water and foods, especially cereal grains, spices and vegetable products. In the UK the organism is particularly associated with rice, and one survey identified Bacillus cereus on over 80 per cent of the samples tested.

Symptoms and illness
Bacillus cereus can cause two different types of food poisoning. The type that occurs in the UK is associated with rice, has a short incubation period (1–6 hr), with vomiting, nausea and diarrhoea as its main symptoms. The duration of the illness is normally 7–24 hr. Rice involved in food-poisoning incidents has usually been cooked in advance of requirements and has then been left at room temperature and *not* been refrigerated (refrigerated rice tends to clump and stick together). In the delay period between cooking and consumption, spores of the organism that have survived the initial cooking germinate on the warm, moist rice to produce bacteria which in turn produce toxin. Consumption of this rice will lead to food poisoning. In one recent outbreak the offending rice was found to have over 3.5×10^8 bacteria per gram.

In the United States and parts of Europe Bacillus cereus produces a different type of food poisoning with an incubation period of 8–16 hr and abdominal pain and diarrhoea as the main symptoms. This type of food poisoning is usually associated with cornflour, vegetables or minced meat dishes.

12.6.6 CAMPYLOBACTER

Incidence

Campylobacter jejuni have only recently been identified as a common and important cause of stomach upsets and there is some evidence to suggest that other species aid the development of stomach ulcers. Figures relating to Campylobacter infections have only been published separately since 1980. Currently the number of reported cases of *Campylobcter* infections is about 35 000 per year although not all these cases involved food. Its actual incidence may be far higher as it can be isolated from between 5–8 per cent of people suffering diarrhoea, making it the commonest bacterium associated with diarrhoea in the United Kingdom.

Campylobacter *bacteria*

These are curved rod-shaped mesophilic bacteria which have a relatively high optimum temperature for growth (43 °C). *Campylobacter* have only limited powers of survival and are particularly sensitive to drying. Initial research has shown that, unlike typical food-poisoning bacteria, *Campylobacter* tend not to grow very well on the surface of foods and that only relatively small numbers may be needed for infection (only 500 organisms in some cases). Of the foods examined, milk seems to provide the most suitable environment for their survival. However, recent surveys found 70–80 per cent of poultry to be contaminated. The organism survives freezing well and the increasing use of frozen poultry and poultry pieces may have contributed to an increase in its incidence.

Distribution, origins and sources

Campylobacter like *Salmonella* is a zoonosis and is found in the intestines of a variety of animals including farm animals and domestic pets. *Campylobacter* can also be isolated from the gut of humans but as the organism does not survive well on the hands (a few minutes only), food handlers are unlikely to be an important source of the organism. In addition to outbreaks involving food, direct transmission to humans, especially from infected children or pets, may occur.

Disease and symptoms

The incubation period is normally between 2–10 days and the main symptoms are diarrhoea and abdominal pain, both of which may be severe, and a flu-like malaise with fever. The illness normally does not last more than 5 days but some exceptional cases have lasted up to 3 weeks. The victims do not remain long-term carriers and the mortality rate is usually low. An exception occurs in elderly people when in some outbreaks the mortality rate has approached 11 per cent. Foods most often associated with *Campylobacter* are raw or improperly pasteurised milk and poultry. More research is needed to clarify the role of *Campylobacter* in causing enteritis.

12.6.7 OTHER BACTERIA CAUSING FOOD TRANSMITTED DISEASES

A number of other types of bacteria, e.g. *Shigella* species, *Yersinia enterocolitica* and *Listeria* species can cause food-borne diseases and while some are a significant factor in other countries, they are of relatively minor importance in the UK. Yersinia and Listeria bacteria can grow at refrigeration temperatures and unless adequate care is taken may give rise to concern in cook chill products. Yersinia enteritis is particularly commonly reported in Scandinavian countries and it may be far more common in the U.K. than previously realised. *Listeria* has recently been associated with Swiss cheese made from unpasteurised milk.

12.7 STATISTICS RELATING TO FOOD-BORNE DISEASE

Figures relating to food poisoning and cases of Campylobacter enteritis have increased dramatically in the 1980's. This could be due, in part, to greater consumer awareness of food borne disease and the better reporting of such illnesses. Undoubtedly a substantial part of the increase is real and could be due to a combination of different factors. These include:

Types of Food Eaten
The type of food we eat and the way in which this food is produced could have contributed to the "real" increase. We eat a greater variety of "unusual" or more "exotic" foods including, for example, soft cheeses made from unpasteurised milk. We now tend to want fewer preservatives and prefer food "rare" or undercooked, e.g. lightly boiled eggs, rare steaks, etc. We also tend to use more prepared meals and rely on microwave regeneration. Battery farming methods and the high throughput in abattoirs and poultry plants have contributed to an increase in carcase contamination. Another major factor must be the increased consumption of poultry meat and products. Consumption of poultry meat has increased by 41% in the past ten years. This might

be beneficial from the nutritional perspective (less saturated fat) but we do know that poultry is an important source of human gastrointestinal infections.

Changes in Lifestyle and Habits

More people now eat out and there has been an increase in "snacking", i.e. the consumption of snack meals rather than more formalised meals. Much greater use of fast foods and takeaways means that fewer meals are eaten in the home. The public tends to shop differently, often only once a week or even less. This practice places great demands on food, especially if combined with overloaded, faulty or incorrectly set refrigerators, Inadequate cooking at barbecues may also have contributed to the increase.

Lack of Hygiene Awareness

This applies to all people handling food at all points in the food chain from farmers, manufacturers, wholesalers, retailers, caterers and the consumer. This lack of knowledge highlights the need for training. Remember a hygiene mistake at home may make 2 or 3 people ill, a hygiene mistake in food manufacturing or large scale catering may make thousands ill.

International Trade and Travel

Food now travels all over the world and this is likely to increase. Some cases of illness are also imported from abroad.

TABLE 12.7 Formally Reported Cases of Food Transmitted Disease England and Wales (OPCS) data

Year	Food Poisoning	Campylobacter	Listeriosis
1985	19242	23572	149
1986	23948	24809	137
1987	29331	27310	259
1988	39713	28761	291
1989	52557	32590	251

When looking at reported cases of food poisoning it must be remembered that this represents the tip of the iceberg, the vast majority of cases are never reported. Estimations of the number of cases actually being reported vary from 1 in 10 to 1 in 100.

12.8 FUNGAL FOOD POISONING AND MYCOTOXINS

Undoubtedly bacterial food poisoning is the most important type occurring in the UK but increasingly evidence suggests that fungi contaminating certain foods are also capable of causing food poisoning. Fungi, the study of which is known as 'mycology', can grow and yield toxins (mycotoxins) in food. *Aspergillus flavus* produces aflatoxins and these have been detected in ground-nuts, cereals and a variety of other foods. Consumption of aflatoxin-infected foods has caused outbreaks of illness in humans. Ergotism is a disease caused by the eating of mould-infected rye. Consumption of rye bread is more common in other parts of Europe and the USA where ergotism is, therefore, more of a problem. Undoubtedly greater attention should be given to the dangers of using or eating mouldy food and the possible consequences of food poisoning. This particularly applies to crops imported from tropical climates with a high humidity. Mycotoxins may contribute to some of the symptoms of Kwashiorkor, a nutritional disease seen in Africa.

12.9 INVESTIGATION OF A FOOD POISONING OUTBREAK

It is to be hoped that no reader of this book would ever be responsible for an outbreak of food poisoning. It is possible, however, for a caterer to become involved either directly or indirectly (as a result of someone else's poor management) in such incidents. Thus it is necessary for all caterers to know what to do on these occasions. The catering manager will become involved when staff or customers start to show signs of illness or when contacted by the local Environmental Health Officer. It is important to keep calm and carry out the correct procedures. It is in your own interest to have the outbreak investigated immediately. Prompt action will lead to:

(a) Preventing its spread.
(b) Identifying the causative food.
(c) Identifying the cause of the food contamination.
(d) Tracking down victims and carriers.
(e) Identifying poor catering procedures.
(f) Preventing further outbreaks.

Action to be taken	Reason for action
1. Stop any more food being served.	The causative food will not be known and to prevent further cases occurring no food should be eaten/prepared.
2. Arrange medical care.	Customers may be quite seriously ill and prompt medical attention could be life saving.

3. Contact the local Environmental Health Officer (EHO).

Delay in informing the authorities increases the risk of more food-poisoning cases and could hinder tracking down the cause. It is better for you to notify the authorities than for investigators to contact you as a result of a victim's illness. **Do not be tempted to hide the outbreak from the authorities.**

4. Contact your immediate superior and/or the owner of the business.

They may wish to take charge of the situation, implement prepared company policy or bring in company hygiene inspectors/outside experts.

5. Try to have as much relevant information as possible for the EHO.

This will save time and, hopefully, speed up the resolution of the problem.

Useful information to have is listed in 6, 7, 8 and 9.

6. The victims.
   (i) Where possible check on symptoms, incubation period, duration and severity of symptoms.

Can help to decide on the type of food poisoning (see Table 12.6) and the most appropriate remedial action, see 11.

   (ii) Collect names, addresses, ages, etc., and any other relevant details.

Can help the authorities to contact relatives, etc.

   (iii) Collect names, addresses, etc., of people not yet ill who may have eaten contaminated food.

Incubation periods vary for individuals. This action can help to identify people who may yet become ill or become carriers.

7. The food.
   (i) Retain for analysis any remaining food portions, meals, cans, cartons, etc., which could be implicated.

Relevant samples speed up the process of identifying the causative organism and the mechanism of food poisoning.

(ii) Try to identify the food involved. Examine menus, food eaten by the victims to identify common food items.

Identification of the causative food can speed up resolving the problem, appropriate preventative measures and an early return to normal work.

(iii) If an item of food is suspected, make full enquiries about it, e.g. make, brand, batch numbers, sell-by date, origin, supplier, receipts, any evidence of abnormality, etc.

Such details rapidly obtained may prevent food-poisoning outbreaks elsewhere.

(iv) Take/collect full details of the history of the suspected food from the time of arrival on the premises to serving, i.e. storage times, locations, temperatures, defrosting times, cooking times, storage after cooking, etc.

Pin-points mistakes in catering practices allowing the food poisoning to take place on the premises.

(v) Do not sell any more suspected food and try to recover any food which has been sold but not yet eaten.

Prevents further spread and speeds up identification. Note: EHO has the power to seize infected food.

(vi) If the suspect food is a composite one made on the premises, then make all these checks on each one of the food ingredients, e.g. chicken, egg, etc.

See (iv), above.

8. The staff.
   (i) Check if any members of staff show signs of food poisoning.

   (ii) Warn staff members not to 'clean up' until necessary bacteriological investigations have been carried out.

Vital evidence concerning the outbreak may be removed.

(iii) Prepare a list of names and addresses, etc. of all food handlers and individuals employed plus any absent including the reasons for absence.

Helps the EHO to know how many people are employed and where they can be contacted.

(iv) Details particularly required of staff members handling the suspected food, e.g. general health, recent medical history (stomach upsets, open cuts, etc.), smoking habits, recent return from abroad.

Helps to identify if a human carrier is involved.

(v) Advise staff members that they may be questioned about their medical history, required to fill in a questionnaire and/or provide samples for laboratory analysis, e.g. nasal swabs, faecal samples, etc.

Good management practice to keep staff members informed of what is expected of them.

9. The premises.
  (i) Check standards of general hygiene – construction and cleanliness.

The EHO will do this and it will give you an idea of what any reports will mention.

(ii) Look for any evidence of pest problems, etc.

(iii) Find copies of hygiene or pest control contracts cleaning programmes.

May be required by the EHO.

(iv) Make notes of any premises/plant malfunctions including when the malfunctions were reported and the action that was taken.

May be required by the EHO.

| (v) Check equipment, e.g. refrigerators, *bains-marie*, etc. to ensure correct working/usage. | To identify if equipment malfunction may have been responsible for the outbreak. |
| (vi) When the investigation is complete, with advice from the EHO thoroughly clean and disinfect. | Marks the initial stage of a return to normal working. |

10. The EHO.

(i) Cooperate fully with the EHO – be available to provide him with the necessary information.	Speeds up the return to normal working and the prevention of further attacks.
(ii) First step taken by the EHO is to decide if food poisoning, food-borne infection or other cause (e.g. Legionnaire's disease).	Initial steps in solving the outbreak.
(iii) The EHO will decide if a detailed microbiological analysis is required.	May help to identify the causative organism and prevent further outbreaks.
(iv) The EHO will question members of staff and victims and inspect the premises. Particular attention will be paid to any staff members who have suffered recent illnesses.	See (iii) above.
(v) The EHO will try to decide on the causative organism and how the incident occurred. If chemical food poisoning is suspected then checks will be made on storage of disinfectants, insecticides, etc.	

(vi) The EHO may give advice on how any future outbreak could be prevented and if prosecution is likely to be forthcoming or if the premises are to be closed.

11. Likely specific preventative measures – these vary depending on the type of food poisoning organism and the particular conditions but are likely to include:

(i) Staphylococcal food poisoning, review of personal hygiene practices – hand washing, smoking, etc., plus review of food storage.

Nearly always has a human source coupled with a mistake in personal hygiene.

(ii) *Clostridium perfringens*
Review of post-cooking storage and serving of cooked meat items.

Typical outbreaks involve spores surviving cooking and germinating in poorly cooked meat dishes.

(iii) *Bacillus cereus*
Check all procedures involving rice, especially post-cooking.

Typically involved with poorly cooled, part-cooked rice dishes.

(iv) *Salmonella*
Review cooking and defrosting procedures (especially of poultry). Food suppliers, food storage plus personal hygiene and health of staff members.
Investigate for mechanisms of cross-contamination.

Can be caused by cross-contamination, human carriers or not cooking food correctly.

12.10 NON-FOOD TRANSMITTED INFECTIOUS DISEASES IMPORTANT IN CATERING

Some disease-causing organisms use food to get from one host to another, other microorganisms use different methods. The well known phrase 'coughs and sneezes spread diseases' illustrates that some microorganisms have adapted to air-borne spread (e.g. in whooping cough, influenza, etc.). Technically speaking, most diseases that could occur in the home could be acquired or transmitted in catering establishments. It is however beyond the scope of this book to enter the realms of medical microbiology but it is worth briefly examining two illnesses about which caterers should have some knowledge.

12.10.1 LEGIONNAIRE'S DISEASE

This is the name given to a respiratory (pneumonia-type) illness which was first identified at a convention of the American Legion in 1976. Food served at the hotel holding the convention was originally one of the suspected sources but the actual cause was eventually found to be the *Legionella* bacteria (named after the legionnaires attending the conference). *Legionella* bacteria live in water under an extremely wide range of conditions. They have been isolated not only in hot springs and lakes but also in domestic water systems, cooling towers and air-conditioning units. Stationary water and debris in tanks may provide ideal growth conditions.

People seem to catch the disease most readily by inhaling tiny droplets of water containing the *Legionella* bacteria, especially in the form of fine mist or aerosol. Such conditions can be created by showers – rubber washers in showers and taps partially inactivate the chlorine in the water and support the growth of bacteria. When an infected tap is turned on after a period of inactivity, e.g. at the start of the holiday season, after a room has been vacant, or even first thing in the morning, high concentrations of *Legionella* may be released. This may be the cause of isolated cases of legionnaire's disease in some United Kingdom hotels. Fortunately, relatively large doses of the organism are needed to set up an infection, cases of which are more common in people over the age of fifty.

Large-scale outbreaks are more likely to occur from contaminated water in air-conditioning units. This seems the likely cause of the outbreak in the United States of America in 1976 as well as more recent hospital outbreaks in the UK and hotel outbreaks in Spain, Portugal and Northern Italy.

In a report published in 1985 *Legionella* bacteria were found in the water supplies of fifty-five hotels out of a total of 104 hotels examined. The report suggested that the larger the hotel the more likely it was to harbour the organism. Twenty-eight out of forty hospitals similarly tested had *Legionella* in the hot or cold water systems.

Codes of practice designed to minimise contamination rates of water systems include:

1. Thorough cleaning of calorifiers (hot water tanks) after periods of inactivity – the sludge found at the bottom of such tanks may be heavily infected. Correct regular maintenance is required.
2. Raising water temperatures in hot water or heating systems to above 55 °C at the outlets to destroy the organism.
3. Checks to monitor water contamination.
4. Use of commercially available devices to blow hot air at 62 °C through plumbing after use.

Another reason why caterers should be aware of the problems posed by *Legionella* bacteria concerns the increase in the number of whirlpool spas (jacuzzis). These are now commonly installed in hotels, hospitals and leisure complexes and with their associated plumbing can provide an ideal breeding grounds for *Legionella*. Whirlpools differ from swimming pools in that the water is usually hotter (nearer body temperature), the water is artificially aerated at high velocity with the capability of generating a fine aerosol, they have a higher bather load. All these features are likely to increase the chances of a Legionella infection and a hotel whirlpool bath has been implicated in at least one major outbreak affecting 25 people in Brighton. Highlighting the need for special maintenance, operation and cleaning of whirlpool spas is the fact that a variety of other illnesses have commonly been associated with them including:

bacterial skin, eye, ear and nose infections caused by *Pseudomonas aeruginosa* and *Staphylococcus aureus*;

fungal skin infections, e.g. athletes foot;

viral skin infections, e.g. plantar warts.

12.10.2 ACQUIRED IMMUNE DEFICIENCY SYNDROME – AIDS

This disease is caused by the HIV virus (human immunodeficiency virus, also known as HTLVIII). Special types of white blood cells (lymphocytes) which assist in the bodies normal production of immunoglobulins (antibodies) used to fight infection are attacked by the HIV virus. Eventually, as a result of the virus attacking the lymphocytes the body's immune system becomes so affected that the sufferer becomes susceptible to a wide range of infections (most commonly a type of pneumonia). This condition is likely to result in death.

In October 1986 there were 3500 registered AIDS victims in the twelve countries in the European Economic Community but it seems likely that the number of victims is doubling every nine months and there could be more than 100,000 cases in Western Europe by 1990. In addition for every declared AIDS case it is estimated that there are 50–100 unknown carriers (the incubation period for AIDS is between 3 and 10 years). AIDS is therefore a recent and important public health risk.

The virus can spread in two main ways:

(a) by sexual intercourse;

(b) the parenteral route, i.e. direct introduction of the virus, from contaminated material (usually blood) into the blood stream of another person, e.g. in the sharing of needles by intravenous drug users.

Note there is no evidence to suggest that the virus can be transmitted through food or drink, through sneezing or coughing, direct contact, e.g. by touching or through sharing toilet facilities.

It is the parenteral route of spread which caterers must guard against and codes of practice to prevent infection of staff should be incorporated into Housekeeping routines. The main problem arises with the possible spread of the disease through blood (e.g. from cuts) and catering staff should treat any blood spillages as being potentially harmful and observe the following rules:

1. Where there is possibility of contact with blood or other body fluids employees should use disposable plastic gloves and aprons.

2. Disposable paper towels should be used for any mopping up that is necessary.

3. All items to be disposed of should be placed in plastic bags or burned. Clothing may be cleaned in an ordinary washing machine using its hot cycle.

4. An area where mopping up has to be done should be disinfected using one part of good household or commercial bleach, with ten parts of water. Household bleach will kill the AIDS virus but can be harmful to the skin so that care should be taken.

5. Employees should ensure that, wherever there is a possibility of contact with body fluids any abrasions or cuts they might have are to be covered with waterproof dressings. Staff training and hygiene awareness is important for first aiders.

6. Deposits of any type of body fluid on the skin, or other parts of the body, should be washed away with copious amounts of clean water immediately.

7. Toilet articles, such as tooth brushes, shaving kits, electric razors, face flannels or towels which could be contaminated should not be shared. If necessary, disposable items should be provided and used.

8. Employees should avoid contaminating towels with blood. Towels should not be shared – use disposable towels, hot air dryers or automatic roller towels.

9. Sanitary towels or tampons should be disposed of with care.

10. Care should be taken with any instruments for manicure, pedicure, epilation, etc.

QUESTIONS

1. Distinguish, using named examples, between infective food poisoning, toxin food poisoning and food-borne infections.

2. Which food-poisoning bacterium is responsible for the majority of reported food poisoning cases in the United Kingdom? Describe three categories of people who can 'carry' this group of bacteria.

3. Describe how the majority of cases of *Clostridium perfringens* food poisoning are caused.

4. List the normal sources of food-poisoning staphylococci. Describe the symptoms of a typical outbreak of staphylococcal food poisoning.

5. Explain why ergotism is not common in the UK.

13

FOOD HYGIENE – PREVENTING MICROBIAL GROWTH AND SURVIVAL

13.1 INTRODUCTION

Hygiene is connected with health, for example, good oral hygiene produces healthy teeth and gums. Food hygiene ensures that food is *safe* to eat and of good keeping quality (particularly important with relation to cook chill, see Sect. 13.5.1). Caterers should realise that not all the food that we eat may be good for us and could result in illness and possibly even death. Food poisoning does not happen by accident but is usually caused by ignorance which leads to mistakes in the handling of food. **Food hygiene, therefore, covers all aspects of processing, preparing, storing, cooking and serving of food to make certain that it is safe to eat.**

Food hygiene is more important today than at any other time in the past. Increasingly people are eating foods prepared outside their own homes, either in restaurants, canteens, cafés, hotels or as take-away meals. Over 100 million meals or snacks are purchased per week in the United Kingdom. The number of reported cases of food poisoning in England and Wales has climbed dramatically since 1972. Food poisoning results in illness and lost working days (estimated at approximately 20 million per year). It is wrong to think that good hygiene costs a lot of money, in fact, the reverse is true, bad standards of hygiene can be extremely expensive. Caterers who operate unhygienic premises are breaking the law and are liable to prosecution which can lead to fines, imprisonment or closure of premises. Court cases dealing with such offences often make newspaper headlines and bad publicity leads to loss of trade and revenue (see Fig. 13.1). Caterers ignoring food hygiene principles run the risk of giving people food poisoning and the victims can claim for compensation. Once again, bad publicity associated with such outbreaks can lead to loss of business. One recent outbreak of food poisoning aboard an airliner resulted in claims for compensation which ran into millions of pounds! **No caterer should have a customer's death on their conscience.** For these reasons students on food-related courses of study should learn the causes of

FIG. 13.1

food poisoning (see Ch. 12) and its prevention (Ch. 13 and Ch. 14). It is an unfortunate fact that some poorly trained staff do not understand the need for, or are prepared to ignore, good hygiene. This should not deter better informed food handlers from maintaining their own high standards and doing their utmost to ensure that all food is prepared hygienically, if possible trying to improve the situation by educating less well informed people.

The reason for food being unsafe has been considered in Ch. 12. Bacterial food poisoning is the most common type occurring in the United Kingdom and Sect. 12.6 considers the bacteria most commonly responsible. However, for cases of food poisoning to occur it is not sufficient for the food to be contaminated, there must also be a period when the harmful bacteria can grow in the food (see Sect. 12.5). Even if the initial contamination of the food with the harmful bacteria is not the caterer's fault, allowing them to grow in the food is! Foods that can support the growth of food-poisoning bacteria are termed 'high-risk foods' (see Sect. 15.2.2). Before bacteria can grow in such foods they need the correct conditions for growth (see Ch. 9). Caterers should *not* allow bacteria the conditions or time for growth. In addition, it has already been mentioned that bacteria can survive in conditions that do not allow their growth (see Sect. 9.3).

The aim of this chapter is to explain to caterers how they can minimise or prevent microbial growth and survival by using correct food-handling procedures.

13.2   FLOW SCHEME FOR CATERING OPERATIONS

In order to see fully how microbial growth, survival and contamination can be prevented it is helpful to visualise the various stages of catering operations by using a simple flow scheme (see Fig. 13.2).

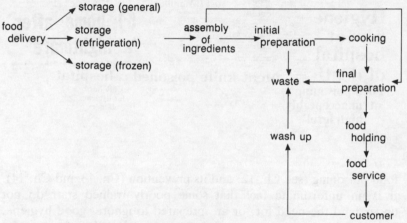

FIG. 13.2 A flow diagram for catering operations

13.3   PREVENTING MICROBIAL GROWTH

The prevention of microbial growth is necessary at all stages in the catering flow scheme and the single most important method of controlling microbial growth is correct use of temperature. Catering errors causing food to be stored at the wrong temperature for a period of time (which can be as short as 1–2 hr) may result in bacterial multiplication and possibly food poisoning. Food-poisoning bacteria normally grow at between 5 °C and 45 °C with an optimum (i.e. best) temperature usually of 37 °C. This means that they will grow quite well at room temperature, especially during the summer when the ambient (i.e. surrounding) temperatures in a hot kitchen can approach 30 °C.

The 'temperature danger zone' in which high-risk foods must *not* be stored is between 5 °C and 63 °C. Below 5 °C food-poisoning bacteria will not usually grow because there is insufficient warmth

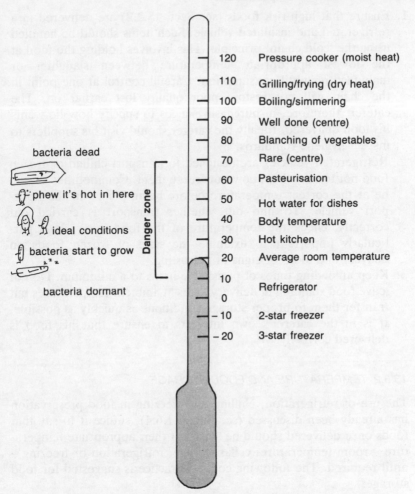

	120 — Pressure cooker (moist heat)
	110 — Grilling/frying (dry heat)
	100 — Boiling/simmering
	90 — Well done (centre)
	80 — Blanching of vegetables
bacteria dead	70 — Rare (centre)
	60 — Pasteurisation
phew it's hot in here	50 — Hot water for dishes
ideal conditions	40 — Body temperature
	30 — Hot kitchen
bacteria start to grow	20 — Average room temperature
	10
bacteria dormant	0 — Refrigerator
	−10 — 2-star freezer
	−20 — 3-star freezer

FIG. 13.3 A thermometer showing the 'temperature danger zone' for the growth of food – poisoning bacteria and a range of temperatures used in catering. Note: it is the amount of heat energy the bacteria are subjected to which is important; this is a function of temperature and time kept at that temperature. Recent evidence has increased the temperature danger zone to between 5 °C and 63 °C.

and the bacteria are inactive. Above 63 °C food-poisoning bacteria, but not spores, are killed by the heat. In catering the rule is to **keep foods hot or cold but *never* warm** (see Fig. 13.3).

13.3.1 TEMPERATURE CONTROL AND DELIVERY

To a certain extent the manner in which food is stored before delivery to catering premises is outside the control of the caterer, however, a few simple checks can be useful:

1. Ensure that high-risk foods (see Sect. 15.2.2) are delivered in a refrigerated and insulated vehicle. Such items should be handled using the 'cold chain' principle. This involves holding the food at the lowest appropriate temperature between slaughter or manufacturer until consumption. Careful control at one point in the chain will not restore poor quality lost earlier on. The caterer, therefore, in purchasing needs to specify how he wants his food delivered. Ideally the caterer should visit his suppliers to inspect hygiene standards.

2. Refrigerated vehicles are designed to transport chilled or frozen food not to cool them down or freeze them. Commodities should be at the correct temperature before being placed in the transport vehicle. To find out whether transport is carried out correctly, check the temperature of the food items. It is particularly important to examine the state of frozen foods on delivery and look for signs of defrosting.

3. Keep unloading times of perishable items to a minimum. Do not leave food standing in delivery areas at ambient temperatures but transfer them to proper storage conditions as quickly as possible. It is in the caterer's own interests to ensure that his food is delivered correctly.

13.3.2 TEMPERATURE AND FOOD STORAGE

The use of refrigeration, chilling and freezing in food preservation has already been discussed (see Sect. 11.6.4), suffice it to say that foods once delivered should be stored at their appropriate temperature – room temperature, cellar storage, refrigeration or freezing – until required. The following code of practice is suggested for food storage:

1. Buy only manageable quantities – buying in excessive bulk is not economical if the food cannot be stored properly.

2. Check operating temperatures of refrigerators and freezers. Food should not be stored in refrigerators and freezers which are automatically assumed to be operating correctly.

3. Equipment should be sited in well ventilated, cool areas, away from sources of heat, e.g. sunshine, cookers, etc.

4. Regular maintenance and service is essential. Equipment should be defrosted and cleaned regularly (otherwise the efficiency is reduced).

5. Check seals on doors of refrigerators and freezers. Minimise periods of time when doors are open.

6. For display equipment, make sure that food is stored below the

'load line'. Food stored above the load line will not be at the correct temperature.

7. Do not overload refrigerators or freezers, store foods to allow circulation of air, and do not store unnecessary foods, e.g. unopened UHT milk, tomato ketchup, at low temperature.

8. Do not expect temperatures in a refrigerator always to be the same even when working correctly – variations will occur depending upon how often it is opened and the type of foods stored. The coolest part of most domestic-type refrigerators is near the bottom (but above the salad area) and warmest near the top. Temperatures within a fridge may vary by as much as 2–3 °C.

9. Use special cooling cabinets of blast chillers to cool food. Use blast freezers or other appropriate equipment to freeze foods (see Sect. 11.6.4 and 18.7.3). Do not use domestic equipment containing stored foods, to cool large items of hot food. Such practices lead to reduced efficiency (due to ice formation on the cooling coils) and temperature fluctuations.

10. Larger establishments should invest in 'walk-in', butcher's type refrigerators or cold rooms with fan-distributed cold air.

11. Rotate stock. The rule is **first in, first out**.

13.3.3 TEMPERATURE CONTROL AND FOOD PREPARATION

Food-preparation areas are often hot and therefore the time that high-risk foods are kept there should be minimised. The following precautions should be taken:

1. Never remove food from cooling units until it is required.

2. Once food preparation has been completed do not leave high-risk foods lying about. Cook them where necessary or return them to a cooling unit.

13.3.4 TEMPERATURE CONTROL AFTER PREPARATION PRIOR TO SERVING

High-risk foods, if not served immediately, should be stored below 5 °C or above 63 °C (a legal requirement, see Sect. 15.2.2). Large-scale food-poisoning outbreaks have occurred owing to food being left unnecessarily in food-preparation areas. In one outbreak in Wakefield meat was left for 7.5 hr in a food-preparation area prior to service. A number of useful rules are:

1. Cooked hot foods to be stored at reduced temperatures should be cooled in special cooling units and be refrigerated within 1.5 hr. Rapid cooling of foods is especially important in the

summer (most cases of food poisoning occur then) when ambient temperatures are high and cooling times are long (see Fig. 13.4). Correct cooling and storage of cooked meat products is essential to prevent *Clostridium* (spores of this bacterium can survive cooking) food poisoning. Similarly, cooling of rice products is essential to prevent *Bacillus cereus* food poisoning.

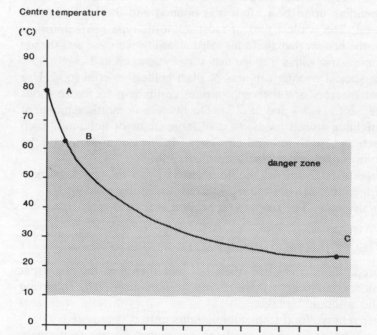

FIG. 13.4 Cooling curve for the centre of a joint of meat stored at room temperature (A) centre temperature of joint of meat after removal from an oven prior to storage at room temperature, +25 °C (B) centre temperature of joint 1 hr later; food entering the danger zone (zone of possible bacterial growth), for legal purposes, 63–10 °C (C) centre of joint reaches room temperature 15 hrs after removal from oven.
Note: temperature danger zone now 5 °C–63 °C.

2. Greater use should be made of refrigerated display units for customer self-selection (see Fig. 13.5).
3. Be vigilant for mistakes made in temperature control, e.g. use of a traditional sweets trolley kept at room temperature. A cream gateau prepared by a chef with food poisoning staphylococci on his hands could be contaminated. If the gateau is then stored on an unrefrigerated sweets trolley in a restaurant for several hours

it is potentially lethal. Similarly, the habit of laying out food well in advance, e.g. at wedding receptions, is not good catering practice (quite a number of food-poisoning outbreaks have been traced back to wedding receptions).

4. The alternative to cooling prepared foods is to maintain hot foods hot. This is one of the functions of hot cupboards, e.g. for pies, and these should be capable of maintaining an internal temperature of 70–85 °C. *Bains-maries* are wells containing hot foods and are heated by steam or hot water. Note, hot cupboards, infra red lamps and *bains-marie* should **never be used for heating up cold foods**, since they would only become warm and could be a health risk. Many cases of food poisoning can be traced back to incorrect storage of food between final preparation and serving! However, nutritional and organolephic quality (see Sect. 5.4) are compromised by long term warm holding of foods.

13.4   COOKING AS A MEANS OF MICROBIAL CONTROL

Food is cooked to make it more appetising (in terms of colour, texture, etc.), easier to digest and to make it safe. These objectives will only be achieved if the cooking is carried out correctly. Incorrectly cooked food is unsafe, unappetising and of reduced nutritional value. Cooking works on the principle that heat energy is transmitted from the cooking environment (air, oil, water) to the food. One consequence of the heat energy is that harmful organisms are destroyed. Note that the outside temperature of the food will not necessarily be the same as the internal temperature. Proper cooking for safety depends on four considerations:

(a) Sufficiently high cooking temperature.
(b) Sufficient time of cooking.
(c) Size of the food being cooked.
(d) Initial temperature of the food.

13.4.1 TEMPERATURE OF COOKING

Not all methods of cooking employ the same cooking temperature. Simmering, stewing and braising tend to be at lower temperatures. Roasting, baking and grilling require higher temperatures and are considered safer. Pressure cooking employs moist heat; owing to higher pressure the boiling point of water is increased and it is both an efficient method of cooking and a means of killing microorganisms rapidly. Frying involves the use of cooking oil, which is a

(a)

FIG.13.5 Display units for customer self-selection (a) refrigerated display for cold buffet (b) cooled marble slab for cold buffet (c) refrigerated display for gateaux and other sweet items (d) refrigerated display for self-selection of items in 'eat-in' or 'take-away' restaurant

more efficient heat-transfer medium and can have an operating temperature up to 220 °C (should be below the smoke point, see Sect. 3.4.1).

The greater the heat differential (temperature outside relative to

(b)

(c)

(d)

the temperature of the food), the quicker the heating process. Forced air convection ovens increase the temperature of the food more rapidly and offer more efficient and even cooking, without having to use higher oven temperatures. Microwave cooking works on a different principle, generating heat internally. Although increasingly employed in the catering industry, care needs to be taken in the use of microwaves, especially in cooking raw and frozen foods. Poor heat penetration can cause uneven heat distribution leading to 'cold spots'. This is particularly likely with frozen foods which should be initially treated using a defrost cycle (pulses of microwaves to break down ice crystals). A rotating turntable also helps to ensure a more even distribution of energy. Microwaves can also be combined with forced air convection.

It is important to ensure that a sufficiently high temperature is used in cooking. Thus, for instance, care needs to be taken with so-called slow cookers to ensure they are not overfilled – otherwise the food will not reach a sufficiently high temperature. Also caution is needed with multiple rotisserie spits seen in a number of fish-and chip-shops. Such establishments wishing to display the food cooking for a long time, set the temperature at a low setting to prevent overcooking. This has, in the past, resulted in food poisoning because the food never reached a sufficiently high temperature. Similar care is needed in barbecueing foods. Note bone is a better conductor of heat than meat muscle therefore meat cooks more quickly with the bone in rather than bone out. Metal skewers have the same effect.

13.4.2 TIME OF COOKING

Food that is being cooked does not instantly reach the same intensity of heat as the cooking environment, time is required for the heat to penetrate the food. The period needed to heat the food to safe levels is closely related to the temperature employed as well as the size and the initial temperature of the food (see Table 13.1). The internal or centre temperature of the food will vary but for rare meat it is only about 63 °C, medium done it is at about 71 °C, and well-done meat is at about 78 °C. The destruction of micro-organisms in food is a consequence of heat energy transferred to the food, thus for food to be safe it must be cooked for an adequate period of time to allow the centre temperature to reach a sufficiently high level. This is of particular importance where it is suspected or known that the centre of the food is contaminated (see Sect. 13.4.5).

TABLE 13.1 Guidelines for cooking and thawing times for different turkey sizes

Turkey weight		Cooking time	Thawing times	
		[180 °C, Gas Mark 4, 350 °F]	20 °C*	4 °C†
(lb)	(kg)	(hr)	(hr)	(hr)
5	2.25	2.5	15	24
10	4.5	3.5	18	36
15	6.75	4.75–5	24	48
20	9.0	5.75–6	30	50

* Room temperature.
† Refrigerator.

13.4.3 SIZE OF FOOD

Food itself is a poor conductor of heat, therefore larger items of food will need longer cooking times than small ones (see Table 13.1). This is to ensure that the centre temperature is the same whether the pieces of food are large or small. In some cases it may be more convenient to joint or segment larger items of food. This would not only ensure greater safety but could also be more economical in the use of heat energy.

The maximum size for safe cooking of joints of meat has been put at between 2.5 and 2.7 kg (5–6 lb). In the case of poultry particular care should be taken with larger catering size birds and the body cavity should not be stuffed prior to cooking as this hinders the destruction of microorganisms by reducing the efficiency of heat transfer. It is customary, in the cooking of large portions of food, to add extra time to allow for heat penetration.

Smaller items of food have the additional advantage of cooling down quicker than large ones after cooking, important when the food is not to be served immediately.

13.4.4 DEFROSTING/THAWING

Some frozen foods need to be defrosted prior to cooking, otherwise the internal or centre temperature will never be sufficiently high to kill any microorganisms present (see Sect. 13.4.5), the heat energy being needed to melt the ice crystals instead.

Defrosting is particularly important with frozen poultry which can have a high contamination rate with *Salmonella* (see Sect. 12.6.1). Thawing can be carried out at room temperature or in a refrigerator (see Table 13.1), although it must be noted that defrosting in the latter takes longer due to the reduced temperature differential, but has the advantage that once thawed the food is still stored at a reduced temperature. Poultry which has defrosted at room temperature (approximately 20 °C) has to be checked frequently otherwise once thawed surviving salmonellae could be actively growing and multiplying. Note that poor conductivity of food results in long thawing times.

Care is needed to check that poultry is defrosted properly – this is not achieved by prodding the outside of the carcass but by checking that the body cavity is free of ice crystals, the legs are flexible and the body pliable.

Raw meat is best thawed slowly in a refrigerator, allowing 5 hr per 0.5 kg (1 lb). Thawing at room temperature is faster (2 hr per 0.5 kg) but is not advisable for all types of meat, e.g. pork. For optimum quality, the meat is best left wrapped during thawing to minimise loss of colour and juices.

Small cuts of meat, including sausages, beefburgers, chops, etc., can be cooked from the frozen state because, being small, there is little delay in heat penetration and adequate cooking is possible in a fairly short period. However, this practice may result in tougher meat. It is not advisable to cook joints (especially larger sized ones) from frozen, they take approximately twice as long to cook, resulting in greater energy requirements and costs. Also when a frozen joint is cooked, the outside may appear done but the inside may be raw. For this reason rolled and boned joints of meat should never be cooked from frozen (see Sect. 13.4.5).

13.4.5 IMPORTANCE OF CENTRE TEMPERATURE

This centre temperature concept is particularly important and can be illustrated by a number of catering examples:
1. Steak can usually be served rare safely because, provided the meat came from a healthy animal, any microbial contamination occurs on its outside surface. These microorganisms are destroyed by the high temperature to which the surface of the meat is exposed when grilled or fried. The inside of the steak can be red (uncooked) but safe because no harmful microorganisms should be present.
2. The same is not true for beefburgers which are made from minced meat and contain microorganisms in the centre as well as on the surface. While it is acceptable to have steaks rare it is not safe to eat rare beefburgers (see Fig. 13.6 a and b).
3. Similarly, doner kebabs served in Greek and Turkish restaurants are made from hand-moulded lamb or beef. These need par-

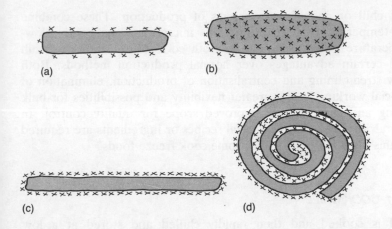

(a)

(b)

(c)

(d)

$\overset{\times}{\underset{+}{\overset{\times}{\times}}}\overset{\times}{\times}$ contaminant bacteria

FIG. 13.6 Diagram to show the distribution of contaminant bacteria on (a) steak (b) beefburger (c) joint before rolling (d) joint after rolling

ticular care in cooking as the outside *only* is cooked slowly on a rotating spit. Microorganisms can be present all through the piece of meat and the chef needs to take great care to serve cooked portions only.

4. The practice of preparing stuffed rolled joints of meat needs special attention in the cooking programme. Microorganisms, originally on the surface of the piece of meat find their way into the centre of the rolled joint (see Fig. 13.6 c and d). Time must be allowed in the cooking for the centre to reach over 70 °C.

Proper cooking should destroy all vegetative bacteria but may well leave behind bacterial spores; for this reason once cooked, foods should be stored hot, or cooled quickly. Food left out to cool in a kitchen can take hours to cool down (see Fig. 13.4). Such foods after cooling and prior to serving, should be reheated thoroughly not just warmed through! Soups and stews must be allowed to boil and simmer for 15 min while meat and poultry must be raised to a temperature of 70 °C. On no account should meat dishes be reheated more than once.

13.5 FOOD-PRODUCTION SYSTEMS

If it is known that there is likely to be a considerable delay between food production and consumption the caterer can choose to adopt cook chill or cook freeze systems of production. These combine high-temperature destruction of microorganisms with low-temperature growth prevention. Both cook freeze and cook chill offer certain advantages over normal production methods. Both allow streamlining and centralisation of production, elimination of unsocial working hours, greater flexibility and possibilities for bulk buying and storage, and improved scope for quality control. In general, for cook chill no special recipes or ingredients are required but this may be necessary for some cook freeze foods.

13.5.1 COOK CHILL

Food is cooked and then rapidly chilled and stored at a low temperature, between 0 and 3 °C. Foods are then reheated prior to serving. In the case of such systems the initial cooking should be adequate to destroy vegetative bacteria. The chilling process should start within 30 min and be completed within 1.5 hr. Such food, if prepared in clean conditions, has a life of 5 days (including the day of production and the day of consumption). Reheating should take the temperature of the food above 70 °C for 2 minutes and it should be consumed within two hours. Foods, once reheated if not consumed must be discarded. If for any reason the temperature of the food during storage exceeds 10 °C then it should be discarded (cold chain broken).

The storage temperature zone of between 0–3 °C should be sufficient to prevent the growth of food poisoning bacteria. However, fears have been expressed that unless temperature is strictly controlled then some species of Staphylococci and Salmonellae, capable of growth at 6.7 °C, or *Clostridium botulinum* capable of growth at 3.3 °C could cause food poisoning. Moreover, two other pathogens *Listeria monocytogenes* and *Yersinia enterocolitica* are psychrotrophic. Surveys have shown that up to 20% of cook chill meals may be contaminated with *Listeria*. Particular care needs to be taken, especially when regenerating using a microwave, that the meals are thoroughly reheated. Such possibilities mean it is essential that cook-chill units are properly designed, manned by staff with adequate training and incorporate quality control procedures of the type used by food manufacturers. The system recommended is one based on Hazard Analysis and Critical Control Points (HACCP) and involves close monitoring of the food process and the food environment. Catering units of the cook-chill type are really food manufacturing units, are best housed in purpose-built premises and are known as central production units (CPU).

Points to Note in a Cook Chill Operation

(a) Always buy good raw materials. Purchase to specifications otherwise 'rubbish in, rubbish out'.

(b) Cooking can be carried out in hygienically-designed production areas using traditional – type heavy duty catering equipment or on a larger scale, with food manufacturing equipment, e.g. large steam-jacketed kettles.

(c) Chilling
The function of the chilling phase is to reduce the temperature of the food to prevent/slow down microbial growth and enzyme activity (see sect. 11.6.4). The main method of chilling is blast-chilling and involves blowing cold air (at least $-4\ ^{\circ}C$) over the food (air velocity not less than 244 metres/min). In order that the food is cooled to below 3 °C within 1.5 hours (DHSS Guidelines) the depth of food should not be greater than 50 mm (food should cool at a speed of 15 mm/hour). The exact rate of chilling will depend on many factors including type and performance of the chiller, type of food (size, shape, thermal conductivity) as well as the temperature of the food entering the chiller. Alternative forms of chilling are likely to find increasing use including cryogenic chilling using liquid nitrogen or carbon dioxide and water immersion chilling (circulating water at +2 °C). Whichever method of chilling is used it should be as rapid as possible (without freezing the food) to maximise nutritional, organo-, leptic and microbiological quality. A complete time temperature record during chilling should be retained.

Generally speaking no special precautions need to be taken with recipe formulation for cook chill (unlike cook freeze). Sauce stability in cook chill should not present a problem although sauces thicken slightly as a result of cooling and are best made thinner than normal. Sauces may be best made separately from the food to prevent skinning. Care should be taken in the arrangement of the food for chilling to maximise surface area or to insulate delicate products from the base of the dish. Food temperatures should be checked during chilling with a probe thermometer.

(d) After chilling, food can be stored for up to five days (including day of production and day of consumption). Some systems based on water chilling, e.g. the Capkold system potentially offer much longer shelf life, up to 45 days. However, it is unlikely that such a long shelf life will be accepted in the

United Kingdom and it is more likely that 21 or 28 days (accepted in France) will be permitted. To avoid mistakes during storage a good system of labelling and stock rotation is required.

(e) Distribution

In its chilled form the food can be safely distributed, if required to a number of satellite units (i.e. regeneration sites served by the CPU). The distribution method must ensure that a temperature of below 3 °C is maintained. Should the distribution temperature exceed 5 °C the food should be regenerated and served within 12 hours. If the temperature were to exceed 10 °C the food should be discarded. When the distribution period is short and it is to be followed by immediate reheating insulated containers (with or without eutectic plates to help maintain low temperatures) can be used. For longer distribution journeys a refrigerated van is required.

(f) Prior to serving the food has to be regenerated (rethermalised) to a minimum centre temperature of 70 °C. This process can be carried out in regeneration kitchens of various sizes (from whole hospitals to ward level). Such kitchens require less equipment than traditional kitchens. The process of regeneration is integral to producing good quality food. Various methods of regeneration exist including infra-red, microwave (for small portions only) although increasing use is being made of combination ovens (combine convection cooking with low pressure steam).

13.5.2 COOK FREEZE

This system involves food being cooked then frozen (blast freezing) to −20 °C. The food is then stored at this temperature. When required it is rapidly heated thoroughly (regenerated) up to 80 °C at the centre and then served. Regeneration is best achieved by forced air convection ovens – microwave regeneration can leave 'cold spots'!

QUESTIONS

1. You are asked at an interview for a catering manager's job to explain the meaning of the term 'food hygiene'. Give a brief account of what your reply would be.

2. List four reasons why poor hygiene costs more than good hygiene.
3. Explain what is meant by the temperature danger zone in food storage.
4. Construct a ten-point code of practice for storage of food at refrigeration temperatures.
5. Proper cooking of food for safety depends on four key considerations. List and briefly describe each of these.
6. Briefly outline the cook chill system of catering and how it should be operated.

14

FOOD HYGIENE – PREVENTING CONTAMINATION OF FOODS

14.1 INTRODUCTION

Food hygiene is concerned with ensuring that food is safe to eat. Therefore, apart from preventing the growth of microorganisms in food (see Ch. 13) the aim is to avoid contamination of the food with anything that might make it unsafe or undesirable. Contamination can occur by toxic chemicals (see Sect. 12.4.2) or foreign bodies, e.g. glass, hair, plasters, metal splinters, paint, cigarette ends/ash, etc. More usually in catering, contamination worries are concerned with pathogenic microorganisms. It is essential before considering how food-poisoning organisms can pollute food to understand their sources and mechanisms of spread.

14.2 SOURCES OF FOOD-POISONING ORGANISMS

The sources, places where microorganisms commonly grow and multiply, have been discussed for the individual food-poisoning bacteria (see Sect. 12.6) but Fig. 14.1 summarises the main sources of food-poisoning organisms and how they can be spread to foods. Note that sometimes the harmful bacteria pass directly from the source to the food; more commonly they are transferred indirectly via an intermediate or vehicle of infection such as equipment, work surfaces, cutting boards, kitchen cloths, etc. Cross-contamination occurs whenever microorganisms are transferred from something that is infected to something that was previously uninfected with those organisms – the sequence of events being known as 'the route of infection':

source or   intermediate
  contaminated ⟶ surface, cloth ⟶ food
  object   or hands

For example,

gut of carrier ⟶ hands ⟶ cream

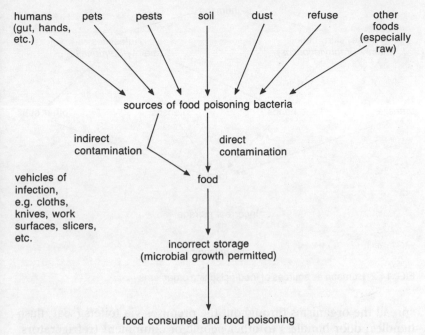

FIG. 14.1 Main sources of food-poisoning bacteria and their transfer to food

Surface of raw ⟶ knife ⟶ ham
 poultry

In any case of food poisoning the Environmental Health Officer will try to establish the route of infection and identify the source of the outbreak (see Sect. 12.9). Such investigations are also likely to expose any incorrect techniques in food handling practices on the part of the caterer.

14.2.1 HUMANS AS SOURCES OF FOOD-POISONING BACTERIA

All living things, plants and animals, harbour microorganisms. Staphylococcal food poisoning can nearly always be traced back to a human source. In addition, humans can also be important as a source of salmonellae which are harboured in the intestines. *Campylobacter* and *Clostridium perfringens* can also be isolated from the human gut and it is possible that human sources are important in some outbreaks.

Hands can contaminate food but arguably **the brain is the most important part of the anatomy in relation to food poisoning.** Lack of thought allows the hands to do the contaminating. Humans can

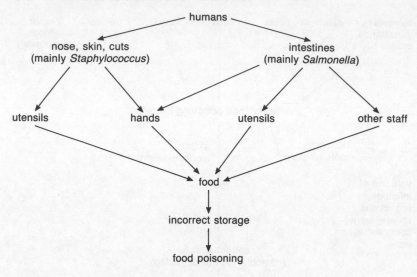

FIG. 14.2 Humans as sources of food-poisoning organisms

spread the organisms throughout the premises via toilets (seat, flush handles, door handles) to other people or equipment (refrigerators, handles, dishcloths, etc.). These intermediates may in turn contaminate food. It is not uncommon to find in an outbreak of food poisoning that a number of members of staff harbour the offending organism. **The function of good personal hygiene (see Sect. 14.4) is to prevent humans from contaminating food with harmful organisms.**

14.2.2 PETS

Cats and dogs are not taught the rules of hygiene and by their very nature sniff and touch contaminated material (soil, refuse, faecal material). The same animals, if permitted, could then lick and touch food, utensils and work surfaces – in this sense cats because they can jump up and walk on work surfaces pose more of a problem than dogs. Such behaviour potentially allows cross-contamination of food not only with food-poisoning bacteria but also other food-borne infections (see Sect. 12.3). Therefore pets should be barred from kitchens and people preparing food should take care to make sure that their hands are scrupulously clean before they start work if they have touched any animals.

14.2.3 PESTS

Pests can include insects (e.g. flies and cockroaches) and rodents (mice and rats). Flies can alight on contaminated matter, e.g. rubbish bins, animal excreta, etc., where they can pick up large numbers of microorganisms on their bodies. If they subsequently land on food, they can physically transfer pathogenic microorganisms on to it (cross-contamination), at the same time possibly polluting it with excreta or contaminated saliva.

Cockroaches, apart from infecting food with food-poisoning bacteria or other organisms causing food-borne infections, can contaminate it with moult cases (they possess an exoskeleton which has to be shed to allow growth) and taint it with an objectionable odour.

Rodents often live in sewers and may even feed on infected waste. Thus they can also contaminate food with a variety of harmful organisms. Rodents, in addition, can pollute food with droppings, urine and hair, as well as damaging the fabric of buildings by gnawing. This is not confined to gnaw holes in skirting boards (seen in many cartoons) but can extend to pipework and electric cables. Damage to the latter can lead to short circuits and a fire risk.

Though not generally considered as pests, some species of birds, including pigeons, sparrows and particularly in coastal areas, gulls, are nevertheless potential hazards. Scraps should not be put out to attract and feed birds as this will increase the chances of roosting and subsequent contamination of premises and food by droppings or feathers as well as causing a general nuisance.

Pest attacks are responsible for:
(a) A significant proportion of cases where food has been declared unfit (see Sect. 15.2.1).
(b) Many of the Emergency Closure Orders and prosecutions brought by Environmental Health Officers (see Sect. 15.1).

Pests, whatever their origin, can harbour and transmit food-borne disease organisms and so to prevent them from contaminating food, caterers are obliged, for legal and economic reasons, to ensure that they are absent from catering premises.

14.2.4 SOIL, WASTE, REFUSE

Soil contains many millions of microorganisms per gram. Caterers should realise that soil entering a kitchen on vegetables is likely to be heavily contaminated with microorganisms some of which may be harmful. *Salmonella* from animal faeces can survive more than a year in soil. Dust also contains large numbers of microorganisms, including bacteria and yeasts as well as bacterial and mould spores. Over 80 per cent of household dust is derived from dead skin cells, and open food should always be covered when cleaning operations are carried out. In some instances quite high numbers of *Salmonella* have been isolated from the inside of vacuum cleaners.

Refuse and waste often contain scraps of raw foods and other contaminated material as well as being an ideal breeding ground for flies and attracting other pests. Waste should not be allowed to accumulate in food rooms, it is far better to **clean as you go** and then clean up thoroughly at the end of each working day. If left until the following morning pests could have had a nocturnal banquet.

14.2.5 OTHER FOODS

Foods (other than salt) start off by being derived from living things. It is therefore inevitable that to a greater or lesser extent all food is contaminated. Even canned foods, which are heat processed, are usually only commercially sterile (see Sect. 11.6.3). Raw foods constitute the greatest problem (see Sect. 11.5.1) having a greater microbial load than cooked or processed foods. Vegetable/plant products start off by being polluted from the soil, air or from animals. Subsequent contamination occurs from equipment and handling. Figure 14.3 illustrates the range of food animals that can be infected with *Salmonella, Campylobacter* and *Clostridium perfringens*. Contamination starts at the time of slaughter when the hide and intestines are removed. Spillage of gut bacteria on to the carcass frequently occurs followed by further pollution from surfaces, equipment, air, water or from handling.

The actual rate of contamination of particular food products will vary according to the number of individuals in a herd or flock infected, the hygiene standards of the abattoir or processing plant,

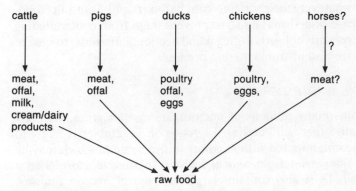

FIG. 14.3 Food animal reservoirs of food-poisoning bacteria.

and the degree of processing the food receives. Modern methods of intensive farming may increase the opportunity for individuals within a herd to infect others, e.g. one Salmonella-infected chicken in a battery hen house may soon infect many others. Infected animals may subsequently contaminate the abattoir, which in turn can infect animals from other herds (cross-contamination). Milk is now largely pasteurised to prevent it being a source of harmful bacteria; similarly all supplies of liquid, dried or frozen egg are heat treated.

The most hazardous items of raw food are likely to be red meat and offal, poultry, shellfish, raw milk and bulked egg.

Food animals themselves may be infected from other animals, contaminated feed or from the general environment (sewage, infected water, soil, pests, etc.) thus setting up a cycle of infection and re-infection which has proved difficult to break. Imports of meat and animal feed from abroad can introduce new types of *Salmonella* into the United Kingdom, further complicating the issue.

14.3   PREVENTING CONTAMINATION OF FOOD

The prevention of contamination of food is important at all stages from delivery of raw materials to service of final product (see Fig. 13.1).

14.3.1   PREVENTION OF CONTAMINATION PRIOR TO DELIVERY AT CATERING PREMISES

Caterers purchasing food have no way of knowing if the items delivered to them are contaminated with harmful microorganisms or not (unless a full microbiological analysis is carried out). They can, however, use their knowledge of hygiene to predict if this is likely. Therefore, they should observe the following, especially for high-risk food items.

1. Always buy from a reputable supplier. People with a good reputation have more to lose if they supply heavily contaminated foods.
2. Check that the delivery vehicle is clean and hygienically constructed (i.e. can be cleaned properly).
3. Note whether the delivery person is hygienically dressed with good personal habits, i.e. not smoking, has clean hands and nails (see Sect. 14.4).
4. Check that the food is hygienically stored in transit. Bad loading

for transport can lead to contamination. Avoid mixed loads where possible – one food could contaminate another. Carcass meat should always be transported separately. Segregate products to avoid cross-contamination. Sufficient space should be allowed between items to allow circulation of cold air.

5. Ensure that unloading is carried out quickly and hygienically with no depositing or stacking of open foods directly on the ground.

14.3.2 PREVENTION OF CONTAMINATION DURING STORAGE

Different foods will need to be stored in the most appropriate manner. Stored foods should be date marked clearly and a strict system of stock rotation should be operated.

Dry food stores

These should be well lit, cool and well ventilated. They should be fitted with proper storage racks, and stored foods should be examined regularly for signs of deterioration, i.e. rusting, mould growth, etc. Foods should be stored in appropriate containers, these should have tightly fitting lids, be easily cleaned and be stout enough to resist vermin attack. Goods should be inspected on arrival and regularly checked thereafter for signs of pest contamination. It has been known for pests brought in on a new consignment of food to spread out and infest other parts of the building.

Goods in dry stores should be stacked to allow access for cleaning and circulation of air, preferably at least 450 mm (18 in) from the ground.

Refrigeration and freezing

Refrigerators and freezers should be cleaned and defrosted regularly preferably with the stocks run down at the time of defrosting (see Sect. 18.7.2).

Ideally there should be separate refrigerators for raw and for cooked foods. In large walk-in refrigerators such foods should be well segregated. Cooked foods should be well covered, and protected from touching or dripping from defrosting foods. It is best to keep cooked and prepared food items at the top, i.e. the coldest part, of domestic-style refrigerators to minimise growth and contamination since such foods will receive no further treatment to reduce the microbial load. Ordinary cardboard or paper are not suitable packaging materials for refrigerated storage, and plastic or glass are superior. Strongly smelling foods, e.g. mackerel, should not be stored near foods that absorb odours easily, e.g. butter. Once opened, if needing refrigeration, tinned items should be removed from the tin and stored in glass or plastic containers to avoid any reaction between the tin and the food (especially acid foods).

14.3.3 PREVENTION OF CONTAMINATION IN FOOD PREPARATION AND SERVICE

The whole process of food preparation exposes food to the risk of contamination. Thus the following guidelines should be implemented.

Food handlers
Good standards of personal hygiene (see Sect. 14.4) should be observed by food handlers (see Sect. 15.2.2) and actual 'handling' of food should be minimised.

Food-preparation areas
These areas should be well designed and constructed and should be frequently and properly cleaned. A comprehensive account of correct design and construction is beyond the scope of this book. Generally speaking, correct design involves separation of preparation areas into 'clean zones' (i.e. those areas where foods nearly ready for consumption are finally prepared, e.g. cooked foods, cream trifles, etc.) and 'dirty zones' where raw food is prepared. The terms 'clean' and 'dirty' are not to be used literally but in a bacteriological sense, raw foods having a much higher microbial load. This arrangement of clean and dirty zones involves organising a logical work flow, i.e. work progresses in a single direction from raw material to finished product, this prevents 'backflow' or prepared foods being taken back into areas used for raw foods. Backflow increases greatly the possibility of cross-contamination. Work flow can be arranged in a number of different ways. Figure 14.4 suggests ways in which this could be organised in (a) a galley-type kitchen and (b) a squarish kitchen.

Environmental Health Officers, while being concerned with all parts used for food production, will be particularly anxious to see that the 'clean' areas are well looked after.

Correct construction and design of food-preparation areas is essential to facilitate proper and thorough cleaning. Walls, floors and ceilings should be constructed so that they can be quickly cleaned and are unlikely to allow pests harbourage or entrance. The choice of constructional materials for food premises will depend on the use to which they are to be put, the type of food being handled,

TABLE 14.1 Constructional materials for catering areas

Area	Materials/Finish	Advantages	Disadvantages	Comments
Ceiling	Absorbent acoustic tiles e.g. fibreboard fixed to metal lattice	*light in colour and weight	*difficult to clean *deteriorates if wet or attacked by vermin	*should be as free as possible from ducts, beams, etc. *preferably no opening to outside, skylights, etc. *light colour reflects light *good local ventilation may be necessary to prevent condensation *good insulation or hot blowers at ceiling height minimize condensation
	paint on plaster	*light in colour *easily cleaned	*condensation can collect and drip onto food	
Work surfaces	Wood	*none – not to be used	*porous. *can crack *difficult to sanitize	*should have vertical upstanding approximately 200 mm high to reduce soiling of walls and food particles contaminating floors and rear of work surfaces
	Stainless steel	*durable *impermeable *easy to clean	*expensive	
	Laminated plastics, e.g. formica	*cheap *impermeable when new	*can deteriorate *can be scored by knives *can crack *susceptible to intense heat *care needed to seal edges	

	Material	Advantages	Disadvantages	General notes
	Marble	*impervious *easily cleaned *good for pastry	*not suitable for chopping/cutting *expensive *care required when setting up	
Walls	Glazed ceramic tiles	*durable with careful treatment *waterproof if mastic or silicone grouting is used	*lots of joints *can crack/be damaged by trolleys, etc. *need to be carefully applied – no air pockets in adhesive *corners/walls may need protection by metal or PVC angle pieces or rails *difficult to repair when damaged	*should be light in colour. *should be of solid construction (brick or block) Stud partitions not suitable for food preparation areas *finish needs to be at least 6 feet in height *window sills, etc. in walls should be sloped to prevent debris accumulating and facilitate cleaning
	Glazed masonry blocks	*see ceramic tiles	*expensive *care required in fixing and jointing to prevent trapping of dirt	
	Metal sheeting – stainless steel or food quality aluminium	*impervious *hardwearing	*care needed with fixing *relatively expensive	
	Plastic wall cladding, many varieties including PVC and polypropylene.	*impervious. *joints filled with silicone sealant *polypropylene joints can be welded		

TABLE 14.1 Contd

Area	Materials/Finish	Advantages	Disadvantages	Comments
	Polymer coating, e.g. epoxy resin – see floors, or resin bonded fibreglass.	*can be applied over existing finish *impervious *tough finish *impermeable *impact-resistant surface	*expensive	
	Paints, various types. Only use heavy duty washable paints in food areas.	*cheap *can incorporate fungicides to inhibit mould growth. *see code of practice on food quality paints	*expensive *only usable in areas not subject to heavy wear *can flake and get into food *ordinary emulsion paints not suitable	
Floor	Quarry tiles	*hardwearing if laid correctly *care needed with grouting *can be made non slip *coved tiles available	*numerous joints which can collect dirt if not properly cleaned *can crack and lift *can be noisy to walk on	No one surface is suitable for all areas of a catering establishment, but: *floors should be non-slip *should be sloped to allow easy drainage (1 inch in every 10 feet) *angle between wall and floor should be coved
	Thermoplastic tiles	*cheap *variety of colours and patterns	*numerous joints can harbour dirt *not hardwearing	

Terrazo tiles	*attractive finish *hardwearing	*see tiles in general *care needed in laying *subject to certain types of chemical attack
Welded vinyl sheets	*smooth sheet material *range of colours and patterns *vinyl cove skirtings available	*small number of joints *not so hardwearing *subfloor needs to be smooth and particle free to minimise wear *can be slippery
Epoxy resin (similarly polyester)	*hardwearing *resistant to chemicals *non-slip unless very wet. *joint-free *varied colours	*food may need protection/be absent during application *high initial cost *can absorb moisture if constantly wet
Concrete	*low initial cost *can be improved by the addition of granite chippings (granolithic concrete) and use of sealers	*not suitable for wet areas *can crack *can generate/attract dust *subject to chemical attack
Mastic ashphalt	*joint-free *impermeable *can be coved to form skirting	*can be slippery when wet *can be susceptible to some chemicals *can be damaged by heavy equipment

the type of food soil which is likely to occur and the preferences of the architect-hygiene consultant. Each type of constructional finish has its own advantages and disadvantages.

To facilitate cleaning surfaces of walls, floors, ceilings and work

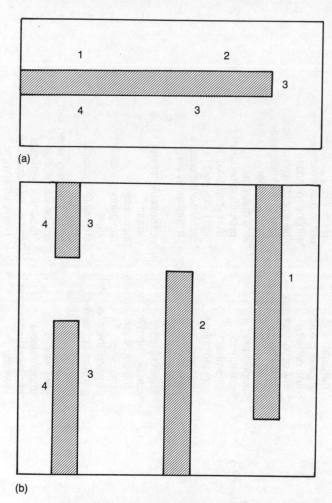

(a)

(b)

1 : Initial preparation area–dirty
2 : Further preparation of raw foods
3 : Cooking areas
4 : Final preparation of cooked items, sweets, etc.–clean

: Partitions at least 4 ft high of solid construction and covered with smooth, impervious, easily cleaned material

FIG. 14.4 Plan for the layouts of: (a) galley-style kitchen; (b) squarish kitchen

surfaces should be smooth, impervious to water, resistant to cleaning chemicals, durable and as economic as possible in installation and maintenance. Table 14.1 illustrates some of the main type of finishes in use with some of their advantages and disadvantages.

Lighting and ventilation should be good (see Chs. 18 and 19). Adequate washing facilities should be provided in food-preparation areas to encourage good standards of personal hygiene, e.g. sinks for hand washing in areas for the handling of raw meat.

Cleaning

Premises should cleaned correctly using appropriate materials (see Ch. 8) according to a written cleaning programme. This should state how often cleaning is to be carried out, the details of the cleaning methods and the person responsible. Thorough cleaning reduces the number of microorganisms in the food environment and the opportunity for contamination of food. The rule in catering is **clean as you go.**

Equipment and work surfaces

It is vital that work surfaces are microbially clean before they are used for food preparation. **Failure to observe this rule will lead to cross contamination.** All surfaces that are likely to come into contact with food should be smooth, impervious, joint-free and easily cleaned. Equipment should be constructed with the rules of hygiene in mind, should not permit accumulation of food debris and should be sited for ease of cleaning. In addition to being easily cleaned, the surfaces should be durable, non-toxic and resistant to heat and chemicals. The most frequently used materials are stainless steel and plastic laminates as they meet most of the above requirements. Wood is porous, tends to crack and traps moisture and micro-organisms in a layer near the surface. Consequently, proper cleaning is difficult, e.g. a butcher's chopping block requires considerable effort to clean. In wholesale butchery wooden blocks have now been replaced with synthetic ones. Cutting boards should be of hard synthetic rubber, polyethylene or polypropylene as these are easily sanitised.

Separate work surfaces and equipment should be used for the preparation of raw and cooked foods **this is essential to prevent cross contamination.** Equipment for raw foods should either be of a different colour (e.g. knife handles) or be clearly marked in some way to identify them as being for raw food only. Never use equipment for preparing cooked foods if it has previously been used for raw food. The use of colour-coded chopping boards is now considered mandatory in National Health Service catering. Cross contamination associated with incorrect use of chopping boards is now recognized as a cause of food poisoning. Where it might be impracticable to duplicate equipment, e.g. a slicer, then slice cooked foods first, then raw foods and then clean the slicer. Take particular care with equipment and surfaces touching raw poultry. Salmonellae originating from poultry can survive for hours on work surfaces and equipment long after the original bird has been eaten.

Catering dishcloths are breeding grounds for millions of micro-organisms and have been implicated as vehicles of cross-contamination in a number of food-poisoning outbreaks. Disposable cloths are best, failing that, cloths should be sterilised properly and frequently. The catering practice of partially drying dirty wet cloths on the top of hot cupboards and then re-using them is, needless to say, unhygienic and dangerous!

In the service of food, clean tongs, spatulas, etc., are to be used minimising the use of hands. The practice of licking fingers to separate paper sheets, or blowing into bags to facilitate wrapping of food, is also unhygienic.

Food on display should also be protected from contamination by the customer, e.g. coughing, sneezing or touching. Precautions should be taken to eliminate flies or other pests.

14.3.4 WASTE DISPOSAL

Considerable quantities of refuse are produced as a result of catering procedures. This should be stored correctly to avoid attracting pests, producing unpleasant odours, as well as to reduce the risk of contaminating food.

Short-term storage is best in foot-operated (reduces risk of contamination of hands) bins with plastic lining sacks (paper disintegrates when wet). Longer-term storage should be in bins with tight-fitting lids (avoids entry by pets or pests) and stored out of direct sunlight in an area raised off the ground for ease of cleaning. Much taller cylindrical metal bins on castors are suitable for businesses producing larger amounts of refuse. Plastic sacks given out by many local authorities may be cheaper to use but suffer attacks by roving pets and pests that scatter their contents over roads and pavements. For larger quantities of waste, refuse compactors can be used to reduce bulky items to a more convenient size.

Another approach to the problem of getting rid of refuse is to install a waste disposal unit. Food is macerated and then flushed into the drainage system. Domestic units are not usually powerful enough to cope with catering waste, and it is better to have a separately plumbed and drained commercial waste disposal unit. These units should not be fed too quickly and sufficient water should subsequently be allowed to enter the drains to flush away any residue which might collect and cause a blockage. Whichever method is used, waste should never be allowed to accumulate and should be disposed of quickly.

14.4   PERSONAL HYGIENE

Food handling is an important function of all aspects of the catering flow system. For this reason personal hygiene must be good in order to prevent pathogenic organisms passing from humans to food. It is up to the management of all catering establishments to foster good attitudes towards hygiene and to provide good facilities for it to be implemented.

14.4.1 HANDS

We have already stated that hands are the most important part of the body (after the brain!) in relation to food poisoning. It therefore follows that they should be washed correctly and as frequently as is necessary (see Table 14.2). After washing, hands should be dried using disposable paper towels, hot air driers or continuous automatic roller towels. Even when hands are washed properly, it would be unwise to assume that they were free of all micro-organisms (hence the need for good personal habits). Salmonellae are relatively easy to wash off but staphylococci have adapted to living on the skin and are difficult to remove for other than relatively short periods.

Frequent hand washing, common in catering, removes the skin's natural oils and an antiseptic barrier cream is useful to prevent the hands drying out.

Finger-nails should be short and clean as millions of bacteria could be trapped underneath. Nail varnish, or false finger-nails, should not be worn. The only jewellery that catering workers should wear is a plain gold wedding ring. Rings with clasps, stones, settings, etc., can harbour dirt, and stones may become detached and lost in food. Any cuts, spots, abrasions, burns or infected areas of the skin should be protected by an adequate waterproof dressing. These should, preferably, be brightly coloured with a fine metal

TABLE 14.2 Rules for hand washing

Rules for hand washing	Why it is important
Wash hands before handling food	Bacteria already on the hands could cause food poisoning
Wash hands after visiting toilet	Potential food-poisoning bacteria from gut and faeces get on to the hands
Wash hands after blowing the nose, coughing or sneezing	Many people harbour a particular type of food-poisoning bacteria in their noses
Wash hands after smoking; never smoke in food-preparation areas	Bacteria from the nose and lips are transferred on to the hands during smoking
Wash hands between handling raw foods and cooked foods	To prevent transfer of bacteria from heavily contaminated raw foods to uncontaminated cooked foods, i.e. to prevent cross-contamination
Wash hands after handling refuse or similar 'dirty' jobs	To prevent cross-contamination

Hand washing should be thorough and involve the use of plenty of hot soapy water!

strip, both of which make detection in food easier, should this be necessary.

14.4.2 HEAD: HAIR, NOSE AND MOUTH

The heads of catering workers should have adequate protective covering, and long hair should be tied back. The protective headgear should be functional as well as decorative and hair nets may need to be worn. The use of hair clips should be avoided in case they should fall out and get into food accidently. Touching, combing or alterations to hair should be carried out in the staff rest-room and be followed by hand washing. There should be no coughing or sneezing over food, and disposable paper handkerchiefs should be used when necessary, followed by hand washing. Although never mentioned in hygiene manuals, moustaches, common amongst chefs, probably constitute more of a health risk than long hair as they filter out nasal discharges as well as trapping food particles. Many people with moustaches have developed affectations, e.g. touching or twirling them while deep in thought. Staff who have moustaches should take care not to bring about cross-contamination.

Good manners as well as hygiene demands no chewing of gum or spitting while food is being prepared. Workers suffering from any nose, eye or ear discharges should report to their supervisor and not handle open food. No false eyelashes or dangling ear rings should be worn in case they fall into food.

Personal habits should be good with no nail-biting, touching of spots, etc., while food is prepared. When food is tasted, as it inevitably is in catering, a clean spoon should be used each time. Never taste food and return the spoon to the food without cleaning.

Smoking, of course, is illegal in food-preparation areas as it increases the likelihood of contamination of fingers as well as possible pollution of food with ash or cigarette ends. It is often possible to see burn marks in formica work surfaces (from left cigarette ends) in kitchens where staff have been illegally smoking!

14.4.3 PROTECTIVE CLOTHING

Catering staff should wear clean, light-coloured, easily washable protective clothing for preparing food. Clothing should preferably have no top pockets (items can fall out of pockets into food). Short-sleeved overalls should not be worn over long-sleeved garments. 'Whites' should not be worn in areas other than the staff rest-room or food-preparation areas – this would defeat the prime objective of clothing not contaminating food with 'outside' organisms.

14.4.4 GENERAL HEALTH

Staff members with eye, ear or nose discharges, infected cuts, abrasions, styes or whitlows should not handle open food. The same rule should apply to personnel with unexplained stomach upsets, as these could be caused by a food-transmitted organism and there could be a risk spreading the infection to food and to other people.

Many of the rules of personal hygiene for food handlers are of course legal requirements (see Ch. 15).

14.5 FACILITIES TO BE PROVIDED TO ASSIST GOOD HYGIENE

Good hygiene is a management responsibility. It is in the manager's interests to ensure his staff are hygienic and therefore should do his best to provide a hygienic working atmosphere and show his commitment to hygiene.

14.5.1 EDUCATION

Education of staff as to the importance and reasons for food hygiene is essential (see Table 14.3) in order that food be prepared in a safe manner. Adequate notices to remind staff of the requirements of food hygiene should be provided (a legal requirement in toilet areas). It is a good idea to issue personnel with attractive, free, protective clothing as an incentive. Relevant hygiene training should be given to all new staff before they pick up bad habits. Numerous appropriate courses in hygiene are available either in Colleges or Environmental Health Departments. Staff are to be encouraged to pursue these courses and gain Certificates or Diplomas in Hygiene.

TABLE 14.3 Reasons for rules of personal hygiene

Rule	Reason
Personal habits should be good, for instance nail-biting, spitting, touching of ears, hair or nose, dipping of fingers into food and returning of licked spoons into food should not be allowed	The human body can harbour food-poisoning bacteria which can be transferred to foods
Any cuts, spots, burns, etc., should be protected by waterproof dressings	Infected areas store potential food-poisoning bacteria in large numbers
Finger-nails must be short; do not wear nail varnish	Bacteria can be trapped under finger-nails in large numbers
Always wear clean, protective overalls and head coverings; do not wear short-sleeved overalls over long-sleeved jumpers, etc.; outdoor clothing must be kept well away from food production areas	Many bacteria can be trapped in the outer and inner layers of ordinary clothing which could contaminate food
Do not wear hair clips, loose jewellery, rings (other than a plain gold wedding ring)	Jewellery can fall into foods; large numbers of bacteria can be trapped next to the skin under jewellery and can be transferred on to food
Tell your superior if you are suffering from a stomach upset (diarrhoea, vomiting, abdominal pain), skin or throat infection	Any of these conditions can be caused by bacteria capable of causing food poisoning and, therefore, there is a greater possibility of food being contaminated with harmful organisms just by your presence

14.5.2 SINKS

Sufficient, correctly sited sinks solely for the purposes of food hygiene (i.e. not for washing food or equipment) should be provided. Ideally such sinks should be foot-operated, leverage taps, correctly used, are the next best) and be provided with hot water, soap, nail-brush and a means of hand drying.

14.5.3 STAFF FACILITIES

Suitable staff facilities including toilets, lockers, changing facilities and even showers should be provided. These should all be kept clean and in good working order. Ideally, toilets should be foot-operated (reduces cross-contamination) and approximately one for every fifteen members of staff. Syphonic-type toilets are more hygienic than the 'wash down' variety and all toilets should be ventilated and separated from a food-preparation area. Notices reminding staff about hand washing should be clearly evident. Staff members should be provided with a locker suitable for the storage of outside clothes. First-aid kits should be available and contain scissors and antiseptic as well as an assortment of dressings, including waterproof ones. Sometimes fingerstalls are included but these can become detached and get into food.

QUESTIONS

1. Explain, using examples, the terms 'cross-contamination' and the 'route of infection'.
2. Construct a five-point code of practice you would suggest a caterer should follow to deal with a delivery of meat.
3. Explain the use of the terms 'clean zone' and 'dirty zone' in describing a food-preparation area.
4. You are asked as a catering manager to explain, to a recent school leaver who has just started hotel work, the principles and practice of personal hygiene. Give a brief account of your explanation and produce a list of key rules the school leaver should obey.
5. Construct a diagram showing the main sources of food-poisoning bacteria and how they might contaminate food.

15

FOOD HYGIENE – LEGISLATION

15.1 INTRODUCTION

The consequences of food poisoning can be serious and sometimes fatal, because of this successive governments in the United Kingdom have decided that legislation is necessary to ensure that the public is not exposed to undue risk from food. Therefore there is a legal obligation on those people who prepare and sell food to ensure that it is safe to eat. Caterers not adhering to relevant legislation, or found to be quilty of causing food poisoning, face prosecution which can result in fines, imprisonment or closure of premises.

To ensure that the legislation is correctly implemented, local authorities employ teams of Environmental Health Officers (EHO, these used to be called Public Health Inspectors, PHI) whose job it is to regularly inspect food and food premises. Environmental Health Officers have the right to inspect food premises at any reasonable time and without prior warning or notification. The officer has the power to remove, for analysis, samples of food which he feels could lead to food poisoning or are unfit for human consumption. In addition to knowing about how microbial growth and contamination of food can occur (see Chs. 13 and 14) caterers, for the following reasons, should be acquainted with the various Acts of food hygiene legislation:

(a) To understand what the law expects of them.
(b) To know how to maintain premises under their control in a legal manner.
(c) To handle and store food in a legal manner.
(d) To organise staff in legal hygienic food handling and to prevent illegal work practices.
(e) To educate and inform others about food hygiene legislation.

Note: the person in charge of any food premises is guilty of an offence if he fails to take reasonable steps to ensure that the food legislation is obeyed.

15.2 FOOD LAW

There is now more legislation concerning food than any other commodity. The two main principles underlying food law are the prevention of deception and the maintenance of food safety. Other important features of new food legislation are the requirement to register all premises, and the requirement that all food handlers receive hygiene training.

Types of Legislation
The caterer will encounter different legal terminology:

Acts	these are passed by Parliament and set out the main principles of the Law, e.g. Food Safety Act, 1990.
Regulations	these give more detail than the Acts which they support, e.g. Food Hygiene (General) Regulations 1970 or the Food Hygiene (Amendment) Regulations, 1990.
Local Acts	Bylaws made by local authorities
E.C. Directives	made by the European Parliament
Codes of Practice	give guidance as to how the law will be interpreted and are intended primarily for Environmental Health Officers and Trading Standards Officers. Codes of Practice are of interest to specialists in hygiene within larger catering organisations, e.g. Codes of Practice on Food Hygiene Inspections.

15.3 SPECIFIC LEGISLATION

15.3.1 FOOD SAFETY ACT, 1990

This is a wide ranging law which strengthens and updates the law on food safety and consumer protection. Besides revising and strengthening the main offences in previous food acts it contains a number of new features. The Act itself is divided up into sections.

The Act defines the word food and for the first time includes products such as slimming aids, chewing gum and water used in food production.

The main offences under the Act are:
* selling, or possessing for sale, food which does not comply with the food safety requirements, i.e. food unfit or so contaminated that it would be unreasonable to expect it to be eaten;

* rendering food injurious to health, i.e. intentionally adding something to food to make it harmful or inadequately heat processing food;
* selling to the purchasers prejudice food which is not of the substance, nature or quality demanded by the consumer, e.g. selling cod described as haddock;
* falsely or misleadingly describing or presenting food, e.g. when statements or pictures concerning food are untrue.

Although the law is passed by central government it will usually be enforced on caterers by local authorities, either by Trading Standards Officers or Environmental Health Officers. These officers can enter premises to investigate possible offences, inspect food to see if it is safe and detain and seize food. Any seized food is taken to a Justice of Peace (J.P.) and if he agrees that the food is unsafe then it will be condemned and destroyed.

In the course of these duties E.H.O.'s must be allowed entry at all reasonable times and during the inspection can examine records or take photographs. If an E.H.O. believes that a food business does not comply with hygiene or processing regulations he may:
* issue an improvement notice requiring the proprietor to put matters right;
* impose a prohibition order (if he feels the public is at risk) which closes all or part of a business;
* issue an emergency prohibition order, if he thinks that the premises give rise to an imminent risk to health.

If a caterer is charged with offences under the Act he can defend himself in court. The principal defence which can be used is that of due diligence. This defence enables a person to be acquitted of an offence if they can prove that they took all reasonable precautions and exercised all due diligence to avoid committing the offence. This part of the legislation is potentially very important for the caterer because in order to prove due diligence they will usually need to have some form of quality assurance programme in operation, i.e. some record keeping of how the food was stored, handled, cooked, etc.

The penalties for food companies/caterers found guilty of an offence have been greatly increased. Crown courts will be able to send offenders to prison for up to 2 years and/or impose unlimited fines. Magistrates courts will generally be able to impose fines of up to £2000 per offence and a prison sentence of up to 6 months, although for some offences the maximum fine may be £20,000.

15.3.2 FOOD HYGIENE (GENERAL) REGULATIONS 1970 (as amended 1990 and 1991)

This is probably the single most important set of regulations of concern to caterers. A useful guide to these regulations is produced (free of charge) by the Health Education Council. This guide can be distributed to staff but catering managers would be well advised to get a copy of the actual regulations and having read it make it available for staff inspection.

Scope of the regulations

The food hygiene regulations apply to all premises where food is produced, e.g. clubs, cafés, etc., except those where other regulations apply (e.g. in dairies). The hygiene regulations cover people owning, managing or working in food premises. Included in the regulations is a description of a food handler as 'anyone who is involved in any process or operation in the sale of food'. This includes people who clean equipment coming into contact with food as well as cashiers touching food in supermarket check-outs.

The regulations apply to all types of food except cream and milk. Particular emphasis is made concerning open food, i.e. food which is not protected from contamination.

Premises

The regulations state that food premises must be constructed properly, kept clean, well lit and ventilated and be maintained in good condition. The food premises must allow for good hygienic practices to be operated and thus must have:

1. Adequate clean and wholesome hot and cold water.
2. Sufficient sanitary conveniences with a notice saying, – '**Wash your hands**' clearly visible. Toilets must be clean, must not be in, or open directly into, a food room and must be in good working order.
3. Sufficient sinks and washbasins. Sinks used for equipment should be clean and must not be used for hand washing. Washbasins should be sited for easy access and use and should be provided with soap, nail-brushes and a means of hand drying.
4. Proper facilities for staff welfare including a first-aid box and cupboards and lockers.
5. Proper facilities for storage of food and protecting it from contamination.
6. Efficient facilities for waste disposal.

278 FOOD HYGIENE – LEGISLATION

Food storage requirements
1. Foods, considered as high-risk foods, i.e. those allowing the growth of food-poisoning bacteria, must be stored correctly. Examples given of high-risk foods include meat and meat products, game, poultry, fish, gravy, imitation cream, cream and milk products. Such foods, unless they are put out for sale or are about to be served, must be stored above 62.8 °C or below 8 °C (or 5 °C for highest risk foods).
2. Possibilities for food contamination should be kept to a minimum. Raw food should be stored separately from cooked foods and neither should be stored where there is a risk of contamination. Food should not be wrapped or placed in a container likely to lead to contamination. Live animals, pets or pests, should be excluded from food-handling areas. Food on display should be correctly screened or covered.

Personal hygiene
Personal hygiene for food handlers should be good:
1. Hands should be clean.
2. Personal habits should be good.
3. No smoking or spitting should be allowed.
4. All open cuts or infections to be protected by a waterproof dressing.
5. Adequate clean protective clothing to be worn.
6. Staff health should be good and any unexplained stomach upsets (diarrhoea and vomiting), septic cuts, knowledge of being a carrier of certain illnesses or discharges, e.g. from the eye, ear or nose, should be reported.
   Food handlers themselves have a legal responsibility for complying with the rules on cleanliness but supervisors or managers who fail to take reasonable steps to ensure that the regulations are carried out are also guilty of an offence.

In addition to the legislation mentioned the government also publishes a number of Food Hygiene Codes of Practice relating to specific situations, e.g. Hygiene in the Retail Fish Trade, Hygiene in Microwave Cooking, Hygiene in the Operation of Coin Operated Food Vending Machines.

The Food Hygiene (Amendment) Regulations 1990 have altered the temperature at which certain foods must be kept. The old regulations specified high risk foods to be stored below 10 °C, this has been further reduced to 8 °C and from April 1st 1993 some high risk foods will have to be kept below 5 °C. Foods falling into the second category, e.g. portions of ripened soft cheeses, cooked products containing meat, fish, eggs, etc. are those foods which are especially prone to contamination by psychotrophic organisms.

QUESTIONS

1. List five reasons why it is important for caterers to have some knowledge of food-hygiene standards.
2. Explain the series of events likely to take place if a caterer is thought to be selling food that is 'unfit'.
3. Produce a brief summary of the Food Hygiene Regulations, 1970.
4. A catering establishment is so badly run that the Environmental Health Officer considers it to be an imminent danger to public health. Which item of legislation could be used to deal with the problem and what is likely to happen.

ILLUMINATION

16.1 INTRODUCTION

The efficiency, comfort and safety in which caterers can perform a specific task will depend on how well they can see to do it! Lighting requirements will depend on the particular area being lit, e.g. kitchens require greater illumination than bedrooms, recommended minimum illumination levels are quoted in Table 16.1 for a range of hotel situations. In addition to improving lighting standards in a hotel, illumination can often be used to create a particular atmosphere using a combination of lighting and décor. Absorption and reflection of light in light fittings and from the décor of a room will give rise to varying colours of illumination which, if used properly, can greatly enhance the appearance and attractiveness of food, e.g. in display cabinets.

16.2 LIGHT

Light can be explained using two theories, both of which can be proved experimentally:
1. Light consists of streams of particles or packets of energy travelling at a speed of 3×10^8 m s^{-1}.
2. Light consists of a wave motion with a pattern similar to ripples on a pond. Light is an electromagnetic wave and visible light (which the eye can detect) has a wavelength of $(4-7) \times 10^{-9}$ Hz in the electromagnetic spectrum. White light consists of seven colours: red, orange, yellow, green, blue, indigo, violet; violet light has the shortest and red light the longest wavelength.

Electromagnetic waves with wavelengths shorter than those in the visible are termed 'ultra-violet' (UV) and those just longer 'infra-red' (IR) light. Ultra-violet light has bactericidal properties and can be used in food manufacturing establishments for the surface sterilisation of products prior to packaging, although its use in catering *per se* is somewhat limited. Infra-red radiation is widely used in catering for its heating effect in cookers. Infra-red lamps can commonly be seen above serving counters where they keep plated meals warm.

16.2.1 UNITS OF LIGHTING

Earliest standards involved candles as the source of light power but differences occur according to candle size. Not surprisingly the candela (cd) was chosen as the SI unit of luminous efficiency. The usual unit used for a source as an everyday measurement is the lumen (lu) where:

1 candela $= 4\,\pi$ lumen

The intensity of illumination received from a given source at a particular surface is measured in lux (lx). One lux is the illumination produced in one square metre per second by a source of one lumen.

16.3 RECOMMENDED ILLUMINATION LEVELS

There is a recommended minimum illumination level for any particular hotel situation (see Table 16.1). The values specified are to ensure maximum comfort but are for people with good eyesight enabling them to work free from eye-strain. Illumination levels

TABLE 16.1 Recommended minimum illumination levels

Area	Level of illumination (lx)
Bedrooms	50
Cloakrooms/toilets	100
Corridors/passageways	100
Stairs	100
Dining room	100
Lounge	100
Entrance halls	150
Food stores	150
Lifts	150
Bedhead	150
Restaurant, at table	200
Reception	300
Restaurant, at counter	300
Study	400
Kitchen (general and food preparation)	500
Cash desk	500
Display in supermarket	900
Bright sunlight out-of-doors	100 000

quoted in the table are minimum values and many people, particularly older people, prefer a higher level.

16.4 CALCULATION OF LIGHTING REQUIREMENTS

Two formulae can be used for determining the number of filament or fluorescent lamps necessary to provide the correct illumination level for any catering area (see Table 16.2). The floor area must be measured in square metres and the minimum illumination necessary obtained from Table 16.1.

Specimen calculations are illustrated below (see Table 16.2).

TABLE 16.2 Methods of calculation of approximate total wattage for rooms

1. Using Table 16.1 for recommended minimum illumination levels.
Formula 1

wattage = factor × illumination level × floor area
    (F)   (lx)   (m²)

F is used to convert the approximate lamp wattage to lux. (lx).

Light fitting	type	Factor for room areas (m²)		
		up to 11.5	11.5 to 24	over 24
Direct, semi-indirect	filament	0.37	0.32	0.26
General diffusing, semi-indirect	fluorescent*	0.085	0.065	0.045
Indirect	filament	0.7	0.6	0.5
	fluorescent*	0.13	0.12	0.1

* Assuming high efficiency fluorescent tubes.

Typical calculations
Small food store, recommended minimum illumination level (from Table 16.1) 150 lux. Area 3 m × 3 m = 9 m².
Fittings – fluorescent tubes.

Total wattage = 0.085 × 150 × 9
              = 114 W

If 40 W tubes were used, three 40 W tubes would be required.

2. Using the formula:
Formula 2

$$N = \frac{E \times A}{F \times M \times U}$$

Where N = number of lamps of specified wattage and type,
       E = illumination at surface in lux (lx),

Table 16.2 Contd

A = area of working surface in square metres (m^2),
M = maintenance factor,
U = utilisation factor,
F = lamp power in lumens (lu).

The utilisation factor will depend on:
(a) The particular light fitting.
(b) The shape of the room.
(c) The height of the fitting above the work surface.
(d) The reflectance of the surface.

Values of U range from 0.3 to 0.7 and an average value can be taken as 0.5. The maintenance factor depends on the light lost due to dirt in fittings, room surfaces and is normally taken as 0.8.

Formula simplifies to:

$$N = \frac{E \times A}{F \times 0.4}$$

Using 40 W fluorescent tubes which give 1160 lx (see Table 16.5).

$$N = \frac{150 \times 9}{1160 \times 0.4}$$
$$= 2.90$$

Therefore, three lamps of 40 W are required, as obtained with formula 1.

16.5 MEASUREMENT OF ILLUMINATION

This can be determined using a suitable light meter. It is important to measure the light actually at the working surface. In a typical kitchen the level can vary from 1500 lx at windows to 150 lx on the working area furthest away. A typical pocket meter (see Fig. 16.1) has a range of from 0 to 2000 lx with a set of range factors. The light window on the meter containing the photoelectric cell must be 'unhinged' so that it is horizontal to receive illumination.

Any area in a hotel which does not meet the lighting requirements listed in Table 16.1 must be modified by increasing the lamp wattage or using a different fitting, etc.

16.6 DAYLIGHT AND ARTIFICIAL LIGHT

Hotels rely on a combination of daylight and artificial lighting. Artificial lighting is controllable and uniform in all parts of a room

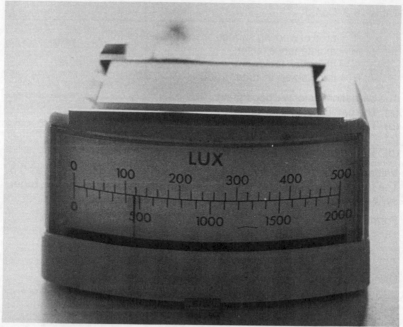

(a)

(b)

FIG. 16.1 A light meter (a) a typical pocket light meter (b) using a pocket light meter to assess illumination levels in a kitchen

whereas daylight varies with weather conditions and window size and location. The lighting requirements of various areas within a hotel must be carefully considered at the design stage. Integration of daylight and artificial light is particularly important in those rooms with limited window area.

16.6.1 DAYLIGHTING

The initial design and spacing of buildings plus surroundings are affected by daylight considerations. In most environments a lighting level of 300–500 lx is acceptable (see Table 16.1) but direct sunlight can give illumination of 60 000 lx. The amount of light received in a room is composed of:

1. Direct light in the room.
2. Reflected light from any external surfaces and the internal surfaces (walls, floors, ceilings).

   These will depend on the following factors:
   (a) Sky conditions: time of day or year and weather conditions.
   (b) The size, shape and position of the windows.
   (c) The type of glass used and whether the window is double glazed.
   (d) The cleanliness of the windows. Dirty windows can reduce light transmission by about 20 per cent. The cleaning of windows (inside and outside) should take place approximately every 2 weeks.
   (e) The effect of any obstruction.
   (f) The reflectance of the décor in the room interior.

Colour, texture and pattern influence the level of illumination; dark colours absorb light, light colours reflect light. In view of the variation of daylight levels, a standard was chosen for daylight analysis as 5000 lx at ground level. Daylight factors were then applied to give minimum daylight standards for various areas; For example for kitchens the value is 2 per cent, i.e. 100 lx, for bedrooms the value is 0.5 per cent, i.e. 25 lx. The daylight factor is the ratio (expressed as a percentage) of the illumination received indoors to the illumination received simultaneously at an unobstructed point out of doors. Where integrated light (daylight plus artificial) is necessary, the artificial light must blend with daylight. The types of lamp which can be used to provide artificial lighting are described in the next section – the lamp which provides the best blend with natural light is a fluorescent light with appropriate colour rendering (see Sect. 16.6.4).

16.6.2 ARTIFICIAL LIGHTING

Filament lamps

When an electric current is passed through a high-resistance wire it produces a heating effect. This is the basis of heating elements where high-resistance nichrome is used as the element material. In a filament lamp the filament is made of tungsten wire sealed in a glass bulb filled with inert gas (argon). The current causes the wire to reach a temperature of almost 3000 °C at which level of heat it produces incandescence (i.e. it gives out light). The pressure of the inert gas reduces evaporation of the filament and enables the bulb to operate at a higher temperature to give increased light output without reducing lamp life.

Standard bulbs have a rated life of approximately 1000 hr and the most likely cause of lamp failure is vibration. Bulbs can differ physically in size and type of connection to the holder but fall into three types of finish:
1. Clear glass, giving a harsh light.
2. Roughened inside surface, termed a 'pearl' bulb and giving a softer, more diffused light. This is the best type for general purpose use.
3. Coated internally with a powder (silica) to give an even greater light diffusion than for pearl bulbs.

Clear and pearl bulbs provide an almost identical illumination but silica – coated lamps give less light (approximately 10 W). A typical filament lamp is illustrated in Fig. 16.2.

Discharge lamps

A current is passed through a gas or vapour to produce a luminous arc. Typical examples include sodium and mercury discharge lamps. This type of lamp is used in street lighting and for commercial interiors or displays and for hotel car parks. They take several minutes to reach full light output.

Fluorescent light fittings

Materials which emit visible light when ultra-violet light is shone on to them are said to be 'fluorescent'.

Fluorescent lamps contain low-pressure mercury vapour which produces ultra-violet radiation when a voltage is applied (see Fig. 16.2). The inside of the tube is coated with a material which fluoresces on exposure to ultra-violet light thus emitting visible light. The exact colour of the light emitted depends upon the choice of the coating material. The colour is important in selecting the

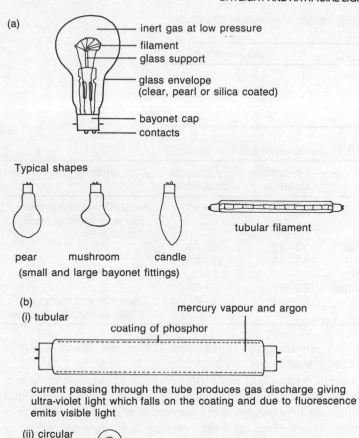

(a)
- inert gas at low pressure
- filament
- glass support
- glass envelope (clear, pearl or silica coated)
- bayonet cap
- contacts

Typical shapes

pear   mushroom   candle
(small and large bayonet fittings)

tubular filament

(b)
(i) tubular
mercury vapour and argon
coating of phosphor

current passing through the tube produces gas discharge giving ultra-violet light which falls on the coating and due to fluorescence emits visible light

(ii) circular

FIG. 16.2 Types of lamps (a) filament (b) fluorescent

correct tube for a particular application, e.g. a tube which emits a more reddish light enhances the appearance of the food and would be most appropriate for illuminating food displays. Fluorescent lamps have two advantages over filament lamps:

(a) They give four times the light output with less radiant heat.

(b) They provide a light compatible with daylight.

The length of tube is usually related to watt (W) output (see Table 16.3), e.g. 15 W tubes are 45 cm long, 65 W tubes are 150 cm long.

16.6.4 CHARACTERISTICS OF LIGHT FITTINGS

This is defined in terms of the way light fittings allow light to be

TABLE 16.3 Length of fluorescent light tube and wattage

Wattage (W)	Tube length (cm)
15	45
40	60
65	150
125	240

TABLE 16.4 Characteristics of light fittings

Type	Percentage upwards	Percentage downwards	Comments
Direct	0–10	100–90	Most efficient illumination of work surface; strong contrasts
Semi-direct	10–40	90–60	
General diffusing	40–60	60–40	
Semi-indirect	60–90	40–10	
Indirect	90–100	10–0	Least efficient method of illumination; no shadows

emitted: (a) upwards; (b) downwards. These are listed in Table 16.4 and illustrated in Fig. 16.3.

The way in which light is distributed by a fitting will obviously affect the proportion of light reaching the working surface. The final choice of fitting depends upon the particular situation in which it is to be used. If efficiency of light reaching the working surface is the main criterion, as in a kitchen, then unscreened light sources would be used since light is lost by absorption in the fitting. Where it is better to sacrifice lighting efficiency to achieve a better visual environment without glare decorative fittings can be used to blend with hotel décor.

Proper use of colour is vital in hotel furnishing and decoration. Colours are usually classed as warm (reds) or cool (blue). Dark colours absorb light, light colours reflect light. Virtually all artificial light sources distribute colour. The colour of the light emitted by a particular light fitting is called the 'colour rendering' and can enhance or detract from the atmosphere in a room or the appearance of food. Reflection from the décor of a room can also affect the colour quality of light. The caterer should be aware of these effects and use them to his advantage. If a dining room has green walls, an unpleasant greenish cast will be given to plates and food. Dark colours, e.g. reds and yellows, appear to reduce room space and ceiling height.

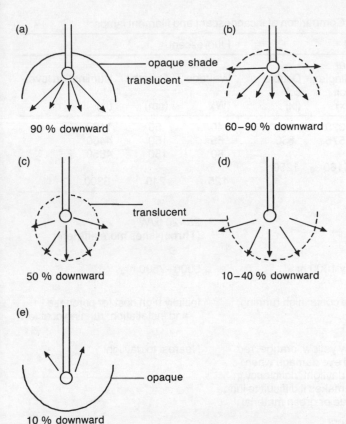

(a)

opaque shade

translucent

90 % downward

(b)

60–90 % downward

(c)

translucent

50 % downward

(d)

10–40 % downward

(e)

opaque

10 % downward

FIG. 16.3 Diagrams of a range of light fittings suitable for applications in catering (a) direct (b) semi-direct (c) general diffusing (d) semi-indirect (d) indirect

A comparison of incandescent and fluorescent lamps is given in Table 16.5. The fixtures and light fittings chosen for a particular area will depend on the level of illumination necessary, glare and contribution to décor.

Adequate lighting is necessary for a safe pleasant environment. The effect of light on carpets and curtains is important to note. A reaction between dyes and light causes deterioration of fibres, for examples, in carpets it produces fading and in curtains it can have a yellowing effect on cotton, linen and rayon.

16.7 GLARE

Glare is caused by contrast between the light source and the surroundings, and will dramatically affect the general comfort of a

TABLE 16.5 Comparison of incandescent and filament lamps

Incandescent			Fluorescent		
1. Light output					
Wattage	Single coil	Double coil	Wattage	Length	Illumination level
(W)	(lx)	(lx)	(W)	(cm)	(lx)
40	320	390	40	60	1160
60	575	650	65	150	4400
			80	150	4850
100	1160	1250			
			125	240	8300

2. Efficiency
8–14 lx/W

25–20 lx/W
(**Three**! times more efficient)

3. Lifetime
Approximately 1000 hr

5000–7500 hr

4. Cost
Low purchase costs; high running cost

Initially high cost for purchase and installation; running cost low

5. Colour
Predominantly yellow, orange, red, light; cause eye damage when mixed with daylight; deficiency in blue/green makes it difficult to judge colour of blue or green material

Nearest to daylight

6. Replacement
Easy

More difficult – especially with longer tubes

7. Heat emission
Mostly as radiation; temperature of filament can be as high as 3000 °C

Mostly by conduction and convection

room. A bright sunny day produces daylight glare. Glare occurs when part of the room is relatively excessively bright.

There are two types of glare:
(a) disability glare.
(b) discomfort glare.

16.7.1 DISABILITY GLARE

Disability glare is noticeable immediately, and reduces visual efficiency. It is produced by a light source if there is sufficient brightness close to an object being viewed, or if an object is

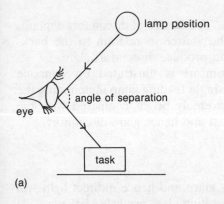

(a)

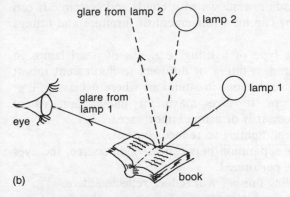

(b)

FIG. 16.4 A schematic representation of the angle of separation to show how glare
and eye-strain can be reduced (a) angle should be as large as possible (b) reflected
glare from pages of book – the lamp should be as high as possible to ensure that glare
is not reflected into the person's eyes

silhouetted against a very bright light. It can also occur by reflection
from shiny surfaces, such as mirrors, polished furniture, gloss-
painted walls, even pots and pans. This type of glare is very
dependent upon the brightness of the source and the angle between
the source, the eye and the object being viewed, known at the
'angle of separation' (see Fig. 16.4). A good example is a person
trying to read a glossy menu where the angle of the lamp can
produce a reflected glare from the surface of the menu.

16.7.2 DISCOMFORT GLARE

This is not immediately noticeable and does not stop a task being
performed. It becomes obvious after a time and gradually produces

eye-strain, fatigue and headaches. The degree of discomfort depends on the size and brightness of the source in relation to the background. Clear unshaded bulbs can produce discomfort glare.

One example of glare discomfort is illustrated by someone reading a book in a room with a single reading lamp illuminating the pages. The resultant page is extremely bright compared with the background, creating high contrast and hence glare discomfort.

16.7.3 GLARE CONTROL

In general, direct light produces glare and hence indirect light will reduce glare. Some ways of controlling glare are listed below:

1. Daylight glare control will not be continuously required and can be reduced by shading windows with blinds and curtains. It can also be reduced by careful arrangement of furniture and fittings in a room.

2. Choice of correct type of lighting, e.g. use of pearl lamps in unshaded lamp fittings; fitting of diffusers to fluorescent tubes; only use bare filament lamps in situations where necessary, e.g. kitchens, workshops to give maximum illumination where comfort is not necessarily of prime importance.

3. Increase background lighting to reduce contrast.

4. Alter the angle of separation between the light source, the eyes and the task to be performed.

5. Matt wall and ceiling finishes will reduce reflected glare.

6. Different colours and texture of furnishings absorb varying amounts of light and can produce diffused lighting. Dark colours absorb light.

7. Reduce the brightness of the source by using a lower wattage lamp, or alternatively screen the lamp.

16.8 EMERGENCY LIGHTING

Most large hotels have emergency lighting in case of failure of the public electricity supply. This consists of a calculated number of low-voltage lamps powered by either a small diesel generator or a battery installation.

In a battery-type installation the batteries must be maintained in a charged state from the normal operation of the mains supply. The size of the installation will depend upon the number of lamps and hence the total current required. Care must be taken with the housing of batteries to avoid any chemical corrosion of floors, etc., and to provide adequate ventilation.

For larger hotels, stand-by generators are normally used which are automatically switched on in the event of a power failure of the mains supply.

QUESTIONS

1. Calculate the minimum number of 60 W light fittings which would be required to illuminate:
   (a) a reception area 6 m × 10 m;
   (b) a lift 2 m × 1.5 m;
   (c) a dining room 10 m × 15 m.
2. What is meant by the term 'colour rendering'? How can this be used to the advantage of the caterer?
3. (a) What is meant by the term 'daylight factor'?
   (b) List four variables which contribute to the daylight factor.
   (c) Which type of artificial lighting provides the best blend with natural daylight?
4. Which light fittings would be best for each of the following situations:
   (a) a kitchen;
   (b) a hotel car park;
   (c) a hotel reception;
   (d) a dining room?

17
SOUND

17.1 INTRODUCTION

Sound is a form of mechanical energy and is produced by a source which is vibrating and causing a compression or pressure wave in a medium (usually air). These sound waves transfer the energy from the source to the ear as shown in Fig. 17.1.

The energy of a sound wave refers to the intensity or loudness of the sound when received. This intensity is measured in decibels (dB) and some examples are given in Table 17.1. The decibel scale is logarithmic and the zero point is chosen as the lowest intensity sound that the human ear can detect – the threshold of audibility.

TABLE 17.1 Sound intensity in decibels (dB)

120	_____	Threshold of feeling
		Rock concert
110		Thunder
100		Jet aeroplane
90		Permitted upper
		industrial limit
80		Car; telephone bell
		at 1 m
70		Typing at 1 m
60		Normal conversation
50		
40		Vacuum cleaner
		Quiet office
30		
20		Whisper
10	_____	Threshold of audibility

If the intensity of a sound is doubled, the loudness does not increase in proportion. For the loudness of a sound to double, the intensity must increase ten times. Intensity is the amplitude of the sound wave as shown in Fig. 17.2. Sound can be 'carried' by solids, liquids and gases since the vibrating particles transfer the energy, thus it cannot pass through a vacuum. The speed of sound in various media is listed in Table 17.2.

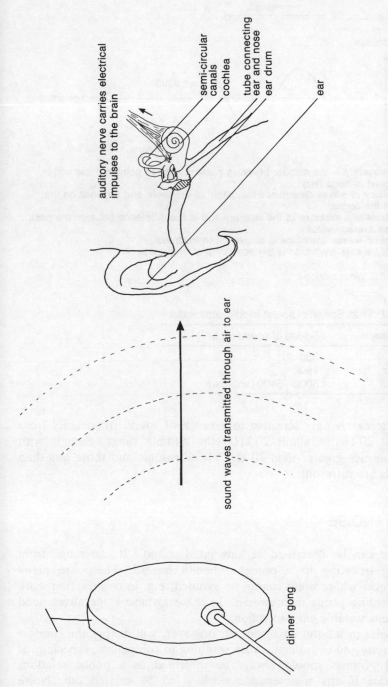

FIG. 17.1 Sound waves are carried through the air from a source of sound to the ear where they are converted into an electrical impulse which is carried to the brain

auditory nerve carries electrical impulses to the brain

semi-circular canals

cochlea

tube connecting ear and nose

ear drum

ear

sound waves transmitted through air to ear

dinner gong

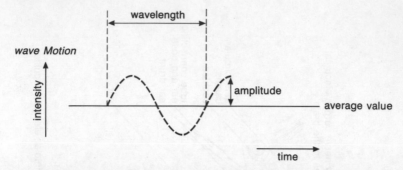

The frequency is the number of waves passing a given point in 1 sec and is measured in hertz (Hz).
Frequency of waves determines the 'pitch' of the wave and depends on the size of the source.
Amplitude is a measure of the intensity and is the difference between the peak and the average value.
For sound waves amplitude is equivalent to loudness.
For light waves amplitude is the equivalent of brightness.

FIG. 17.2 Wave motion

TABLE 17.2 Speed of sound in different media

Medium	Speed of sound (m s^{-1})
Air	330
Water	1500
Metals	5000–6400 (approx.)

The ear is only sensitive to a range of sound frequencies from about 20 Hz to about 20 kHz, the audible range. Sounds with frequencies greater than 20 kHz are ultrasonic and those less than 16 Hz are infrasonic.

17.2 NOISE

Noise can be described as 'unwanted sound'. It can range from being irritating to a potential health hazard. There are many instances where noise cannot be avoided, e.g. in construction work or bottling plants in breweries. In these instances operatives need to wear suitable ear protection.

Noise in a hotel environment, however, will disrupt the comfort of guests and cause annoyance resulting in complaints, especially at night. Guests should always be informed as a public relations exercise if any maintenance work is to be carried out. Noise pollution can be a major problem and 'discos' can produce noise levels as high as 120 dB. Prevention of noise involves some method of sound insulation. It is necessary to identify the cause and then develop a method of reducing the noise. Consequently the acoustic design of rooms in buildings is of great importance.

Sound transmission in a hotel can be divided into five main categories:
1. External air-borne noise.
2. External structure-borne noise due to services and mechanical plant.
3. Internal air-borne noise.
4. Internal structure-borne noise.
5. Impact noise.

17.2.2 EXTERNAL AIR-BORNE NOISE

This can be reduced by suitable screening effects, landscaping, etc., but many hotels are located on busy roads so this is not possible. The initial hotel design should take any excess noise, such as high traffic flow, into consideration. The windows of the building facing the sound should be double glazed to reduce sound transmission with a gap of at least 150 mm between sheets of glass recommended. This gives an insulation value of about 40 dB compared with 20 dB for a closed single-glazed window. For maximum insulation, the double glazing units should be sealed and this can reduce problems of condensation. External cavity walls give a 50 dB reduction in noise. Door and window frame surrounds should be sealed with a suitable material (e.g. mastic).

17.2.2 EXTERNAL STRUCTURE-BORNE NOISE

This is effectively vibrating noise transmitted from source to building via the ground and is not really significant.

17.2.3 INTERNAL AIR-BORNE NOISE

This can be reduced in the design stage of the hotel by locating noisy areas, such as parts used for entertainment and delivery, away from the guest quarters. Reduction in the passage of air-borne noise involves consideration of:
  (a) Doors.
  (b) Ceilings.
  (c) Floors.
  (d) Walls.

A normal hollow door will give a reduction of about 15 dB and this is suitable for many areas. Where necessary, a heavier acoustic door can be used. Suspended ceilings, which are completely airtight, will reduce noise. The construction should not be too rigid and should be reasonably heavy to prevent the ceiling transmitting vibrating sounds. If the floor has a concrete finish this provides good sound insulation. Wooden floors should have an arrangement of battens and insulation to give a floating surface of boards supported on insulated wood joists (see Fig. 18.4). Partition or cavity walls reduce sound transmission. Another common practice is to arrange the room so that cupboards, fitted wardrobes, etc., act as a 'buffer' in sound transmission.

17.2.4 INTERNAL STRUCTURE-BORNE NOISE FROM EQUIPMENT

This is usually noise produced by operating services in a hotel, e.g. boilers, pumps, ventilation plants, lifts, refrigeration equipment and dishwashers. Vibrations from these machines can travel via the floor, etc., throughout the building.

Noisy equipment, such as generators, is best sited in a separate building so that vibrations are not transmitted through the main hotel rooms. If it has to be sited in the hotel it should be insulated by the use of a suitable anti-vibration mounting to dampen the vibrations and absorb the energy. The equipment should rest on a substantial base fitted with vibration-resistant pads.

Service installation which produce structure-borne noise include:
(a) Ventilation plant (which also produces air-borne noise).
(b) Flow of water in pipes for baths and water closets.
(c) Central heating pipes, etc.

In the case of ventilation, the air flow should be reduced to an acceptable level and the lining of ducts can be fitted with absorbent material. In water closets, ball valves produce noise during flushing and can be replaced by silent filler valves (e.g. Torbeck). Plastic pipes reduce noise compared with metal ones.

17.2.5 IMPACT NOISE

Air-borne sound is direct transmission of noise from part of the structure of the room being set into vibration due to impact. These can be caused by people moving furniture, dropping objects, slamming doors or a group of people dancing at a party, etc. Impact noise mainly applies to the floor and basically the efficiency of sound transmission depends on the mass and design of floor and wall construction. This type of noise is reduced by providing suitable insulation to absorb the impact energy, for example, 'floating floors' (filled with a suitable absorbent material) or heavy carpeting. Doors can be fitted with dampened springs to avoid them banging.

17.3 ROOM ACOUSTICS

The previous section has dealt with the ways of reducing noise in a room. In normal rooms the internal acoustics are not that important, but in larger spaces in a hotel, e.g. conference rooms, ballrooms, etc., they become critical. Two sounds are actually produced:
  (a) Direct sound from the source.
  (b) Reflected sound from the walls and ceilings.

If multiple reflections are too large, this obscures the direct sound-producing reverberation. Conversely, too little reflected sound gives a 'flat' direct sound. The design and insulation of the walls, etc., should aim at producing the correct balance.

17.4 FACTORS WHICH POTENTIALLY ENDANGER HEARING

Loud music has led to the number of complaints of noise from entertainment 'places', increasing from 400 in 1973 to 1200 in 1980. For the same period, the rise was only from 300 to 550 for complaints about industrial noise. Walls reduce sound by only 6 dB for every doubling of the mass of the wall so in an adjoining room there is a considerable problem.

The present permitted upper limit for noise levels is 90 dB (average) for 8 hr but this varies for individuals, and many experts would prefer a limit of 80 dB. Noise from the variety of sources mentioned earlier can damage the delicate structure of the ear. For some people prolonged exposure to noise in excess of 80 dB will endanger their hearing.

Short-term exposure to noise levels higher than 90 dB (e.g. at a 'disco') can cause hearing fatigue which usually corrects itself once the person moves away from the source of the noise. Too much exposure to sounds of 110–120 dB can result in permanent damage and hearing loss. It is relatively easy to measure the noise level using a sound-level (decibel) meter.

In many food-processing plants, where the operators have to work in an environment with noisy equipment, some form of ear-guard is essential, e.g. ear-muffs and mouldable plugs (cotton wool is of limited value). Other areas where there can be high noise levels include typing pools and computer rooms.

Noise is recognised as a major stress factor responsible for such problems as fatigue (resulting in accidents), absenteeism from work, psychological pressure (e.g. objections to major road works through built-up areas), and even has an effect on mental health.

QUESTIONS

1. (a) How is sound transmitted?
   (b) List five ways in which sounds can be transmitted through a hotel.
2. (a) What is meant by the 'threshold of audibility?
   (b) In what units is sound measured?
   (c) What are the long-term effects of working in high-noise areas?
   (d) How can damage to hearing be avoided in a noisy environment?
3. (a) What is meant by the term 'noise'?
   (b) List five situations in a hotel which produce noise.
   (c) How can hotel design minimise noise problems.

18

HEATING SYSTEMS, VENTILATION AND REFRIGERATION

18.1 INTRODUCTION

A hotel, or indeed any catering establishment, consists of a number of separate and different microenvironments whose temperature and humidity characteristics have to be carefully controlled. The atmosphere within a kitchen would not be acceptable in a lounge or dining room. The concept of 'thermal comfort', i.e. the control of the environmental conditions to suit guests and staff, has important implications, not just in financial terms. A kitchen has a range of separate and extremely different temperature levels, from the very low, e.g. a deep freezer, down to −20 °C, to the very high, e.g. an oven, up to 250 °C. Maintenance of these temperature levels requires a range of highly specialised units, some of which will be discussed in this chapter.

18.2 FACTORS AFFECTING THERMAL COMFORT

Maintaining correct 'thermal comfort' is of great importance in a hotel and depends on:
1. Correct environmental temperature, produced by radiant conditions from heating installations and aided by minimisation of heat losses through effective insulation.
2. Rate of movement of air and air temperature, i.e. ventilation.
3. The amount of water vapour in the air, i.e. humidity

It is the object of heating systems in hotels to provide the correct environmental temperature. More sophisticated systems also control humidity and ventilation. A body loses heat to the environment and gains heat from it by three methods, radiation, conduction and convection. The overall aim is to obtain a satisfactory thermal balance in terms of heat lost and gained. Thermal balance in a room is illustrated in Table 18.1.

TABLE 18.1 Thermal balance in a room

Heat gained	Heat lost
Radiation from sun (solar heat gain)	Conduction, convection through exterior walls, ceilings, windows
Heating appliances (local and central heating)	Conduction via floors to the ground
Electrical and lighting appliances	Refrigeration units
Radiant heat from occupants	

18.3 CONTROLLING ENVIRONMENTAL TEMPERATURE

Methods of providing hot water and heating can be divided into two main groups:
(a) Central systems.
(b) Local systems.

In central systems, the heating source is a (central) boiler which distributes hot water, steam or warmed air. Fuel for the boiler can be electricity, gas, oil or solid fuel such as anthracite (smokeless fuel) and coke. Increasing use is being made of solar energy via heating or solar panels, but lack of constant sunshine makes economic storage of heat difficult and such systems are used as a 'backup' to the main central heating installation.

In local systems, the water is heated adjacent to the appliance and heating is provided directly to it.

The choice of system, or combination of systems, will depend on the exact needs of the hotel, e.g. hotels with a constant high demand for hot water would be best served with a central boiler. An intermittent demand from mainly scattered hot water points (flats, etc.) would be best served with local water heating.

18.3.1 CENTRAL HEATING SYSTEMS FOR HOT WATER

Several different types are available depending on whether the hot water supply is separate from, or connected to, the heating system.

Direct system
This system, illustrated in Fig. 18.1, involves circulation of hot water between the central boiler and an insulated hot water cylinder, with direct 'take off' from taps and other appliances. This system is used either if:

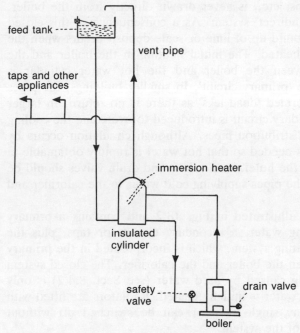

FIG. 18.1 A schematic representation of a direct system of hot water supply

(i) Hot water supply is *not* combined with central heating.
(ii) The water supply is soft. Use of hard water in a direct system leads to a deposit of scale (furring). The boiler should be treated (rust-proofed) with easy access for cleaning.

The advantages of a direct system are that it is relatively inexpensive and only one cold water feed is received (from the cold water feed tank). An expansion or vent pipe is needed since water expands when heated; the vent pipe discharges to the cold water tank.

Indirect system

This system is used when the hot water supply is combined with a heating system. The insulated hot water cylinder contains an inner heat exchanger and this arrangement is termed a 'calorifier'. Water from the boiler circulates through the heat exchanger thus heating the water in the cylinder. To minimise heat losses the boiler should be situated fairly close to the calorifier but at a slightly higher level to allow for gravity circulation.

The boiler and the heat exchanger form a self-contained system and water for taps, etc., is never drawn directly from the boiler, hence the term 'indirect' system. As a consequence of this closed system, the only build up of lime or scale deposit occurs when the water is initially heated. The initial heating in the boiler and the pipe system between the boiler and the hot water cylinder is referred to as the 'primary circuit'. In smaller buildings, the pipes and outlets are termed 'dead legs' as there is no return. In larger buildings, a secondary circuit is introduced to overcome the cooling of water in the distribution pipes. Although circulation occurs by gravity, a pump is needed so that hot water is rapidly obtainable in different parts of the hotel. Stop valves and drain valves should be fitted to each of the pipes supplying cold water to the calorifier and the boiler.

This system is illustrated in Fig. 18.2 and contains a primary system for heating water, a secondary circuit for taps, plus the closed central heating system, which is incorporated in the primary circulation between the boiler and the calorifier. The closed system means that scaling caused by hard water (see Sect. 8.4.2) is only present when the water is initially heated. Radiators are fitted with valves so that any single radiator can be switched off without affecting the rest of the system.

18.3.2 LOCAL SYSTEMS FOR PROVIDING HOT WATER

This involves either instantaneous heaters or storage heaters. Instantaneous heaters consist of a coiled water pipe heated either by an electric element or by gas jets which are automatically switched on or lit when the water tap is turned on. In this system *no* hot water is stored. A simplified diagram of an instantaneous gas heater is shown in Fig. 18.3. This illustrates the water pipe which is effectively a small heat exchanger. The final part of the pipe has metal fins to allow for heat dissipation. Effective ventilation is essential for gas fired water heaters.

A typical electric water storage heater consists simply of an insulated storage cylinder with a heating element immersed in the water, i.e. an immersion heater.

The advantages of local heating systems compared to a central heating system are that less pipework is involved, no separate boiler house is needed, no pump is required and for small separate units, e.g. holiday flats and flatlets, this is ideal. Disadvantages are that since there would be many more gas or electrical connections the fire risk is increased.

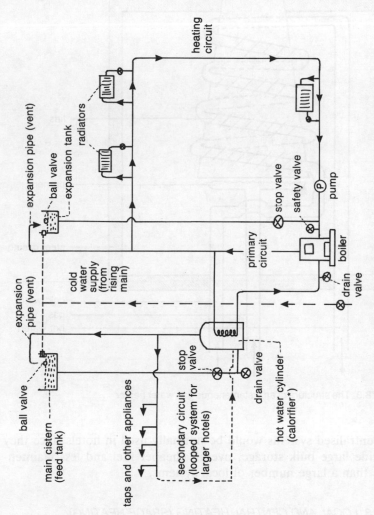

FIG. 18.2 A schematic representation combined heating and hot water supply (indirect system)

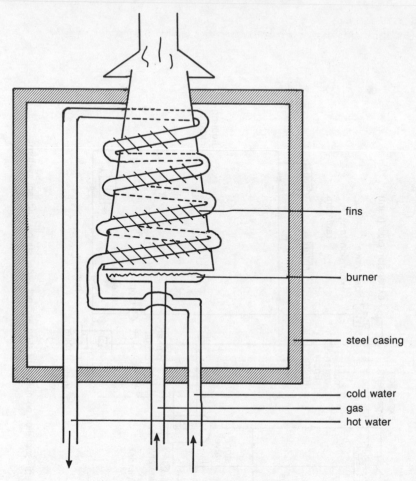

FIG. 18.3 The structure of an instantaneous gas water heater

Centralised systems would be normally used in hotels since they provide large bulk storage, overall cheaper fuel and less maintenance than a large number of local systems.

18.3.3 LOCAL AND CENTRAL HEATING (SPACE HEATING)

Most homes have a combination of individual space heaters, such as gas or electric fires plus a central heating system. The latter tends to be used in the winter months to provide background heating, with fires supplying extra heat if required. In summer, normally individual space heaters only are necessary.

Local heating

Local heating systems can involve the use of four types of fuel:
- (i) Solid fuel.
- (ii) Oil.
- (iii) Electricity.
- (iv) Gas.

They can be of the direct type such as an electric fire, or the indirect type such as a storage radiator.

Solid fuel

This is of limited use in hotels although open fires can be a considerable attraction and are highly decorative. They are, however, an inefficient method of heating, smokeless fuel is necessary in many areas, grates have to be cleaned daily and regular flue sweeping is essential. A new range of fires and stoves are designed to stay alight overnight and operate with little trouble. Many fires can be easily fitted with a back boiler to combine space heating with water heating.

Oil

Portable oil heaters are frequently used to provide a very inexpensive method of heating. Larger heaters have fans to give a better circulation of warm air. Flueless oil stoves give off fumes as combustion products and so must be used only in properly ventilated areas.

Electricity and gas

The main types of local heating systems involve gas or electricity. Electrical space heating appliances have the advantage of being clean and silent, there are no combustion fumes, no flue is required, there is no risk of leaks, and they are readily portable wherever power points are available. They are easy to install and no pipework is required. Gas fires have the advantage of being more economical and often more controllable.

Examples of direct heating by electrical and gas appliances are listed in Table 18.2 and examples of indirect heating in Table 18.3.

Central heating systems

Fuel is converted to heat using a central unit and the heat is then distributed throughout the hotel. This involves a central boiler (solid fuel, oil, gas or electricity) and an appropriate heat transfer medium such as water or air. Since water has a much higher heat capacity than air it is the more efficient medium for heat transfer. Most hotel

TABLE 18.2 Space heating by electricity and gas – direct systems

Appliance	Comments
Electrical	
Radiant electric fire	High-resistance wire or rod provides electric heating element: (a) with parabolic reflector gives a conventional electric fire – high temperature; (b) enclosing element in quartz tube gives 'infra-red' heaters usually mounted on walls – medium temperature
Convector fire	Utilises heating element but with air re-circulated; economical and can be made more efficient by the use of a fan
Electric radiator	Oil-filled and thermostatically controlled; mobile, heated by immersion heater, 80 % convected heat, 20 % radiated heat
Tubular heater	Hollow tubes containing a resistance element (20–30 W/m); 30 % radiant heat, 70 % convected heat
Fan heaters	Resistance element with heat distributed by fan
Radiant panel	Heating elements (medium-temperature) mounted at a high level and inclined towards the floor
Electric wallpaper	Low-temperature heat source used in walls and ceilings
Gas	
Radiant fire	Consists of bars (radiants) made of fireclay heated to about 900 °C by gas jets; small heaters, need no flue provided the room is well ventilated; larger heaters *must* have a flue; the radiants are usually mounted on a panel and surrounded by a steel reflector plate
Radiant convector fire	Most common type of fire with circulation of air utilising heat from the flue gases; many convector heaters have a room-sealed combustion unit using a balanced flue; balanced flue units are essential for rooms with no chimney outlet
'Living flame' gas fires	Popular alternative to coal or log fire avoiding dirt and hard work aspects, e.g. removing ash; some models use gas inefficiently
Warm air units	Self-contained units combining heating with ventilation by convection only

systems use either gas or oil as fuel, with a radiator system, circulation being via a suitably sized centrifugal pump.

Certain electric storage heaters can also be envisaged as providing central heating by distributing heat through several rooms, e.g. by

TABLE 18.3 Space heating – indirect systems

Appliance or method	Comments
Electric storage heaters	Operated by 'off peak' supply and therefore cheaper than direct heating; heating element is enclosed in high thermal capacity refectory blocks in an insulated metal casing; approx. 35 % radiant heat and 65 % convected heat; heated during night and heat given off through the day; very little control therefore unless a thermostatically controlled fan is included; fan storage heaters can be used to provide a **warm air system** by forcing air through ducts into rooms
Underfloor heating	Grid of heating cables are laid in suitably designed concrete floors; care must be taken that cables do not interfere with other services and that appropriate insulation is used; usually operated on an 'off peak' supply and thermostatically controlled by a time switch

placing a powerful fan-operated heater in a strategic position where it can heat several rooms.

Warm air systems (ducted air systems)
Air is forced over a heat exchanger by a fan and the heated air is then distributed via ducts and grills into individual rooms. The

TABLE 18.4 Insulators

Material	Conductivity, k (W m^{-1} °C^{-1})
Asbestos	0.36
Brick	0.84
Concrete	1.0
Cork board	0.02
Glass	1.02
Glass wool	0.05
Hardboard	0.10
Plaster board	0.16
Plaster	0.50
Plastic (expanded polystyrene)	0.03
Plywood	0.14
Roofing felt	0.20
Roofing tiles	0.90
Slates	1.80

TABLE 18.5 Examples of insulation in buildings

Location	Insulating material
1. Floors	
(a) Solid (concrete) floor	Insulating layer of polystyrene incorporated in floor construction (see Fig. 18.7a). Above floor level insulation includes the use of mineral wool or glass fibre, wooden blocks, carpets, etc.
(b) Timber floors	Air gap between floor construction and ground required to prevent dry rot (see Fig. 18.4b); insulation draped over joists
2. Walls	
(a) Exterior walls	Plastic foam, polystyrene beads or 'Rockwool' 'cavity wall insulation'
(b) Interior walls	Plaster or plaster board on walls
3. Windows	Air gap
4. Doors	Air gap
5. Ceilings	Plaster, plaster board, polystyrene tiles. Air gap
6. Upper floors or roof space	Mineral wool or glass wool
7. Roofs	Felt, slate or tiles
8. Water pipes	Glass wool, rock wool, cork, mineral wool
9. Hot water boilers	Aluminium foil
10. Ovens	Glass wool
11. Refrigeration units	Glass fibre, polystyrene, cork

system involves warm air ducts and ducting for the return of cool air. When the air reaches the heater it is filtered and its temperature increased to 30–50 °C then recirculated. The advantages of this system are ease of control, fast response and no radiators in rooms to take up a lot of space. It has the disadvantage of humidity problems and high running costs.

Comments

Building regulations require addition of
   insulating material between concrete and
   screed

Floor boards on supports give pallet-type
   construction

25 % of heat loss is through
   walls
Fixed either to brick or to a timber
   framework

Double glazing with suitable air gap between
   panes (20 mm recommended)

Used in hollow doors; solid timber doors are
   better insulators but are more expensive

Attached to floor joists
Suspended or false ceilings use an air gap;
   better to use a fibreglass quilt in the air gap

Placed as a layer (40 mm thick) on joists

Typical pitched roof consists of battens
   fixed to rafters with roofing felt as
   insulation covered by slates or tiles

Insulation/lagging to prevent loss or gain of
   heat

Minimise heat losses

Used for doors and sides in cabinet units and
   for floors, walls, etc., in walk-in cold stores

18.4 INSULATION

Heat losses in a hotel are expensive because of high fuel costs, and
since the current trend in these establishments is for higher temperatures, heat conservation is extremely important. Minimising heat
losses involves various forms of thermal insulation (see Tables 18.4
and 18.5 and Fig. 18.4), although good planning in the initial

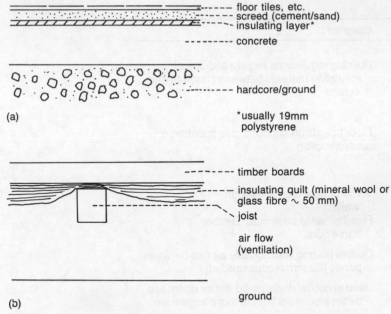

(a)

*usually 19mm
polystyrene

(b)

FIG. 18.4 A diagram to show floor insulation (a) section through concrete, ground
floor construction (b) section through joisted floor construction

construction of buildings should take insulation factors into consideration. Obvious methods include roof insulation, double glazing of windows and cavity wall insulation but ways should be devised to prevent heat losses via badly fitting windows and doors, unused chimneys (flues) or other means of uncontrolled ventilation.

The overall rate of heat transmission due to three processes of conduction, convection and radiation is known as the 'thermal transmittance', U. This is defined as the heat transferred, in watts (W) through an area of one square metre when there is a temperature difference of one degree Centigrade on each side of the material. For example,

for a single-glazed window, $U = 5.60$ W m^{-2} °C^{-1}
for a double-glazed window, $U = 2.57$ W m^{-2} °C^{-1}
(with a 20 mm air gap)
i.e. a factor of 2.

The equation for the rate of heat loss, Q_f, is given by:

$$Q_f = \text{thermal transmittance} \times \text{area} \times \text{temperature difference}$$

e.g. for a single-glazed window area 4 m $\times$ 2 m, outside temperature is 0 °C, inside temperature is 20 °C:

$$Q_f = 5.60 \times 8 \times 20 \text{ W}$$
$$= 896 \text{ W}$$

For a complete building an allowance must also be made for draught and ventilation losses.

18.5 VENTILATION

Adequate ventilation is necessary in many catering situations and essential in food-preparation areas. Ventilation disposes of:
(a) Food and body odours.
(b) Fumes, smoke and combustion products.
(c) Water vapour and carbon dioxide.
(d) Excess heat.

These are replaced with fresh air. The rate of air change is important because too slow an air movement makes the room 'stuffy'. Recommended air changes for various areas are listed in Table 18.6.

TABLE 18.6 Air changes and minimum temperatures for catering areas

Area	Recommended air changes per hour	Minimum temperature (°C)
Kitchen	20–60	18
Sculleries and wash-up areas, laundries	10–15	
Restaurants	10–15	20–24
Internal toilets	6–8	13–18
Bathrooms	6	13–18
Offices	4–6	19–20
Bedrooms	3	13–16
Corridors and stairs	2	13–18

Good ventilation is essentially linked with comfortable conditions for any given catering area. Fresh air not only provides an adequate supply of oxygen and reduces stuffiness, it also maintains bacterial contamination at an acceptable level. Inefficient ventilation can result in increased humidity, producing bodily discomfort and condensation problems for the building, and soilage due to dust and grease not being removed. Ventilation systems can be linked with heat exchangers to recover and reuse heat energy. In such systems incoming cold fresh air is heated by outgoing hot stuffy air. Cooker hoods provide extraction specifically over cooking areas and reduce the problems of excess water vapour and cooking smells caused by the boiling and frying of foods. The efficiency of cooker hoods can be increased by the use of filters which extract dust and grease from the air. Grouping of cooking ranges under cooking hoods provides a more efficient means of ventilation than extractor fans in walls and windows.

18.5.1 VENTILATION SYSTEMS

There are three types of ventilation system:
    (i) Natural.
    (ii) Mechanical.
    (iii) Air conditioning.

Natural ventilation

This depends on a combination of wind pressures and the convection effect caused by and the temperature difference between the interior and the exterior of buildings which results in convection currents.

There is very little control with this type of system which depends entirely on weather conditions via open windows, etc., and it is difficult to filter the air to remove dust and grease. The extent of window opening depends on the location, for example, for natural ventilation of habitable rooms and sanitary accommodation the window opening must equal one-twentieth of the floor area.

Mechanical ventilation

Electrically operated fans provide the required volume of air change and in addition the air can be filtered. The most common method involves a fan expelling the stale air (mechanical extraction) and replacing this with fresh air from a natural inlet. This is a requirement in toilets with no window, the fan being turned on with the light switch.

Air conditioning

This is really a sophisticated system of mechanical ventilation. In addition to the heating or cooling of the air, humidity control is involved. Maintenance of the filter screen is essential and these must be regularly checked and cleaned to ensure that no blockages occur. Standards of filtration vary enormously and in a computer room would require an efficiency of 85 per cent.

An automated air-conditioning system will improve the working environment thus increasing the efficiency of staff, enjoyment of customers and reduction in money spent on cleaning and decorating buildings. Care needs to be taken in the maintenance of air conditioning systems to prevent outbreaks of Legionnaire's disease (see Sect. 12.10.1).

18.6 HUMIDITY

The presence of moisture is a critical factor in ventilation. The actual amount of water vapour present in the air is known as the 'absolute humidity'. Much more important, however, is the 'relative humidity' (RH) which relates the saturation of the air as defined below:

$$RH = \frac{\text{mass of water vapour present in a given volume of air}}{\text{mass of water vapour needed to saturate the given volume of air at the same temperature}}$$

Relative humidity will obviously depend on the temperature since the hotter the air is, the more water vapour can be absorbed in it. Conversely, when the temperature falls water vapour condenses out as dew.

Saturation values for atmospheric moisture (in kilograms of water per kilogram of dry air) vary from 0.0044 kg at 2 °C to 0.0147 kg at 20 °C. A typical calculation shows that at 20 °C if the actual amount of water vapour present in the atmosphere in the atmosphere is 0.0074 kg then the RH would be:

$$\frac{0.0074}{0.0147} \times 100, \text{ or 50 per cent}$$

Relative humidity will depend on exact location in a catering area, for example in a kitchen or laundry area the amount of water vapour present will be quite large.

A 'comfortable' RH for most people is between 30–70 per cent. High RH means that the air contains too much moisture. In hot conditions, such as in a kitchen, breathing becomes difficult and the body cannot lose water vapour by 'sweating'. This in turn means that it becomes overheated, causing nausea and headaches. A high RH in cold conditions will result in the skin pores remaining open, making the body feel colder. If the air is too dry then moisture will evaporate readily from the skin and since the body provides the heat for the process this leaves a 'cold' feeling. Dry air conditions can cause irritation of the eyes, nose and throat.

Humidity can be measured in catering areas using a hair hygrometer or a wet and dry bulb thermometer hygrometer. The amount of water vapour present in the atmosphere can be controlled by a humidifier (see Sect. 18.6.1).

18.6.1 HUMIDITY CONTROL

The main difference between mechanical ventilation and air conditioning lies in humidity control. There is a definite need to humidify or dehumidify the air. If air enters a building at a low temperature and then passes through a heater, its relative humidity is reduced and could fall below the value needed to give comfortable conditions. Conversely, warm air when cooled will have its relative humidity increased. The air-conditioning unit will refrigerate or re-warm air before it enters a particular area.

18.6.2 SELF-CONTAINED AIR CONDITIONERS

These are complete units which are normally used in small buildings, such as hotels and restaurants, and are sited on an outside wall of the room they supply. The unit comprises a heater, refrigerator, compressor fan, condenser filter and humidifier. Fresh air is drawn in, heated or cooled, filtered, etc. and then distributed.

18.7 REFRIGERATION

A number of different refrigerated units are of importance to the caterer, including refrigerators (fridges), chillers, freezers, ice makers, ice-cream makers, food display cabinets and wine storage units. In each of these units the temperature of an insulated cabinet is lowered by a cooling unit, which can be of the compression or absorption types.

The basic principles of a compressor refrigerator involve a cycle of evaporation and liquefaction of a refrigerant (see Fig. 18.5). During evaporation, the refrigerant absorbs heat from the insulated cabinet or freezing compartment, this is called the 'latent heat of evaporation'. The refrigerant is then compressed so that it liquefies and gives off the latent heat to the surroundings.

Refrigerants commonly used include ammonia, Freon, methyl chloride and carbon dioxide. All refrigerants should, of course, be non-toxic to foods and absorb large quantities of heat when evaporating. Ammonia is the most efficient heat remover but it is poisonous and tends only to be used in larger industrial plants. It is, however, widely used in absorption refrigerators.

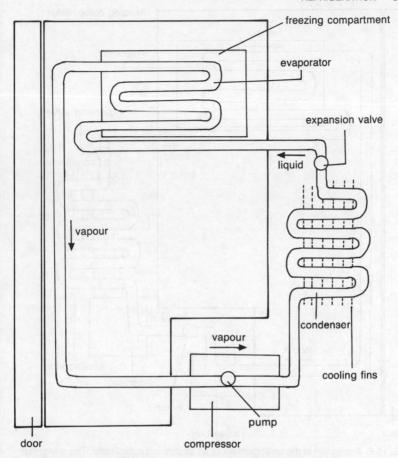

FIG. 18.5 A schematic representation of a compression refrigerator

Freon and methyl chloride are generally used in small and medium-sized refrigerators. Although methyl chloride absorbs two-and-a-half times more heat than Freon when evaporating, it is mildly poisonous and therefore is not as safe.

Absorption refrigerators (see Fig. 18.6) operate on the basic principle that a solution of ammonia can be heated to produce ammonia vapour which is then cooled via an air condenser and the liquid ammonia passes into the evaporator (in the freezing compartment). The evaporator is filled with hydrogen, producing, a vacuum effect and resulting in evaporation of the ammonia. The action is the same as in the compression refrigerator in that latent heat is extracted from the cabinet, producing the cooling effect. Ammonia is more dense than hydrogen so it sinks to the bottom of

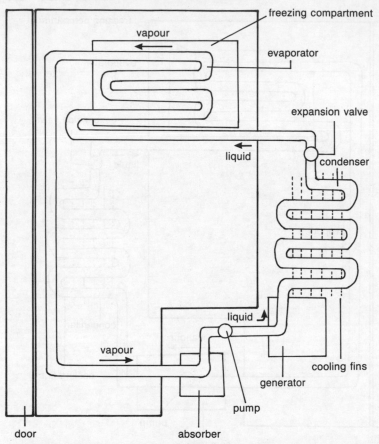

FIG. 18.6 A diagram of the arrangement of an absorption refrigerator. The refrigerant gas is often ammonia which is absorbed into water from the evaporator. Heat is applied in the generator to distil off the ammonia which passes on to the condenser

the evaporator. It is then absorbed by water and returns to the generator.

Compression refrigerators can only be electrically operated, whereas absorption refrigerators can use either gas or electricity as a heating source. Compression refrigerators are cheaper to run (three times as cheap) although absorption refrigerators have no pump or expansion valve and are hence quieter in use and require less maintenance.

Many hotels have large 'walk-in' cold rooms. These are suitably insulated (see earlier section) with use of compression or absorption refrigeration, depending on room capacity. One safety point is that doors *must* be capable of being opened from the inside.

18.7.1 OPERATING TEMPERATURES OF REFRIGERATORS AND FREEZERS

Refrigerators operate at temperatures from 0–+4 °C; this slows down the rate of growth of microorganisms, and perishable foods can be preserved for longer periods of time. Deep freezers operate at much lower temperatures (down to −20 °C). Freezers have a 'star rating' – one-star ($\star$) (−6 °C) indicates that food can be stored for 1 week, two-star ($\star\star$) (−12 °C) means that it can be stored for 1 month, three-star ($\star\star\star$) (−18 °C) means that it can be stored for 3 months (see Sect. 11.6.4). Freezers can be of the upright or chest types, the latter being the most economical, since less cold air is lost on opening the lid. Freezers enable certain foods to be preserved for up to 12 months.

18.7.2 CARE OF REFRIGERATION EQUIPMENT

Both refrigerators and freezers should be sited away from heat sources, such as general heating equipment, boilers, etc. Items like refrigerators, ice makers, ice-cream makers, etc., can be noisy due to the operation of the motor especially when not levelled correctly and should be placed so that their noise causes the minimum amount of inconvenience.

Refrigerators and freezers ought to be inspected and maintained on a regular basis. The inspection should include a regular defrosting schedule and ensuring that the unit is not overloaded. It is important that doors are opened for the shortest time possible to minimise the entry of warm air and loss of cold air from the cabinet. Any moisture entering the cabinet will be deposited on the evaporator, forming an insulating layer of ice and reducing the efficiency of heat absorption. In a compressor-type refrigerator this means that the motor (compressor) has to work that much harder or longer to maintain the thermostatically set temperature. Automatic defrosting is available with most refrigerators and this can keep the ice layer to a minimum.

Overloading occurs when too much food is present or if items which are too hot are stored in the cabinet, causing an increase in temperature which can affect the foodstuffs already present.

18.7.3 OTHER FREEZING TECHNIQUES

Other freezing techniques include using a current of very cold air such as in blast freezing (temperatures of −20 °C down to −40 °C) useful for pre-cooked foods, and fluidised beds for small particles such as peas and diced vegetables. These techniques apply to food manufacturing rather than normal hotel usage.

Large quantities of ice can be used in some hotels and this would necessitate the installation of an ice-making machine. In the common type of appliance, water is frozen by allowing it to flow over a sloping refrigerated plate. When a suitable thickness of ice has been deposited, the plate is warmed, the ice block slides off and comes into contact with a heated grid which breaks down the ice block into cubes. Small amounts of ice can of course be obtained from suitably designed trays in the freezer compartment of a refrigerator.

Apart from ice being used to cool drinks and for the storage of foods such as fish, etc., solid carbon dioxide can be employed as a solid refrigerant. This produces low temperatures and can be of benefit if the food has to be transported in large cold boxes. Since carbon dioxide readily sublimes, insulation must be very efficient.

QUESTIONS

1. (a) What is meant by the term 'thermal comfort'?
   (b) List three factors which determine thermal comfort.
2. Why is good ventilation essential in a busy kitchen?
3. (a) What is meant by the term 'relative humidity'?
   (b) What is the 'comfortable' range for relative humidity?
   (c) What are the effects of: (i) a high relative humidity; (ii) a low relative humidity?
   (d) How can humidity be controlled in a kitchen?
4. (a) List the operating temperatures of: (i) a refrigerator; (ii) a deep freezer.
   (b) What is the meaning of the star rating on a freezer?
   (c) Construct a four-point code of practice to use when operating a freezer.

ELECTRICITY AND GAS SERVICES

19.1 INTRODUCTION

Electricity and gas are the two major fuels employed in hotels and other catering establishments and play an essential role in cooking as well as in the maintenance of comfortable environmental conditions (see Ch. 18). The correct installation and maintenance, not only of particular appliances, but also of the fuel supply to the catering premises and the distribution of the fuel within the premises, are critical to the safety of clients, staff and property. It is imperative, therefore, that *all* catering staff understand:

(a) The safe procedures regarding the use of electrical and gas appliances and their supplies to ensure that no unnecessary accidents occur.

(b) The correct procedure to adopt in the event of an emergency.

Caterers are advised to consult electricity and gas boards concerning any problems with installation, fuel supplies or appliances.

19.2 ELECTRICAL SUPPLIES

19.2.1 ELECTRIC CURRENTS

An electric current can be regarded as a flow of electrons. There are two types of electric current, direct current and alternating current.

Direct current (d.c.) is generated by batteries or d.c. generators. In d.c. circuits the electrons move in one direction only and the current has a constant value (see Fig. 19.1). Direct current supply has very little application in hotels except for emergency supplies (using lead–acid batteries) for use during power cuts, and special equipment such as food hoists.

Alternating current (a.c.) reverses its direction several times per second as shown in Fig. 19.1. The current starts at zero, increases to a maximum, then decreases to zero, increases to an opposite maximum and returns to zero. This constitutes one complete cycle. The frequency is the number of cycles per second (one cycle per

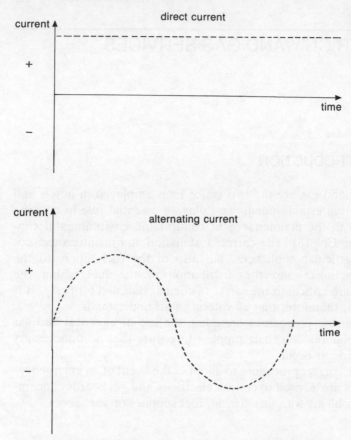

FIG. 19.1 Schematic representation of alternating and direct currents

second (c/s) equals one Hertz (Hz). Normal United Kingdom supplies have a frequency of 50 Hz. Electricity is generated in power stations for public supply as alternating current and it is distributed to consumers using a system known as the 'national grid'. This supply produces alternating current on the three-phase system.

An alternating current is generated when an electromagnet rotates inside a coil of wire (see Fig. 19.2). Single-phase supplies are produced by a generating unit consisting of a stationary single coil of wire inside which is a rotating electromagnet. In a three-phase supply there are three coils of wire in the generating unit with a rotating electromagnet between them. As the magnet rotates three separate currents of electricity are produced as shown in Fig. 19.4. Each current is out of phase by 120 °, one-third of a cycle. A three-

poles of C-shaped magnet

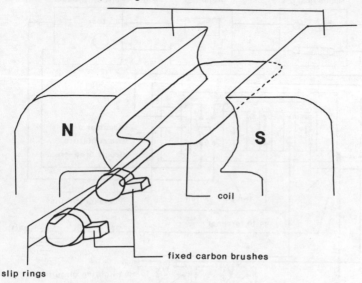

slip rings

FIG. 19.2 Alternating current generator

phase feed wire is supplied via the national grid to local transformer stations (substations). Of the three wires supplied to the substation, the first is a neutral wire earthed at the substation. The voltage between the other two wires, the phase wires, is 415 V. Between any phase wire and neutral the voltage is 240 V.

Hotels can, therefore, take either a single-phase supply (240 V) which is suitable for most domestic purposes, or a three-phase (415 V) supply which is used for high-power appliances such as lifts and kitchen ranges, with a demand of 3730 W or more. The three-phase supply is more efficient than single-phase.

19.2.2 SUPPLY OF ELECTRICITY TO PREMISES

Electricity is usually supplied to a hotel via an underground cable to a boxed distribution board at a convenient location within the building. The supply must pass through the main fuse in a sealed box and meter, both of which are the property of the Area Electricity Board Authority. For domestic supplies the 'box' is now frequently placed outside buildings to allow meters to be read without any need for access to the premises.

A typical distribution system for lighting and socket outlets is shown in Fig. 19.3.

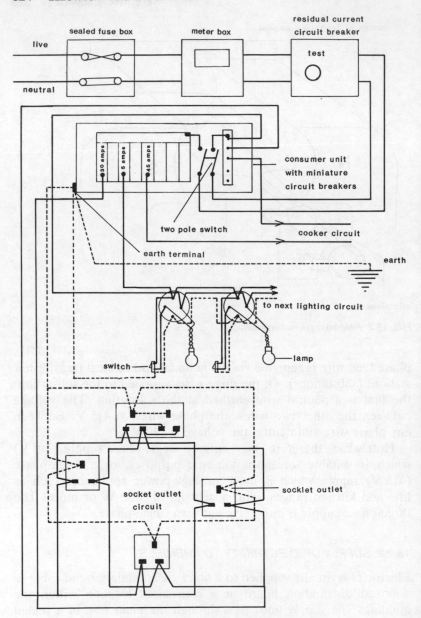

FIG. 19.3 Typical ring main system for lighting and socket outlets

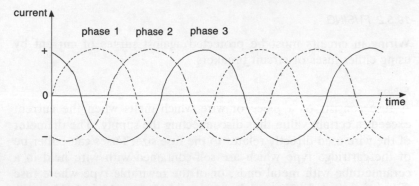

FIG. 19.4 Schematic representation of a three-phase supply, showing each phase 120 ° out of phase

19.3 SAFETY ASPECTS OF ELECTRIC CIRCUITS

19.3.1 EARTH CONNECTION AND ELECTRIC SHOCK

Metal cases on appliances will conduct electricity and become 'live' if the wiring in the appliance is damaged and the live wire comes in contact with the case. If a person touches the 'live' metal case then he will receive an electric shock. Electricity always takes the path of least resistance to earth, which in this case is through the body of the person in contact with the earth. This occurrence can be avoided in two ways:

1. By earthing the case of the appliance to provide an easier path, i.e. one with less resistance to earth, than through the body of the person. The current then flows to earth and the fuse in the plug socket is 'blown'. Earthing of electrical circuits within a hotel is best achieved by using the Electricity Board's metallic cable sheath which is connected to the earth electrode in the substation. Some older buildings use an earth rod sunk into the ground outside the premises. The service pipes, such as gas, water or electricity, should be cross-bonded to the earth to ensure that they do not become 'live' in the case of an electrical fault developing within the premises.

2. By the use of double-insulated appliances. Appliances carrying the symbol, ⬜, have a double insulated casing so that parts of the appliance which are handled by the operator cannot become 'live'.

19.3.2 FUSING

Wiring in circuits must be protected against surges of current by using either fuses or circuit breakers.

Fuses

A fuse consists of a piece of wire which melts when the current exceeds a certain value thus disconnecting the supply. The diameter of the wire used directly relates to the fuse size. Fuses can either be of the cartridge type which are self-contained with wire held in a ceramic tube with metal ends, or of the rewirable type where fuse wire is connected between the terminals of a porcelain holder (see Fig. 19.5).

Circuit breakers

Circuit breakers operate by thermal or magnetic 'trips' and break the circuit immediately when there is any slight difference in current between the neutral and the live wires – these currents are normally

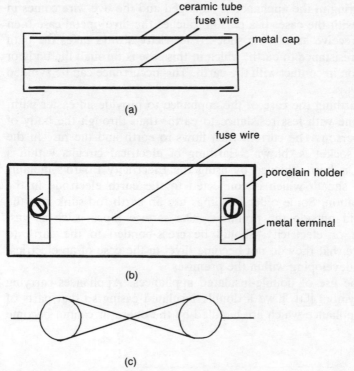

(a)

(b)

(c)

FIG. 19.5 Fuses (a) cartridge fuse (b) rewireable fuse (c) electrical symbol

equal. Differences would occur as a result of current flowing to earth. Circuit breakers can be reset manually and although they are more expensive than conventional fuses they have the advantage of acting as switches in circuits. Residual current circuit breakers (RCCB) are used where the conventional type of earthing is difficult, such as in areas where the soil has a high resistance.

19.4 ELECTRICITY METERS

Modern meters are of the digital type which record electricity used directly in kilowatt-hours (kWh), e.g. if the meter reading at the beginning of a quarter was 13237 and the reading at the end of the quarter was 14929, then 1692 units would have been consumed during the quarter, which at a cost of 7p per unit would be 1692 × 7p, 11 844p or £118.44. Added to this sum would be the quarterly standing charge for the meter, e.g. £11.25 at the current commercial rate, giving a total quarterly bill of £129.69.

19.5 GAS SUPPLIES

19.5.1 GAS METERS

Two types of meter are currently in use, the dial type and the digital type. In the dial type of meter the reading on each of the dials is noted. The important feature is to observe the position of the pointer and record the *lower* of the figures between which it is situated on the four lower dials. In Fig. 19.6 the reading is 1262 × 100 cubic feet (ft^3).

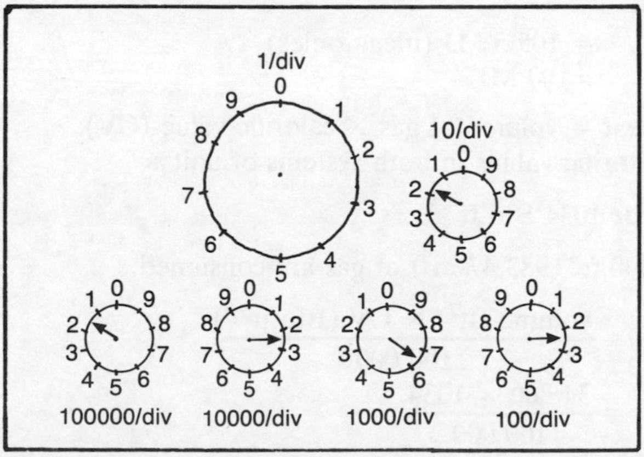

FIG. 19.6 Gas meter: dial type

In the digital type the reading is the four numerals in the rectangular box. There are two more figures as the index registers in 100s of cubic feet. Some meters do register the gas volume in cubic metres (m³) as shown in Fig. 19.7.

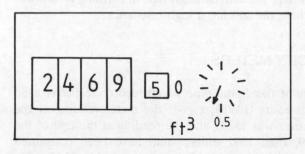

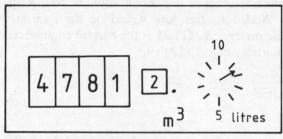

FIG. 19.7 Gas meters: digital types

19.5.2 COST OF GAS

The cost of gas is measured in therms (1 therm was 38.6p in 1988). One therm is 100 000 British thermal units (Btu) or alternatively 1 Btu = 1/100 000 therm.

1 therm   = 105.5 MJ (megajoules)
1 metric therm   =100 MJ

total amount of heat = volume of gas × calorific value (CV)
Gas bills quote calorific values in both systems of units:

i.e. 38.6 MJ m^{-3} or 1034 Btu ft^{-3}

Therefore, if 34 800 ft³ (983.47 m³) of gas are consumed:

$$\text{number of therms} = \frac{\text{volume (ft}^3) \times \text{CV (Btu ft}^{-3})}{100\ 000}$$

$$= \frac{34\ 800 \times 1034}{100\ 000}$$

$$= 359.83 \text{ therms}$$

At 37p per therm $= 359.83 \times 37$p
                    $= £133.14$

In SI units:

number of metric therms $= \dfrac{\text{volume (m}^3) \times \text{CV (MJ m}^{-3})}{100}$

$= \dfrac{983.47 \times 38.6}{100}$

$= 379.62$ metric therms

Although gas bills in the United Kingdom should be calculated in metric therms in line with our entry into the European Economic Community, the therm is in fact still being used and there is currently no prospect of any change. In checking gas bills it is important that megajoules (MJ) and metric therms are converted to therms before multiplying by the price per therm.

19.6   GAS LEAKS

When there is a suspected small gas leak one simple method of detecting the source is to apply a mixture of liquid detergent and water by means of a paint brush. As gas passes through a leaking joint and the detergent solution it creates bubbles – the size of the bubbles is an indication of the extent of leakage.

This method is unsuitable for large leaks which would blow away the detergent solution completely.

19.6.1 PROCEDURE TO DEAL WITH ANY GAS LEAK EMERGENCIES

Gas safety regulations place a legal obligation on customers to turn off the gas and notify the appropriate Gas Board. Telephone numbers are available for 'gas escapes' in all telephone directories.

If there is either escape or smell of gas then the procedure should be to:

1. Ensure safety of people, evacuate if necessary, maximise ventilation of premises by opening all the windows.
2. If possible turn the gas supply off at the mains or a local isolation valve and notify management.
3. Do not smoke and warn others not to smoke. Extinguish naked flames.
4. No electric bells or switches must be used.
5. Ensure safety of property.

6. Notify the Gas Board.

Gas Board engineers will locate and repair a gas escape leaving the installation in a safe condition.

19.7   LIQUEFIED PETROLEUM GAS (LPG)

This is normally used in hotels in rural or outer city areas where a supply of natural gas is not available. LPG usually refers to butane and propane, the latter being the gas normally used in hotels for cooking. Propane is more expensive than natural gas, depending on usage it can cost almost twice as much.

Installation in hotels of systems using LPG from cylinders or bulk (tank) supply for commercial butane or propane is covered in the British Standard Code of Practice BS 5482. This deals with selection of correct appliances, installation requirements, inspection and testing for safe usage.

LPG should be treated in exactly the same way as natural gas once it enters the hotel. For a small public house or hotel using LPG the supply is normally a bank of cylinders, each containing 47 kg (94 litres) connected to a manifold, when one cylinder is empty then there is an automatic change over to a fresh cylinder.

Large users of LPG would require storage tanks. The smallest tank is 1000 litres in volume, but tank sizes can vary. A large hotel (100 beds) could use as much as 50 000 litres of LPG per year with appropriate storage tanks (2000–5000 litres).

Gas supply is computer monitored by suppliers and this means that a constant supply can be maintained by appropriate 'top up' deliveries. The bulk tanks are usually located in a screened area adjacent to the hotel. Storage in cylinders is discussed in Sect. 19.7.2.

The catering manager would require sufficient knowledge of the gas supply so that he could:
1. Appreciate the safety aspects and shut off or isolate the supply if necessary.
2. Monitor gas usage to record energy supply and hence cost of using various appliances.
3. Understand the system sufficiently to give some idea of the work and cost involved in the event of servicing.
4. Be able to install a cylinder, e.g. for an outside barbecue or flambé cooking.

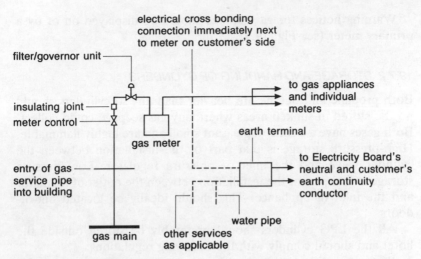

filter/governor unit

electrical cross bonding
connection immediately next
to meter on customer's side

to gas appliances
and individual
meters

insulating joint
meter control

gas meter

earth terminal

entry of gas
service pipe
into building

to Electricity Board's
neutral and customer's
earth continuity
conductor

water pipe

gas main   other services
as applicable

FIG. 19.8 Gas supply to a building

19.7.1 COLOUR CODING OF LPG SUPPLIES

Gas pipes above ground are colour coded with yellow ochre (08C35); below ground they are marked with an orange tape labelled 'gas mains below' (BS 1710). Butane cylinders are colour coded blue, propane cylinders are coded red.

Gas engineers will obviously lay and connect the gas pipes to a hotel (see Fig. 19.8). There can be two meters:

(a) A primary meter connected to the mains service gas pipe and recording the total charge for all gas used.

(b) A secondary meter to measure the gas used in separate appliances or parts of a hotel.

ESCAPES

Open Windows

Do Not Search With Naked Light

Turn-Off Supply at Meter Control Tap

And

IMMEDIATELY Contact Your GAS SERVICE CENTRE

Do Not Turn on Again Until the Escape Has Been Repaired

FIG. 19.9 Escape notice

Warning notices for gas escapes should be displayed on or by a primary meter (see Fig. 19.9).

19.7.2 STORAGE AND HANDLING OF CYLINDERS

Both propane and butane are heavier than air, so cylinders should not be stored in sunken areas where any gas seepage could collect. Both gases have a strong unpleasant smell and are highly flammable. High-pressure storage is that part of the installation between the cylinder valve and the inlet of pressure regulator. Low-pressure storage is that part of the installation between the outlet of regulator and the inlet of appliance. This should ideally be located out-of-doors.

All the LPG cylinders should preferably be stored outside the hotel and should comply with the following regulations:

1. Storage position must be chosen to give ease of access for changing, maintenance and rapid removal, if necessary.
2. They must be properly supported and stored upright with the valve uppermost. Support must give protection from accidental damage.
3. They must not be sited in a position where they cause an obstruction, e.g. a passageway or an exit.
4. There must be sufficient ventilation.
5. They must not be stored near corrosive or combustible substances or near a possible ignition source (in event of accidental gas discharge).
6. They should not be subject to extremes of temperature. Suitable temperature range is 10–30 °C. Under no circumstances should the temperature exceed 45 °C.
7. Propane cylinders must be located outside premises but butane cylinders can be fitted inside, provided suitable fire-resistant housing and adequate ventilation are provided (B.S. 476:8).
8. Flexible hoses and tubing should be regularly inspected. The length of pipe from the gas supply point to the highest rated appliance should be as short as practicable.

19.7.3 CONNECTION OF APPLIANCES

This is normally carried out by the supplier, as is maintenance and delivery. Service and reserve cylinders are usually arranged connected to a manifold fitted with non-return valves and automatic changeover when a cylinder is empty. If a cylinder has to be changed over manually or set up specially for a barbecue, the following procedure must be adopted:

1. Check that the replacement cylinder is of the correct type.
2. Extinguish any source of ignition.
3. Check that a pressure regulator has correct pressure setting (28 mbar for butane, 37 mbar for propane).
4. For a cylinder used for special events, such as barbecues, the connecting tube to the appliance should be high-pressure flexible hose or solid copper or steel tubing.
5. Check connections are gas-tight. The correct spanner must be used and hand-tight is not sufficient.
6. Check the cylinder connection for gas leaks by brushing with soapy water or suitable detergent. Leaks are indicated by the formation of bubbles. **Never check for leaks with a naked flame.**
7. In a manifold system, if the supply is interrupted when the

---

TABLE 19.1 British Standard 5482 : Part 1 : 1979

Model emergency action notice or leaflet for users of liquefied petroleum gas

GAS LEAKAGE* (USUALLY DETECTED BY A DISTINCTIVE SMELL)

DO NOT OPERATE ELECTRICAL SWITCHES

NEVER LOOK FOR A LEAK WITH A NAKED FLAME*

IMMEDIATE ACTION. CLOSE all cylinder valves.

EXTINGUISH all sources of ignition.

OPEN all doors and windows.

If leakage cannot be stopped, REMOVE CYLINDERS to a safe place in the open air and advise the supplier. If this is not possible, evacuate the premises and call the fire brigade.

DO NOT USE THE INSTALLATION until it has been checked by the gas supplier or other competent person.

FIRE*
IMMEDIATE ACTION. IF SAFE TO DO SO, SHUT OFF GAS SUPPLY*. Do not attempt to extinguish gas flame by any other means. *Raise the alarm and call the fire brigade**, stating that a liquefied petroleum gas cylinder is involved and its location.

DO NOT GO NEAR if a cylinder is heated by fire.

ALERT EVERYONE in the immediate area of the fire and evacuate the building.

ADVISE FIRE BRIGADE on their arrival of the LOCATION of the cylinder.

If a cylinder is not involved in the fire and it is safe to do so, close all cylinder valves and remove the cylinders to a safe place.

---

cylinder is about to be changed then turn off the taps on the appliance *before* changing the cylinder.
8. Turn off these appliances and the cylinders after use.
9. If taps or valves are stiff or leak then consult a gas engineer.

19.7.4 PROCEDURE TO BE ADOPTED TO DEAL WITH A LPG LEAK

The action to be taken depends on the precise circumstances but there are three approaches which can be adopted:
1. A leakage of LPG is suspected or detected. This is usually detected by smell or by the 'frosting' of the joint at the point of escape.
2. Gas escape followed by ignition resulting in fire.
3. Where the LPG cylinder is exposed to an external fire.
   The model to follow is recommended in BS 5482 and is outlined in Table 19.1.

QUESTIONS

1. (a) Describe the meaning of the terms: (i) single-phase supply; (ii) three-phase supply.
   (b) Name an appliance which would operate from each type of supply in (i) above.
2. What is meant by:
   (a) earthing;
   (b) double insulation;
   (c) fuse?
3. Calculate the cost of a gas bill in which 45 600 ft^3 of gas have been consumed if the cost per therm is 39p.
4. It is your job as the manager of a large hotel to list the procedures to be followed in the event of a gas leak to a new employee. Briefly explain the reasons behind each of the points in your list.

APPENDIX OF QUESTIONS

1. You are provided with the names of four microorganisms, 1–4, and a list of statements (a)–(x). Study the names and decide which statements apply to which microorganism.

1. *Staphylococcus aureus*
2. *Aspergillus flavus*
3. *Clostridium perfringens*
4. *Saccharomyces cerevisiae*

(a) Reproduces by budding.
(b) Is beneficial to the food industry.
(c) Causes toxin-type food poisoning.
(d) Is useful in brewing.
(e) Causes infective food poisoning.
(f) Forms endospores.
(g) Is an aerobic organism.
(h) Causes food poisoning with a typical incubation period of 1–6 hr.
(i) Is an anaerobic organism.
(j) Causes food spoilage.
(k) Is a round bacterium growing in chains.
(l) A thermophilic bacterium.
(m) Is found in the gut of humans and animals.
(n) Is a round bacterium growing in clusters.
(o) Will not grow below an a_w of 0.91.
(p) Can be found in infected cuts and spots.
(q) Is a rod-shaped bacterium.
(r) Forms endospores.
(s) Causes food poisoning.
(t) Causes food poisoning with

an incubation period of from 12–24 hr.

(u) Is a heterotrophic organism.

(v) Is a curved rod shape.

(w) Is mesophilic.

(x) Can be found contaminating cereal products.

2. (a) Outline the sources whereby *Salmonella* might enter kitchens.

(b) Explain the mechanism of *Salmonella* food poisoning and list the facts you would wish to ascertain in trying to identify a case of *Salmonella* food poisoning.

(c) *Salmonella* food poisoning arose following the consumption of cream-filled profiteroles, but the cream used in the product was free of *Salmonella* when delivered to the restaurant. However, a supply of cheap cracked eggs, used in many products in the restaurant, was found to be contaminated with *Salmonella*. Outline a possible series of events which must have taken place for the food poisoning to occur.

(d) Name two other bacteria which cause food poisoning in a manner similar to *Salmonella*, and what are the usual sources of these bacteria?

3. An outbreak of food poisoning occurs in a hotel and as a result four members of staff are sent for stool tests.

(a) What is a stool test and what food-poisoning organisms are the authorities looking for?

(b) Describe four categories of people who might give a positive stool test.

(c) Name the sort of foods with which this food-poisoning organism is frequently associated.

(d) Describe the symptoms, incubation period and duration of this type of food poisoning.

4. A summer coach party have a day out at the seaside. For refreshments *en route* they take ham sandwiches which have all been prepared by one woman. Some people start to eat the sandwiches soon after departure from their home town. Three hours later, as the coach arrives at the destination these people suffer from vomiting and mild headaches and are taken to hospital.

(a) Suggest, with reasons, the most likely causative organism of the food poisoning.

(b) Explain the most likely way in which the ham could have been contaminated, and how this could have been prevented.

(c) Is the infection likely to be fatal?

5. A small hotel in Scotland opens for Christmas and serves a traditional Christmas day meal including turkey (a 28 lb frozen catering turkey). Fourteen hours after the meal, ten of the guests started to feel ill, having diarrhoea, fever and abdominal pains, within another 2 hr six more guests were ill. Food poisoning was diagnosed and the local public health laboratory discovered that remains of the turkey were contaminated with food-poisoning bacteria.

(a) State, with reasons, the most likely causative organism of food poisoning.

(b) Explain how modern methods of farming could lead to an increase in this type of food poisoning.

(c) State two special precautions that chefs take to prevent this kind of food poisoning.

6. (a) Explain the mechanisms whereby certain bacteria cause food poisoning.

(b) What are the criteria used in identifying the type of bacterial food poisoning?

(c) A group of students visited a hotel and whilst there they were each served with a slice of Black Forest gateau and coffee. This was the only meal consumed by all the students on the day. During the following 2 days all the students went down with food poisoning, the symptoms being severe diarrhoea, fever, and in some cases nausea and vomiting. The symptoms persisted for 3–6 days. Suggest what the causative organism was giving reasons for your deductions. How might the gateau have been infected?

7. Explain each of the following terms used to describe microbial growth:

(a) Some food-spoilage organisms are psychrophilic.

(b) If the a_w of food drops below 0.6 then microbial spoilage will not occur.

(c) Most food-spoilage bacteria are neutrophilic.

(d) Vacuum packaging of foods helps to prevent the growth of aerobic spoilage organisms.

(e) *Salmonella* is a facultative parasite.

8. A coach party set out from London to go for a day at the seaside. *En route* they stopped off at a pub for a meal and were served with stew/hot pot. The stew had been reheated after

originally being served to a coach party the previous day. After leaving the pub and arriving at the seaside one or two people started to feel ill; within 12 hr most of the people who had eaten the hot pot were ill, the symptoms being abdominal pain followed by mild diarrhoea. A doctor diagnosed food poisoning.

(a) Suggest, with reasons, the most likely causative organism.

(b) What mistakes did the kitchen staff make which lead to this case of food poisoning. What special precautions should chefs take to prevent this sort of food poisoning?

(c) How long is the food poisoning likely to last? Suggest the most likely source of the organism.

9. Briefly outline the roles of the following organisms in the production of a named food product:

(a) *Saccharomyces cerevisiae*;

(b) *Acetobacter aceti*;

(c) *Lactobacillus bulgaricus*;

(d) *Penicillium camemberti*;

(e) *Saccharomyces ellipsoideus*.

10. At a catering exhibition a number of disinfectants are on display. One is marked 'bacteriostatic', all the others are marked 'bacteriocidal'. One is based on phenolic derivatives; one is based on hypochlorite; one is based on pine fluid.

(a) Discuss the difference between the terms 'bacteriostatic' and 'bactericidal'.

(b) Discuss the uses/limitations of disinfectants based on phenol, hypochlorite and pine fluids.

11. In November 1987 a well known club in London was fined nearly £7000 on over thirty charges concerning cleanliness and disrepair in its kitchens.

(a) Briefly describe the powers of entry of Environmental Health Officers.

(b) List two items of legislation that deal with the hygiene of catering establishments.

(c) Describe the action you would take if an outbreak of food poisoning occurred in a hotel managed by you.

12. A group of thirty students purchased food from an Indian take-away restaurant. The meals consisted of boiled rice, fried rice, tandoori chicken and chicken curry. After the meal food poisoning resulted but not all students were ill.

Meal profiles:

Group A	Group B	Group C	Group D
Boiled rice	Fried rice	Fried rice	Boiled rice
Chicken tandoori	Chicken curry	Chicken tandoori	Chicken curry

Students who were ill came from Groups A and D. The victims suffered vomiting and diarrhoea 1–6 hr after eating the food.

(a) Suggest, with reasons, the most likely causative organism of food poisoning.

(b) Explain briefly the microbiological chain of events taking place and how this type of food poisoning may be prevented.

(c) Explain how a food-borne infection differs from food poisoning. Give three examples of food-borne infections.

13. Outline the conditions that are required for the growth of microorganisms and explain how by altering some of the conditions we can preserve our food.

14. (a) What is the name of the *Salmonella* bacterium implicated in most outbreaks of food poisoning in this country.

(b) How does *Salmonella* food poisoning differ in principle to staphylococcal food poisoning.

(c) Apart from microbial food poisoning state two other ways in which food poisoning occurs.

(d) Discuss the relative occurrence in this country of the different types of food poisoning.

15. Explain fully the rules of personal hygiene relating to:

(a) hand washing;

(b) jewellery;

(c) make-up;

(d) protective clothing;

(e) smoking;

(f) general health.

16. The temperature at which food is stored and cooked is extremely important in catering. How would you explain to a trainee chef:

(a) Why steak can be served rare but not beefburgers.

(b) Why rolled joints of meat need longer cooking.

(c) Why food not intended for immediate consumption should be stored below 10 °C or above 63 °C.

(d) Why large meat pies need longer cooking than small ones.

(e) The correct use of a *bain marie*.

17. (a) Define the term 'food spoilage'.

(b) Explain why although assessing food spoilage can be a value judgement a concensus of opinion is necessary in catering.

(c) Classify foods into three categories based on ease of spoilage.

(d) Give three examples of how physical spoilage can occur.

(e) Which type of microorganisms would you expect to find

spoiling the following foods, explain your answers; (i) bread; (ii) milk; (iii) oranges.

18. In December 1985, 120 patients and staff of a Scottish hospital contracted food poisoning. Environmental Health Officers inspected the premises after the event and made the following comments:
    (a) Enquiries showed some of the ten frozen turkeys used may not have been completely thawed before cooking.
    (b) 'Hosing out' of the turkey cavities was performed using a tap in a salad preparation sink.
    (c) Turkeys after cooking were returned to the same work surface on which they had been defrosted.
    (d) Dishes of food were put into warm trolleys for storage and delivery prior to service.
    (e) Meat, delivered from a meat packaging plant in a plastic bag and stored on the floor of the chill room, was removed to a wooden preparation table where it was deposited alongside cooled cooked chickens.

    Explain fully how and why each of these events illustrates poor catering and hygiene practices.

19. Distinguish between the following:
    (a) disinfectant and antiseptic;
    (b) pasteurisation and canning;
    (c) bacteriostatic and bacteriocidal;
    (d) hypochlorite disinfectant and phenolic disinfectant;
    (e) heat-sensitive bacterium and thermoduric bacterium.

20. Calculate the energy value of a traditional Sunday lunch using the following information:

Starter
Melon (50 g)
Main course
Roast beef (60 g), roast potatoes (90 g), Yorkshire pudding (50 g), boiled parsnips (20 g), carrots (70 g) and boiled peas (70 g).
Dessert
Lemon meringue pie (100 g)

Composition of nutrients (g/100 g food)

	Carbohydrate	Protein	Fat
Melon	5.0	0.6	0
Roast beef	0	26.6	0
Yorkshire pudding	25.8	6.8	10.1
Roast potatoes	27.3	2.8	4.8
Boiled parsnips	13.5	1.3	0

	Carbohydrate	Protein	Fat
Carrots	4.5	0.9	0
Peas	7.7	5.0	0.4
Lemon meringue pie	46.4	4.5	14.6

Energy value of nutrients (kJ/g)

Carbohydrate	16
Protein	17
Fat	37

(a) List the food group into which each food item falls.
(b) Describe the overall nutritional value of the meal.
(c) Describe how you could modify the meal in order to bring it into line with current nutritional advice.

21. Explain the meaning and the significance to health of the following statement from the top of a carton of a sunflower margarine:

HIGH IN ESSENTIAL POLYUNSATURATES*
Low in saturates : Low in cholesterol
* Natural *cis-cis*-linoleic

22. Breakfast cereals are commonly eaten in the United Kingdom. A typical serving of a popular cereal would be 20 g of cereal and 100 g of milk. Calculate the provision of each of the listed vitamins by the cereals and milk as a percentage of the recommended daily allowance for each vitamin. Discuss your findings.

Nutrients provision per 100 g

	Milk	Breakfast cereal
Niacin	0.08 mg	16.0 mg
Riboflavin	0.19 mg	1.5 mg
Thiamin	0.04 mg	1.0 mg
Vitamin B_6	0.04 μg	1.8 μg
Vitamin B_{12}	0.3 μg	1.7 μg
Vitamin D	0.021 μg	2.8 μg

23. The following is a list of organic compounds, using this list select responses to questions (a)–(h):

Dextrose	Glycogen
Glycerol monostearate	Fructose
Amylose	Sorbitol
Butyric acid	Linoleic acid
Pectin	Sucrose
Oleic acid	Cellulose
Lactose	Palmitic acid

(a) Name two that are disaccharides.

(b) Name a substance that acts as a sweetener in diabetic products.

(c) Name a substance that is used to enhance the emulsifying properties of fats.

(d) Name two substances found in fibre.

(e) Name two monosaccharides.

(f) Name one substance found as a major component of olive oil.

(g) Name a substance responsible for the smell of rancid butter.

(h) Name a polysaccharide component of starch.

(i) Name four compounds that are found in jams.

(j) Give alternative names for cane sugar and grape sugar.

(k) Name two compounds that are unsaturated fatty acids.

(l) Name two compounds that are carbohydrates of animal origin.

(m) Name two that are found in invert sugar.

24. Calculate the energy value of a meal of fried cod in batter (150 g) and chips (210 g) from the following data. Comment on your result in relation to the energy needs of a 20-year old sedentary female.

Composition of nutrients per 100 g

	Carbohydrate	Protein	Fat
Fried cod in batter	7.5	19.6	10.3
Chips	37.3	3.8	10.9

Energy value of nutrients (kJ/g)

Carbohydrate	16
Protein	17
Fat	37

25. The following are substances that can occur in food materials:

Aspartame	Sodium glutamate
Papain	Myosin
Actin	Collagen
Elastin	

(a) Name one that is a flavour enhancer.

(b) Name two that are major muscle proteins.

(c) Name one that is an artificial sweetener.

(d) Name one that is a meat tenderising enzyme.

(e) Name one that is a dipeptide.

    (f) Name two that are elastic proteins.

    (g) Name one that is an inelastic protein.

    (h) Name one found mainly in ligaments.

    (i) Name one found mainly in tendons.

    (j) Name one that does not contain a peptide linkage.

26. It is likely that legislation will be introduced in the near future concerning fat labelling. This will include total fat and saturated fat.

    (a) Which has the higher total fat content, butter or lard, or are they the same?

    (b) Which has the higher total fat content, soft margarines or hard margarines, or are they the same?

    (c) Which has the higher saturated fatty acid content, soft margarines or hard margarines, or are they the same?

    (d) Which has the higher fat content, lard or cooking oil, or are they the same?

    (e) Which has the higher saturated fatty acid content, olive oil or sunflower oil, or are they the same?

27. (a) Explain, in chemical terms, the difference between the stability of mayonnaise and French dressing.

    (b) Why is butter not a good type of fat to use for frying?

    (c) Why is olive oil used in salad dressing?

    (d) What is meant by the term 'high ratio fats' and where are they used in catering.

28. (a) What is meant by the terms: (i) saturated fatty acid; (ii) monounsaturated fatty acid; (iii) polyunsaturated fatty acid?

    (b) The composition of three fats, A, B and C, is shown below:

	Fat A	Fat B	Fat C
Saturated fat	55	15	10
Monounsaturated fat	23	20	20
Polyunsaturated fat	2	45	10
Water	20	20	60

Identify fats A, B and C and briefly comment on their use in catering.

    (c) Explain the meaning of the term 'palate cling' and how it can be minimised in food preparation.

29. Examine Fig. A.1 and list as many mistakes in personal hygiene as you can.

30. Examine Fig. A.2 and list as many examples of bad catering practice as you can.

FIG. A.1

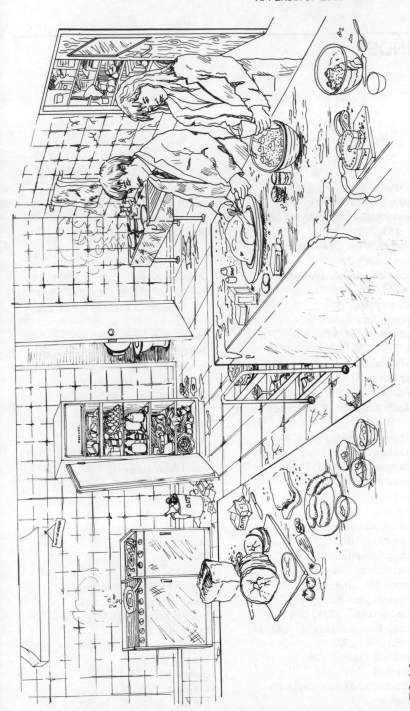

FIG. A.2

INDEX